The complete guide to referencing and avoiding plagiarism

Second edition

The complete guide to referencing and avoiding plagiarism

Second edition

Colin Neville

Open University Press

Open University Press
McGraw-Hill Education
McGraw-Hill House
Shoppenhangers Road
Maidenhead
Berkshire
England
SL6 2QL

email: enquiries@openup.co.uk
world wide web: www.openup.co.uk

and Two Penn Plaza, New York, NY 10121-2289, USA

First published 2007
Reprinted 2007, 2009
First published in this second edition 2010

A catalogue record of this book is available from the British Library

ISBN-13: 978-0-33-524103-3
ISBN-10: 0335241034

Library of Congress Cataloging-in-Publication Data
CIP data applied for

Typeset by RefineCatch Limited, Bungay, Suffolk
Printed in the UK by Bell & Bain Ltd., Glasgow

Fictitious names of companies, products, people, characters and/or data that may be used herein (in case studies or in examples) are not intended to represent any real individual, company, product or event.

Mixed Sources
Product group from well-managed
forests and other controlled sources
www.fsc.org Cert no. TT-COC-002769
© 1996 Forest Stewardship Council

The **McGraw·Hill** Companies

Contents

Preface

The second edition of this book contains an expanded section on electronic sources, which includes social networking sites and virtual learning environment (VLE) sources. It also contains an extended 'Frequently asked questions' chapter, plus a new chapter with an essay titled, 'What's the point of referencing?' This was written by a postgraduate student for an essay-writing competition sponsored by the *LearnHigher* network. It is included because I feel it demonstrates how students can 'find their own voice' in assignments, as well as presenting well-referenced evidence in support of their arguments.

Furthermore, a major new inclusion to this second edition is the result of a research survey looking at the perceptions of UK higher education students on referencing. The aim of this study was to identify how students perceive the roles of referencing in academic writing, to identify the main referencing problems for students and to consider the implications of the findings for higher education institutions, and in particular for staff development.

A total of 278 students across all disciplines and from 14 UK institutions of higher education were involved in the research, and the study has confirmed what many staff in learning support services knew already: that many students find referencing a time-consuming, frustrating and difficult experience. The main practical issues for them are related to understanding when they should reference, the referencing detail required, and the time the whole process takes.

However, their difficulties were compounded by the often bewildering range of referencing styles they encountered; allegedly inconsistent advice and feedback from tutors; and a lack of clarity as to understanding when and how they could integrate their own experiences into assignments. But above all, for many, a fear of being accused of plagiarism was at the core of their difficulties. This latter issue is pursued and discussed further in Chapter 4.

Student 'voices' from this research are quoted extensively, bringing the students' referencing difficulties vividly, directly and unpretentiously to life. In response, the referencing problems they present are directly addressed in the book; in Chapter 1 students troubled by these issues are directed to the relevant chapters, where practical advice and solutions are presented.

So, as with the first edition, this book is aimed primarily at students in higher education, but is likely also to be relevant to pre-degree students in schools and colleges. It tries to do three things.

First, it presents, discusses and gives examples of the main referencing systems found in higher education in Britain. However, it also tries to explain the principles underpinning referencing, as it was clear from my survey that many students were too bogged down by referencing practice detail to think beyond this.

Second, it describes and illustrates the often small differences between the main referencing styles applied in Britain. These may be small, but the individual referencing styles described in this book are often fiercely defended by their academic guardians. In the first edition, I estimated there were nine referencing styles to be found within UK higher education institutions. However, this has proven to be an underestimation, and the total is more likely to be nearer to 14 – or even more if hybridization is taken into account (see later in this preface).

It seems that referencing styles have flourished like mushrooms in higher education. Particular referencing styles have been adopted by subject disciplines, for reasons linked to history, professional practice, or for reasons of personal whimsy by heads of department – and defended thereafter by them, often out of sheer cussedness, against administrators who try to introduce uniformity of referencing practice across an institution. But the range of referencing styles can aggravate a situation where tutors are said to be giving inconsistent advice to students, and where students on combined studies courses may encounter two or more referencing styles – and differences in tutors' interpretation of these.

I would argue, therefore, that the challenge for higher education institutions over the next few years is to review the range of referencing styles that students encounter, and to explore how students can learn to reference in a way that does not stifle their own writing styles and independent thought.

This last point presents particular challenges for academics. If it is accepted that a primary aim of higher education is to encourage students to think and express themselves independently, then referencing should be demonstrated as one of the means to this end. The way institutions present the role of referencing in assignments is, therefore, particularly important: it should not be perceived by students as a clanking suit of armour to be worn against accusations of plagiarism, but as a fine tool for the shaping of knowledge. Students should be the masters of referencing, and not its servants.

Third, the book presents a range of sources, and illustrates how to reference these in a comparative way. In Chapter 9, the name–date (Harvard), APA, MLA, and numerical styles are shown alongside each other to show the differences between styles for each chosen source.

So the book, I hope, may prove particularly useful to students who encounter a range of referencing styles in their journeys through pre-degree, undergraduate and postgraduate studies. Undergraduates on a combined studies course may find themselves having to reference sources in two or more styles as they encounter different disciplines, with each discipline wedded to its own referencing style preference. The graduate may then move on to a postgraduate programme and encounter a completely new referencing regime, where tutors insist that sources are meticulously cited and referenced in line with departmental practice. Only when this situation changes, will the information in this book become redundant.

So the book operates on a number of levels. It offers a practical 'how to reference' guide for students and their tutors. This is important, as clarity and understanding of both the principles and practice of referencing can lead to increased confidence in academic writing. But it also highlights the tensions and contradictions in referencing within institutions, particularly relating to the large range of referencing styles encountered by students. The message from the research is that higher education institutions have ignored these tensions for too long.

Referencing styles in the book

Although the name–date (Harvard) referencing style appears to be the predominant one in higher education in Britain, the American Psychological Association (APA), and Modern Languages Association (MLA) styles, still retain their firm holds in psychology and language disciplines respectively. In addition, numerical referencing styles, including those recommended by the Modern Humanities Research Association (MHRA) and Institute of Electrical and Electronic Engineers (IEEE), still maintain a significant presence in a wide range of humanities, science and technology courses.

However, although the name–date (Harvard) referencing style, followed by the two numerical styles, tend to be the styles adopted by the majority of degree and pre-degree courses in Britain, the benchmark guides for their application, British Standard 'recommendations', are less user-friendly, compared with others, particularly APA and MLA. The referencing style guides produced by the APA, MLA, MHRA and IEEE are all written in clear prose, with easy to follow referencing examples and with the 'rules of the game' spelt out unambiguously to their disciples. In contrast, British Standard (BS) issue guidelines have been subject to interpretation over the years, and have been distilled with the essence of the individual writer. Although most adapters of BS recommendations have kept to BS recommendations for presenting the order of elements in references, you will find subtle variations on BS wherever you look. British Standard, for example, illustrates full source references showing:

- Name (s) of authors or organizations in upper case
- Year of publication not enclosed in parenthesis.

However, institutional variations have emerged. Some institutions, in their referencing guidelines to students, follow British Standard and illustrate author names in upper case, while many others do not; and it is almost universal practice in UK institutions now to illustrate name–date (Harvard) references with the year shown in parenthesis.

What appears to have happened is that Harvard and APA styles, because of their similarities, have merged gradually into a referencing hybrid. There are still differences between Harvard and APA to be observed – as this book will show – but these are akin to parents knowing the difference between their identical twin children. Pity the poor student asked to use both Harvard and APA styles on a combined studies degree, and trying to work out the differences between them!

So faced with the many subtle institutional versions of Harvard, and a lesser number of numeric referencing guidelines to choose from, which one does this author choose? Like most guides to referencing, this one is somewhat of a hybrid too, in that I have followed the BS order of elements in references, but deviated by using the widespread practice of placing the year in parenthesis for Harvard referencing.

On the other hand, I have followed the British Standard examples by using upper case with author or organizational names, as this tends to distinguish and highlight the author from other elements in the source. I have also followed British Standard examples and kept capitalisation in the titles to a minimum, and which is also consistent with the advice given in many contemporary writing style guides.

So it is probably impossible for any writer on referencing to produce a definitive guide to referencing that embraces the Harvard and British versions of the numerical styles, given the subtle variations that abound. The guide is, therefore, as 'complete' as a mortal being can make it in the face of these differences.

What I have done, however, is to try and explain **why** students should reference in the first place, explain the main differences in referencing style, and give examples of the most commonly used sources by students in Britain today – plus a few that are uncommon. Once the principles of referencing are understood, and with some examples to guide them, most students will be able to work out how to reference the sources they encounter.

But surely, a book on referencing is an anachronism when students today can use referencing management software to find sources and organize their bibliographies. You might think so, but it is not yet the case. As I argue in Chapter 3, although the software is often freely available to students within their own institutions, it can be time-consuming to learn to use; and many students simply do not bother: although for those that do, it can save them much time and effort in the longer term. The available software does not yet solve all information retrieval, citation and referencing problems, and a universal, easy to use referencing software management system has yet to arrive on the scene. It may arrive in due course, but for the moment, and perhaps even then, this book has some modest expectations of life. For, despite the advance of software, the book and other printed forms, still retain, for many, the advantages of being flexible, portable and easy to use. However, I would say that, wouldn't I?

Sources and influences

The sources for referencing examples presented in this book are based on guidelines and recommendations from the following:

- For name–date (Harvard), and for the British Standard numerical referencing styles (numeric and running-notes): British Standard Institution (BS) guidelines: 5605: 1990: *Recommendations for citing and referencing published material*; BS 1629:1989: *Recommendation for references to published materials*; BS 5261-1:2000: *Copy preparation and proof correction – part 1: design and layout of documents*; BSO ISO-690-2: 1997: *Information and documentation – guidelines for bibliographic references and citations to information resources*
- For the Institute of Electrical and Electronics Engineers (IEEE style): *Transactions, journals, and letters: information for author* (2006)
- For the Vancouver style numeric system, the International Committee of Medical Journal Editors *Uniform requirements for manuscripts submitted to biomedical journals: sample references (2006)*
- For Modern Humanities Research Association (MHRA style), the 2008 edition of the *MHRA style guide: a handbook for authors, editors and writers of thesis*
- For name–date American Psychological Association (APA style): (2005), *Concise rules of APA style* and the (2007) *APA style guide to electronic references*

- For author–page, MLA style: *The MLA handbook for writers of research papers* (2009)
- For the Chicago style: Turabian (2007) *A manual for writers of research papers, theses, and dissertations*
- For the Council of Science Editors (CSE) style: *Scientific style and format: the CSE manual for authors, editors, and publishers* (2006).

I have also drawn on the guidelines on referencing legal sources produced by the *Oxford Standard for Citation of Legal Authorities*, produced by the Faculty of Law, University of Oxford.

Other publications also consulted and found to be particularly helpful were: Levin (2004) *Write great essays* and Maimon et al. (2007), *A writer's resource*

(See 'References' for full source information of all items mentioned above.)

Acknowledgements

My sincere thanks to my wife, Wendy, for the hours she has spent proof-reading these chapters and for making good suggestions for changing the order of the text.

I am grateful to the following for allowing me to use extracts from their publications, or their work:

- Professor Michael Keniger, Deputy Vice-Chancellor (Academic), University of Queensland for his permission to use his institution's online example of common knowledge in referencing, shown in Chapter 3
- Dr Celia Thompson, University of Melbourne, for her permission to use the referencing example from her article, shown in Chapter 5
- Mr Jonas Juenger, postgraduate student at the London School of Economics, for his winning entry in the 2009 *LearnHigher* Referencing Learning Area essay writing competition, and which is shown, with his permission, in Chapter 8.

I would like to express my appreciation to the following for their help with the research cited in this book:

- Mr Chew Chee Khiang, an Open University student in Malaysia, for his advice on referencing foreign names, which is found in Chapter 7, 'Frequently asked questions'
- Professor Lin Norton, Research Director, and Dr Katherine Harrington, Director, and their colleagues, in the *Write Now* Centre of Excellence in Teaching and Learning, for supporting and approving the award of a mini-research grant to undertake this research
- Particular thanks to Dr Peter O'Neill and Sandra Sinfield of London Metropolitan University for their very generous support and for organizing and publicizing referencing workshops in this institution; it was a pleasure to work there with them
- Similarly, my grateful appreciation to Russell Delderfield and Becka Currant in the Learner Development Unit, University of Bradford, for their support, and their efforts to organize and publicize referencing workshops for Bradford students
- Thanks, too, to Muhammad Khan at Liverpool Hope University for his technical expertise in setting-up and managing the 'Have your say' facility on the *LearnHigher* site.

Finally, my appreciation and thanks go to all the students who have contributed their views to my research; without them it would not have happened.

The book chapters at a glance

Chapter 1: The 'shock' of referencing. This chapter introduces the structure of the book and the result of a research project looking at student perspectives on referencing.

Chapter 2: Why reference? This chapter explains the principles and reasons for referencing in assignments.

Chapter 3: The 'what' and 'when' of referencing. This chapter looks at the 'what' (to reference) issues of choosing sources and when you need to reference – and when it is not necessary. It also includes advice on saving time by using referencing management software and by developing effective note-making strategies and techniques.

Chapter 4: Plagiarism. This chapter discusses the issue of plagiarism – and how to avoid it. It includes two exercises: one to test your understanding of plagiarism, and the other to look at the issue of 'copy and paste' from the Internet.

Chapter 5: Referencing styles. This chapter presents an overview of the range of referencing styles you may encounter on courses in Britain and illustrates the differences between them.

Chapter 6: Name–date (Harvard) style of referencing. This chapter looks in detail at the name–date (Harvard) style of referencing, as this referencing style is the most widely used in Britain. The chapter includes referencing examples and an example report.

Chapter 7: Frequently asked questions. This chapter has 18 of the most frequently asked questions about referencing – and answers to these.

Chapter 8: How to express your own ideas in assignments. This chapter presents you with a sample essay that demonstrates how to integrate your own ideas into an assignment – using references to help you do this.

Chapter 9: Referencing in action. This chapter presents many examples of referencing. You will be presented with a wide range of sources and comparative examples of how to reference these using Harvard, APA, MLA and British Standard numerical styles.

1

The 'shock' of referencing

Student perceptions of referencing • The students who came to the workshops • 'Have your say' comments

Since starting at university, the focus on it has been huge and a shock.

(Undergraduate, Law and Politics)

I find referencing incredibly anal and not very productive to my learning efforts . . . I did not come to university to learn the skills of bureaucratism!

(Undergraduate, Politics and International Relations)

The use of references is vital to explore other avenues of information and previous work. I have come to realise the value of putting references in my own work as a way of seeing which other works I have built my ideas on, or those that contrast with my ideas.

(Postgraduate, Geography)

It is an expected academic practice that students will refer to (or cite) the **sources** of ideas, data and other evidence in written assignments. Referencing is the practice of acknowledging in your own writing the intellectual work of others; work that has been presented in some way into the public domain.

However, the importance given to referencing in Britain is not universal, and students studying in Britain from other countries are often surprised by the emphasis placed on it by UK higher education (HE) institutions. It can often come as a shock to students who have studied in Britain too!

I think that the big issue with referencing is that it is not required at A level to a very high standard and then you are suddenly expected to just know how to do it at university, without anyone teaching you.

(Undergraduate, Philosophy).

Referencing – the basic idea

The basic principle of referencing is to support and identify the evidence you use in your assignments. You direct readers of your work to the source of evidence. This can be done by presenting (or 'citing') either the name of the source, or an identification number, in the main text of your work. The full source detail is given later, either in a footnote/endnote, and/or in an alphabetical list at the end of the assignment.

As you progress through different levels of study in higher education, you are expected to be increasingly more critical of ideas and theories and their application in models and practices. Ideas are often a product of a particular period of history and of the social, economic, and cultural norms and values of that time, and a critical approach demands that you are aware of and able to acknowledge the source of ideas. In so doing you are able to alert the reader to the origins of the ideas, theories, models or practices under discussion.

Education needs ideas, arguments and perspectives to thrive, but these have to be tested rigorously and subjected to the critical scrutiny of others. This is done by researching, preparing and presenting work into the public domain. This is a formidable task for any writer or commentator, and one that can take years to achieve. Referencing is then, about respecting and honouring the hard work of writers and commentators – by acknowledging them in your assignments.

Referencing can also help you to find your own voice in assignments, by helping you write essays and reports that project or reflect the way **you** see or perceive things. Evidence presented and correctly referenced supports and strengthens your opinions – and converts them into arguments.

But, despite all these worthy reasons, many students find referencing a pain, a mechanistic chore and a complete bore – although not all, as can be seen from the comments of the third student quoted at the start of the chapter; but more on this later.

This book presents an overview of the main referencing styles currently applied in British schools and colleges, and in higher education. It is aimed at students: pre-degree, undergraduate and on postgraduate courses, and will explain:

- The **why** of referencing: the academic rationale for all styles of referencing and the principles underpinning the practice
- The **what** of referencing: what to reference; which sources to choose
- The **when** of referencing: when to reference – and when it is not necessary
- And the **how** of referencing. The main differences between referencing styles in Britain will be described, and illustrated with examples of the types of sources that you will undoubtedly want to refer to in your assignments.

It will also discuss (in Chapter 4) the thorny issue of **plagiarism**, and how important referencing is to avoid accusations of cheating.

But, in addition to the three big referencing issues – the 'why', 'when', 'how' of referencing – this book will also address particular referencing issues that students find particularly problematic. These issues were the subject of research, leading to a conference in 2009 and my report *Student perceptions of referencing* (Neville 2009b).

Student perceptions of referencing

During the 2009 academic year, I organized a research project to gather the views of undergraduate and postgraduate students from across a range of UK higher education institutions on the topic of referencing in academic writing. I offered drop-in referencing advice workshops for students at two universities, and set up an online 'Have your say' facility on the *LearnHigher* website (*LearnHigher* is a network of higher education institutions, working together to develop effective learning resources and materials for students and staff).

As a result, I gathered the views of 278 students at 14 UK institutions of higher education. Of this total number, 207 were undergraduates (74 per cent) and 71 postgraduates (26 per cent), drawn from a wide range of subject disciplines. Of the total number, 77 students came to the workshops to ask questions about referencing students; and 201 students sent me their comments on the 'Have your say' facility. The quotations in this book are all taken from comments received from 'Have your say' and provide a real sense of what those students felt about referencing.

So what do students think of referencing? And what difficulties do they encounter?

The students who came to the workshops

Understandably, the students attending the workshops had immediate problems they needed to resolve; these are shown in the list that follows. If you have encountered similar problems yourself, you will find that I attempt to address these in this book, and the relevant chapters are shown next to the problem.

The issues and problems brought to the workshops, in rank order of their recurrence, were these:

1 Secondary referencing – this is when you read author A, who quotes, paraphrases or summarizes author B. You are interested in using the information about B, but are not sure who to reference, or how.
   If this is an issue or problem for you, **read Chapter 7, 'Frequently asked questions', question number 3.**
2 When to reference – students were often quite confused about when **not** to reference; when it was **not** necessary.
   If this is an issue or problem for you, **read chapter 3.**
3 Reference and bibliographic lists – there was confusion or lack of knowledge about how to organize and format a list of sources in a 'References' or 'Bibliography' section of an assignment.

*If this is an issue or problem for you, **read Chapters 5 and 6**, and look at the essay example in **Chapter 8**.*

4 Referencing quotations – students were often unsure how to manage and reference quotations.

*If this is an issue or problem for you, **read Chapter 3:** when to reference 'six scenarios', and the essay in **Chapter 8**, which contains a number of quotations.*

5 Referencing electronic sources – the explosion of information on the web has presented students with difficulties in working out how to reference electronic sources.

*If this is an issue or problem for you, **read Chapter 9, section S**.*

6 Understanding the name–date (Harvard) referencing style – many students had been asked to use this style, but were struggling to understand it.

*If this is an issue or problem for you, **read Chapter 6**, and look at the essay in **Chapter 8**, which uses this style of referencing.*

7 Understanding numerical referencing styles – similar to above comments on the name–date (Harvard) style.

*If this is an issue or problem for you, **read Chapter 5**.*

8 Using 'own voice' in assignments – this was about how one's own ideas and experiences can be integrated into assignments.

*If this is an issue or problem for you, **read Chapter 7, 'Frequently asked questions' numbers 17 and 18, and read Chapter 8**.*

However, underpinning many of the problems and anxieties that brought students to the workshops was the fear of being accused of plagiarism – but more on this later (in Chapter 4).

'Have your say' comments

Comments were sent by 201 students, from 14 HE institutions. Of this total, 155 were undergraduates (77 per cent), and 46 postgraduates (23 per cent). Students were asked to respond to these questions: 'How do you feel about referencing in assignments?', 'What are the "big issues" or concerns about referencing for you?'

From the total of 201 students, 51 of these (36 undergraduates; 15 postgraduates) presented entirely positive views about referencing. This represented 25 per cent of all the 'Have your say' respondents. Comments from these students included the following:

> Referencing is an essential element of the assignment; what academic use is there in saying anything that is unverified or unsupported . . . I wouldn't read an unreferenced piece of work myself – it would have no credibility.
>
> (Postgraduate, Classics)

> I believe that being told that you have to show references within your work and so, therefore, having to look in books and journals for quotes or points to use,

has helped to improve the overall quality of my work and helped the overall grade I receive.

(Undergraduate, Business Studies)

Referencing is essential and learning to do it boosts confidence, not just in writing, but also and primarily in arguing ideas. It is a way of putting my point forward.

(Postgraduate, Communications and Media)

But of the 201 students responding to 'Have your say', 150 (75 per cent) made critical comments about referencing. These tended to break into two groups:

1 'Seriously dislike referencing'

Eleven of the 150 respondents (7 per cent), all of whom were undergraduates, were critical of the whole practice of referencing and could not see or offer any redeeming features. The comments included the following:

In all honesty, I seriously dislike referencing. It is far too troublesome for simply putting forth a point.

(Undergraduate, Accounting, Management and Information Systems)

I hate referencing because I am not very good at it and find I get marks deducted for bad referencing. The thing is, I have never been taught to write an essay, let alone how to reference.

(Undergraduate, Philosophy)

I don't understand why referencing in essays is taken so seriously when you don't even have to think about it when writing essays in exam conditions.

(Undergraduate, Philosophy and Politics)

2 'I can see why we have to reference, but . . .'

However, 139 students (69 per cent of the grand total) expressed views that started typically: 'I can see why we have to reference, **but** . . .' The specific 'but' items amounted to 247 points of criticism that embraced 14 areas of concern or difficulty. Many of the issues arising from the workshops featured in the 'Have your say' feedback, but other difficulties were also raised; these are set out, as follows, and the chapters identified where help with these problems can be found.

1 Time management related issues ('referencing takes too much time').
   *If this is an issue or problem for you, **read Chapter 3**: the sections on saving time.*
2 Anxiety about plagiarism.
   *If this is an issue or problem for you, **read Chapter 4.***
3 There are 'too many referencing styles'.
   *If this is an issue or problem for you, **read Chapter 5** to understand the basic principles and practice of these, and for advice on raising the issue at your institution.*
4 Critical of the detail needed in a reference.

*If this is an issue or problem for you, **read Chapter 3**, particularly the section: 'saving time: using referencing management software'.*

5 Difficulties with referencing particular sources.

*If this is an issue or problem for you, **read Chapter 9**, for many examples of how to reference sources.*

So this book is not just about 'how to reference' – although it is important for your progress through higher education that you **do** know how to reference properly – but it is also about looking at the wider referencing issues that concern many students, and helping you and others to address these.

2

Why reference?

Principles of referencing • Three other student-related reasons

It stops you spouting cow dung.

(Undergraduate, Contemporary Art Practice)

So **why** reference? And **why** is there so much emphasis on referencing? Referencing in Britain has to be seen, not just in an academic, but also in a social and political context. It is part of a societal value system that vigorously supports the idea of the intellectual property rights of others. It has been argued that in countries characterized by individualism, which includes competition, self-interest, self-reliance and personal achievement, the respect for copyright is usually strong (Hampden-Turner and Trompenaars 2000).

However, in societies with a more collective ideology people are often more willing to sublimate their individuality to the benefit of the community as a whole. Ideas are regarded as being more in the public domain: to be shared and used for self or community improvement. In this social context, copying is widely practised as a legitimate form of sharing of ideas with others, without the necessity to refer continually to a named originator (Yang 2005, p.286, citing Kuanpoth 2002). While this may be generally true, there appears to be, even within this cultural context, variations on the practices (see Ha 2006, discussed in Chapter 4 of this book).

Principles of referencing

Why reference? Arguably, referencing in a higher education context is built on three key assumptions:

• **The main purpose of referencing is to facilitate the development and**

transmission of knowledge. This development and transmission is powered by human endeavour and communication; referencing is one element in this communication process.

- As students progress through higher education they are expected, increasingly to become more critical of ideas and theories and their application in models and practices. This critical approach includes the intelligent selection and presentation of ideas and an awareness of their sources; **referencing is a practical manifestation of this engagement with knowledge**.
- The **standardization of referencing practice supports this communication process**. References should be presented in such a way that allows everyone who has learned the practice to recognize and understand the meaning of codes and formulas presented.

These three key assumptions underpin six specific and knowledge-related reasons for referencing.

Six knowledge-related reasons for referencing

1 Facilitates the tracing of the origin of ideas.
2 Helps you to build a web of ideas.
3 Supports your own voice in academic writing.
4 Validates arguments.
5 Helps to spread knowledge.
6 Acknowledges the work of others.

---

1 Tracing the origin of ideas

Academic study involves not just presenting and describing ideas, but also being aware of where they came from, who developed them, why and when. The 'when' is particularly important. Ideas, models, theories and practices originate from somewhere and someone. These are often shaped by the social norms and practices prevailing at the time and place of their origin, and the student in higher education needs to be aware of these influences.

Referencing, therefore, plays an important role in helping to locate and place ideas and arguments in their historical, social, cultural and geographical contexts. As one student in the research study commented:

> It does help to strengthen arguments, as you make reference to current arguments and debates. Without it, it would be impossible to cite the origins of the debate within the essay.
>
> (Postgraduate, Sustainable Development)

Learning builds on learning. However, like trying to discover the 'real' source of a mighty river, there are often many contributory networks to knowledge, and it is sometimes impossible to work back to the beginning and to the origin of an idea. This point is pursued in Chapter 4.

All you can do, sometimes, is to reference **a** source; a source that is immediately relevant to your assignment and particular argument and one that appears to be reliable and valid in relation to the arguments presented by you.

2 A web of ideas

Knowledge connects and spreads: the past connects with the present and has an impact on the future. As you build your argument in an assignment, it is rather like a spider building its web. You build carefully engineered connections between ideas. You advance an argument in one section, but then counter it with another threaded and connected group of ideas, each supported by its own referenced evidence. But you have at the centre your own position, your own place in the scheme of things; your point of view.

3 Finding your own voice

Many students, when they enter higher education, are confused about a gap they perceive between the conventions of academic writing and the need to make their **own** points in essays. Some tutors will, on the one hand, encourage students to develop their own ideas, while emphasizing the need for them to cite and refer to the work of experts in the particular subject area. Other tutors will encourage personal opinions in assignments; others will not. This apparent confusion can sometimes result in assignments that are an unsuccessful blend of the personal and the academic. One student saw it this way:

> setting out author's views one after another, without any of your own thoughts in between . . . leads to your work appearing as a thicket of speech marks and parentheses.
>
> (Undergraduate, Japanese Studies and Politics)

However, you can strive to gain **ownership** of your own work in the following ways:

- You can decide which position or direction to take in an assignment.
- You can select evidence that allows **you** to present a strong set of arguments or descriptions.
- You can summarize or paraphrase in **your** own words what you read.
- You can write in a style that comes from within.

The perspective you take, the ideas you present, the conclusion you reach, can all be your choice; referencing helps this process. The process is summarized in the flow chart (Figure 2.1).

You can read more about this issue of finding your own voice in assignments in Chapter 7, 'Frequently asked questions', sections 17 and 18, and by reading Chapter 8 of this book.

You can present an argument in an assignment by:

1. Stating your point of view early in the assignment and presenting a clear and consistent rationale to support it.

2. Offering **reliable evidence**, or illustrative examples, to support your argument. This is evidence that you have read in reputable and authoritative texts, articles, newspapers, Internet sites and so on.

3. Showing where this evidence has come from: by citing your sources and listing all your sources in the reference or bibliography section at the end of your assignment.

4. Showing that you are aware of, and have considered, arguments that are counter to your own. You will need to summarize counter-arguments in a clear, accurate and undistorted way.

5. Being able to show why the arguments you have chosen to advance are more convincing for you than others.

FIGURE 2.1 Flow chart of argument presentation process

4 Validity of arguments

To be taken seriously, you must present valid evidence in assignments. Aristotle, around 350 BC, argued that persuasive rhetoric included *Logos*: appeals to logic to persuade an audience through sound reasoning. This is done by the presentation of reliable evidence, usually in the form of facts, definitions, statistics and other data that has an appeal to the intelligence of a particular audience. This ageless principle can be applied equally to written arguments. Referencing reliable and valid evidence in assignments has such an appeal to the intelligence of the reader.

Referencing also enables your tutors to check for themselves the accuracy and validity of the evidence presented. In particular, they will want to ensure you are using ideas from the past in a way that is relevant or original to the assignment topic under discussion. Do not assume tutors have read everything on the subject; they may be unfamiliar with the work you cite, so may need to check it themselves.

5 Spreading knowledge

Referencing also presents an opportunity for the tutor and other readers to advance their own knowledge. It gives them the possibility of tracing the sources you cite and using the same evidence for their own purposes. You have probably discovered already how useful bibliographies and lists of references at the end of journal articles can be in identifying other related sources for your own research. Once you start following up sources in bibliographies, it can open up a fascinating trail of knowledge. One source leads to another; you begin to build your own web of learning around a subject.

6 An appreciation

Education needs ideas, arguments and perspectives to thrive. But these have to be tested rigorously and subjected to the critical scrutiny of others. This is done by researching, preparing and presenting work into the public domain, which, as was noted earlier, is a formidable task for any writer, and one that can sometimes take years to achieve. Referencing is, then, also about giving appreciation: a modest genuflection to the work of others. It is about showing courtesy and respect, and about honouring the hard work of writers and commentators – by acknowledging them in your assignments. As one student commented:

> I see it as quid pro quo . . . If you had produced the original thought you would be pretty gutted if someone 'stole' it!
>
> (Undergraduate, Theology)

Three other student-related reasons

From a student perspective, there are three other reasons why referencing is important:

1 Your reading, and influences on your work
2 Marking criteria
3 Avoiding plagiarism.

Your reading, and influences on your work

Tutors will be also interested in your list of references or bibliography to identify what authors or sources have been influential in moulding or shaping the direction taken by you in your research. As one student commented: 'It helps the marker see the evolution of your ideas' (Undergraduate, English and Philosophy). The tutors, may, as a result, offer comment on the absence or inclusion of any particular commentator or theorist in an assignment. Your sources may also occasionally help your tutors, by introducing new authors and ideas to them, thus broadening their own knowledge.

Marking criteria

> During my first year . . . I did not understand why lecturers made such a big deal about referencing and plagiarism. Well, today I understand that it is a crucial part of academic assignments – in fact, [it] is about educating yourself, which means researching, comparing contrasting views, being critical about what you read etc.
>
> (Undergraduate, Events Management and Psychology)

The selection of relevant evidence and accurate referencing is an important element in the marking of assignments, particularly at postgraduate level. Accurate referencing can often make the difference between a pass, credit or distinction. Accurate referencing is also a tangible demonstration to your tutor of your research, intellectual integrity and the care you have taken in preparing to write the assignment.

Avoiding plagiarism

Finally, accurate referencing will help you to avoid being accused of plagiarism. Western concepts of plagiarism are based on an economic model of capitalism and the notion that someone can claim **ownership** of an idea if it has been presented in the public domain in some tangible way. However, the explosion of global communication mediums has created difficulties in identifying original sources of ideas, and there is a grey area between deliberate cheating and carelessness with referencing – or ignorance of it. However, you can read more about this in Chapter 4.

Some milestones in referencing history

- Referencing can be traced back to back to Roman jurists who 'provided very precise references to the earlier legal treatises they drew upon' (Grafton 1997, pp.29–30). In other early manuscripts annotation, glosses, or explanations, were included to connect the finished work to its sources.
- The invention of printing in the late fifteenth century that made ideas more accessible and established the notion of an author. The growth of printing encouraged people to write and to make a living from their ideas and talent for writing. It also encouraged the cult of personality, and the emergence and promotion of artists distinguished by their style of writing (Eisenstein 1983). This led to writers wanting to protect their work against plagiarism.
- The Statute of Anne, passed into law on 10 April 1710, was the first Copyright Act in the world; it established both copyright for the authors of books and other writings, and the principle of a fixed term of protection against piracy for published works.
- The development of printing also standardized the practice of annotation into printed footnotes. These appeared within scholarly works from the eighteenth century onwards. References appeared in textbooks in footnotes and were referred to in the

text by printers' symbols, including asterisks and daggers. These influenced the growth of referencing styles from the nineteenth century onward.

- The development and growth of universities in the nineteenth century in Europe and the USA resulted in the mass examination of student knowledge by way of essays and examinations. There was a rigorous testing of knowledge and, as part of this, students were expected to cite the origins of ideas and offer detailed analysis and interpretation of sources. Citing and analysing the works of authors became a way for students to demonstrate their scholarly engagement with a text.
- In the twentieth century, a range of referencing styles has developed, all building on these earlier foundations.

3

The 'what' and 'when' of referencing

What to reference • Primary and secondary sources • Choosing sources
• References and bibliographies • When to reference • When you do not need to
reference • The big issue for students: time – and lack of it!

> The problem I have with referencing is that I never know when **not** to do it.
>
> (Undergraduate, Economics and Politics)

This section of the book is about the range of sources that can be referenced, and about the criteria for evaluating them, particularly Internet sources. It is also about the occasions when you should reference – and when it is not necessary. It is also about ways of saving time: by more effective note-making, and by the use of referencing management software.

But first, before you read on, try answering the questions in the quiz in Figure 3.1.

To check your responses, you can read the remainder of this chapter and look at the quiz answers in Appendix 1.

What to reference

Most information or other forms of communication, including performance and visual arts, that have been written, recorded, filmed or presented into the public domain in some way to others can potentially be used. This obviously includes an increasing range of Internet sources, but can include unlikely subjects, such as display boards, postcards and advertising – all of which can be of interest to, among others,

Look at the following situations that can occur when writing assignments and decide if a citation is needed.

	Yes	No
1. When you include tables, photographs, statistics and diagrams in your assignment. These may be items directly copied or a source of data collation which you have used.		
2. When describing or discussing a theory, model or practice associated with a particular writer.		
3. When you summarize information drawn from a variety of sources about what has happened over a period, and the summary is unlikely to be a cause of dispute or controversy.		
4. To give weight or credibility to an argument that you believe is important.		
5. When giving emphasis to a particular idea that has found a measure of agreement and support among commentators.		
6. When pulling together a range of key ideas that you introduced and referenced earlier in the assignment.		
7. When stating or summarizing obvious facts, and when there is unlikely to be any significant disagreement with your statements or summaries.		
8. When including quotations.		
9. When you copy and paste items from the Internet and where no author's name is shown.		
10. When paraphrasing or summarizing (in your own words) another person's work that you feel is particularly significant, or likely to be a subject of debate.		

FIGURE 3.1 Quiz on understanding when to reference

historians, sociologists and communication and media studies students. The 'Miscellaneous' section of Chapter 9 illustrates how to reference some of the less obvious areas.

However, there is no point in referencing anything that cannot be read, heard or seen by another who wants to check the same source. So personal conversations on the telephone, and text messages, for example, can be mentioned in the main body of an assignment, but should not be referenced, unless there is some audio or written record of the discussion that can be heard or read by others (see the example of referencing text messages in Chapter 9). Emails, summarized or quoted entirely or partially, can be both cited in the text of an assignment and referenced, providing you save or record them in some form and can make them available to your tutor, if required. Interviews you conduct for research can also be cited in the text, and referenced, provided you have evidence that the interview took place. This can take the form of an audio recording, completed questionnaire, transcript or notes taken at the time.

The important point to bear in mind in selecting evidence for use in assignments is about their **credibility** and **reliability**, and distinguishing between primary and secondary sources.

Primary and secondary sources

What is the difference between primary and secondary sources?

- **Primary source**: this is evidence that comes directly from the people involved in the event or phenomenon in question. This would include theories, models, ideas, interpretations, definitions and practices as described and presented by their originators, rather than their commentators.
- **Secondary sources**: these include material produced about the event or phenomenon, including the commentary or interpretation of others about theories, models, ideas, definitions and practices. They would include, for example, reportage material in newspapers, magazines, reference books and on the Internet.

Try and use **primary** sources whenever possible in your assignments for your central definitions, main descriptions, quotations, key points, arguments and assertions; and **secondary** material for lesser definitions, factual information, illustrative examples, and supporting points.

Choosing sources

The important thing is to choose sources that give credence, authority and support to the ideas and arguments that you present. Your tutor will suggest a range of reliable sources, and this will be your starting point, but you will also be expected to look beyond the recommended reading and to search out relevant information for yourself. If you do this, and connect relevant evidence gained from additional reading to your assignment, this can sometimes make the difference between a pass and a distinction grade.

In this respect, you will find that recommended books and other sources will prove – because of the accurate referencing that has gone into them – to be rich veins of additional information. If you read a particular chapter as a starting point for research into an assignment topic, the references or bibliography will often point you in the right direction of other relevant sources.

There are four main sets of questions (see Table 3.1) you can ask of any source, concerning:

- Relevance and bias
- Currency
- Accuracy
- Coverage.

Table 3.1 Interrogating sources

Relevance and bias	Currency
• To what extent is the source relevant and applicable to the assignment?	• When was the source originally published? Are the ideas, practices, assumptions etc. still valid? You need to ask if the ideas expressed are a product of a particular time and place in history that no longer applies today
• Does the information presented give a partial or restricted view of the subject?	
• How balanced and objective does the language in the source appear to be?	
• Are counter-arguments to the author's own ideas treated with respect? If not, why not?	• Has the author revised or changed his or her views since the date of the original source? If so, when, why, and how?
Authority	**Scope**
• Is the source authoritative enough to be included in the assignment? For example, is the source a credible one, e.g. a reputable publishing company or a peer-reviewed journal?	• How universal or general are the ideas, models or practices described in the source? Do they have a limited geographical or occupational application?
• Do other authors refer to and discuss this source?	• Do the ideas in the source span a range of cultures or are they just applicable to particular groups?
• How credible is the source to you? You can turn your own reservations into a starting point of critical enquiry about it	

The value of using academic journals in your research

The importance and value of using academic peer-reviewed journals in assignments was highlighted in a study by Zeegers and Giles (1996), which analysed essays submitted by over 500 first year undergraduate biology students. A positive correlation was found for the relationship between the number of relevant journal articles referred to in the assignment and the level of mark awarded: 'Most students who were awarded a credit grade or higher used five journal articles or more and spent on average 20 hours reading them' (p.452). The number of relevant journal articles read and the number of hours spent reading generally, and writing the essay, appears also to have been a significant factor in the award of good marks to geography students (Hounsel 1984), and to psychology students (Norton 1990).

(Neville, 2009, pp. 87–8)

References and bibliographies

At the end of your assignment you will produce a list that is headed either **'Bibliography'** or **'References'** (Table 3.2), unless you have been asked by your tutor to include both in the assignment. (Some styles of referencing refer to these lists respectively as 'Works consulted' and 'Works cited'). What is the difference between a list of 'References' and a 'Bibliography'? The terms are often used synonymously, but there is a difference in meaning between them.

Table 3.2 References and bibliographies

Bibliography (or 'Works consulted')	References (or 'Works cited')
If you wish to list the sources you made specific reference to (cited) in your assignment, **and** give details of other sources consulted, (but not directly cited), then you can include all the sources under one sub-heading: **'Bibliography'**.	If, however, you have cited – made specific reference to – all the sources you consulted in the assignment, your list will be headed **'References'**.
	If you make a point of reading selectively, it is likely that you will make use of everything you read and refer directly to it in your assignment. In that event, it will be perfectly correct to just have a 'References' list instead of a 'Bibliography'; it will certainly not go against you.

- **References** are the items you have read and **specifically referred to** (or cited) in your assignment.
- A **bibliography** is a list of everything you read in preparation for writing an assignment. A bibliography will, therefore, normally contain sources that you have cited **and** those you found to be influential, but decided not to cite. A bibliography can give a tutor an overview of which authors have influenced your ideas and arguments, even if you do not specifically refer to them.

When to reference

When to reference? This is a recurring question, and one that can produce, unfortunately, a range of different answers from tutors. Angélil-Carter (2000), for example, found inconsistencies among staff at one higher education institution, particularly in the area of what constituted common knowledge, which does not need referencing. 'Common knowledge' to one tutor, was not always the same as to another, even in the same subject area (more comment on what is common knowledge to come later in this chapter).

Knowing when to reference is as important as understanding how to reference; this can establish your credibility with your tutors.

When to reference: six scenarios

You should reference evidence in assignments in the following situations:

1 To inform the reader of the source of tables, statistics, diagrams, photographs and other illustrations included in your assignment
2 When describing or discussing a theory, model, practice or example associated with a particular writer; or using their work to illustrate examples in your text (this links specifically to the next two items)
3 To give weight or credibility to an argument supported by you in your assignment
4 When giving emphasis to a particular theory, model or practice that has found a measure of agreement and support amongst commentators
5 To inform the reader of the sources of direct quotations or definitions in your assignment
6 When paraphrasing another person's work, which is outside the realm of common knowledge, and that you feel is particularly significant, or likely to be a subject of debate.

See the following examples (in the Harvard Style of referencing) of these six scenarios for when to reference

1 To inform the reader of sources of the tables, photographs, statistics or diagrams presented in your assignment (either copied in their original form or collated by you)

Example

The surface temperatures in the world have increased by 1 degree Fahrenheit, or 0.6 degrees Celsius, since the mid-1970s, and the highest surface temperature ever recorded by the National Aeronautics and Space Administration (NASA) was in 2005. Climatologists generally agree that the five warmest years since the late nineteenth century have been within the decade 1995–2005, with the National Oceanic and Atmospheric Administration (NOAA) and the World Meteorological Organization (WMO) ranking 2005 as the second warmest year behind 1998 (Hansen 2005).

---

2 When describing or discussing a theory, model, practice associated with particular writers; or using their work to illustrate examples in your text. You may, for example, compare and contrast the views of established authors in the field.

Example

A major study of British school leavers by Maizels (1970) concluded that parents had a major influence on the kind of work entered by their children. The children were influenced over a long period of time by the values and ideas about work of their parents. A later study (Ashton and Field 1976), reached the same conclusion, and showed a link between the social and economic status of parents and the work attitudes and aspirations of their teenage children.

3 To give weight or credibility to an argument presented in your assignment.

> **Example**
>
> Handy (1995) has argued that federalism is a way of making sense of large organizations, and that the power and responsibility that drives federalism is a feature of developed societies and can be extended into a way forward for managing modern business. In relation to power, Handy argues that 'authority must be earned from those by whom it is exercised' (p.49). Respect must be earned from employees, and not expected simply because of one's rank.

4 When giving emphasis to a particular theory, model or practice that has found a measure of agreement and support among commentators.

> **Example**
>
> As the behavioural response of communication apprehension (CA) is to avoid or discourage interaction with others, it is not surprising that CA has been linked to feelings of loneliness, isolation, low self-esteem and the inability to discuss personal problems with managers or others (Daly and Stafford 1984; Mc Croskey et al. 1977; Mc Croskey and Richmond 1987; Richmond 1984; Scott and Rockwell 1997).

In the above example, the student cites five sources, all saying much the same thing, to emphasize and give credibility to an important point summarized in the assignment. The use of multiple authors can add weight to a summary, particularly if the idea is a controversial one. However, citing six authors is the suggested maximum for this purpose, and citing two or three is the more usual practice.

5 To inform the reader of the sources of direct quotations or definitions in your assignment.

> **Example**
>
> Cable (2001) argues that Freeman became ever more resentful of the way he was treated by publishers. It appears he felt that his Oxbridge education should have accorded him more respect from his contemporaries. He talked 'bitterly of a certain titled young gentleman who treated him as an equal on The High in Oxford but who, on Saxmundham railway station, refused to acknowledge him' (p.5). However, Cable

> argues that this snobbishness was also in Freeman's own character, so he was particularly sensitive when the snubs were directed at him!

If the quotation is by a well-known person and is included just to add colour and general interest to your writing, it does not need to be given a full reference entry. But if in doubt, always supply a full reference entry for this type of quotation.

If the quote is taken from a printed book or journal, you always need to include the page number in the citation so the reader can go straight to that page to find it. If it is an electronic source the URL address, which will be listed in the full reference, should take the reader to the relevant web page or screen.

6 When paraphrasing another person's idea or definition that you feel is particularly significant or likely to be a subject of debate.

Example

We all perceive the world around us in ways that are often unique to us through a series of personal filters, and we 'construct' our own versions of reality (Kelly 1955).

Note: In this example the student paraphrases an idea that Kelly originally outlined in 1955. The inverted commas around 'construct' suggest this is a significant word used by Kelly to describe a key concept. By citing the source the student is, in effect, saying 'this is **Kelly**'s idea; I am just paraphrasing it'.

When you do not need to reference

However, there are four situations when you do not need to reference sources. These are:

1 When presenting historical overviews
2 When presenting your own experiences
3 In conclusions, when you are repeating ideas previously referenced
4 When summarizing what is regarded as 'common knowledge'.

1 Historical overviews

You do not need to reference information drawn from a **variety of sources** to summarize what has happened over a period of time, when those sources state much the same things and when your summary is unlikely to be a cause of dispute or controversy.

In the example that follows, the student summarizes the topic generally, and has used for this purpose a number of different and reliable sources, which all agreed on the reasons for the growth in call centres.

> The growth in call centres in the West was encouraged by economic and technological factors. From the late 1970s the growth of the service sector focused the attention of large organizations on communication with customers in more cost-effective and streamlined ways. This growth of a service sector economy connected with advances in telecommunications and changes in working practices in Western companies. The logic of call centres was, that a centralized approach and rationalization of organizational operations would reduce costs, while producing a standard branded image to the world.

However, if the student had used just one source for the summary, this should be cited and referenced.

2 Your own experiences and observations

You do not need to reference your own experiences or observations, although you should make it clear that these are your own. For example, you could use the first person term 'I' to do this, although not all tutors encourage this style of personal writing. If you are discouraged from writing in the first person, you could say something like, 'it has been this author's (or this writer's) experience that . . .'. If, however, you have had your work published in a journal, book or other source, you could cite your own published work in support of your own experiences. For more information on these points, see Chapter 7, 'Frequently asked questions', sections 17 and 18, and Chapter 8, 'How to express your own ideas in assignments'.

3 Summaries or conclusions

You do not need to reference again if pulling together a range of key ideas that you introduced and referenced earlier in the assignment. For example, it can be good practice in writing, particularly in a long assignment, to summarize ideas before moving on to another line of discussion. Also, when you reach the concluding sections of your assignment and begin to draw your arguments together, you would not need to cite sources previously referenced, unless you were introducing new material, or introducing a new perspective drawn from previously cited sources.

4 Common knowledge

This is the most problematic of the four, as there can disagreement among academics on what constitutes common knowledge. One definition is:

> Information that is presumed to be shared by members of a specific 'community' – an institution, a city, a national region, the nation itself . . . a particular race, ethnic group, religion, academic discipline, professional association, or other such classification.

> (Hopkins 2005)

Common knowledge has two main elements: common knowledge in the public domain; and common knowledge within a subject area or discipline.

In the public domain, you are using common knowledge when sharing and expressing generally undisputed facts circulating freely, publicly and without the restraint of copyright, and when there is unlikely to be any significant disagreement with your statements or summaries of this information. This would include undisputed information found in reference books and encyclopedias.

However, note the following differences between fact and opinion:

- Thomas Hardy wrote *Tess of the d'Urbervilles*: **Fact**.
- Thomas Hardy wrote *Tess of the d'Urbervilles*, and the poetic beauty of his language raises it above other novels in the rural tradition (Winchcombe 1978): **Opinion**.

The first sentence contains an undisputed fact. However, the second concludes with an opinion, and an author is cited to support the assertion. The wise student would also look for, and include, **other evidence** to support this opinion, by paraphrasing or quoting Winchcombe's reasons for making this assertion, and by seeking evidence from other literary critics to support (or dispute) the view.

Common knowledge also includes general descriptions of folklore and traditions in the public domain, although specific author comment on these would be referenced. For example, you might talk generally about the traditions in a particular area, but would need to reference what a particular author had to say about, for example, the deeper meanings or origins of these.

Common knowledge would also cover commonplace observations or aphorisms on the world, for example, that the dark winters can have a depressing impact on our moods, although if you produced any specific evidence to that effect, this would be cited.

The University of Queensland (2006) include the following six examples of common knowledge when referencing would not be required:

1 That Neil Armstrong landed on the Moon in July 1969 (common fact of history)
2 That Alexander Fleming discovered penicillin (common fact of history)
3 The definition of photosynthesis (common knowledge in the discipline)
4 That humans need food and water for survival (commonsense observation)
5 That Count Dracula lived in Transylvania (accepted folklore)
6 'Life wasn't meant to be easy' (aphorism).

Secondly, there is common knowledge within a **subject area or discipline**. Every subject has its own set of commonly agreed codes, assumptions, jargons, formulas or symbols that you will not need to define, explain or reference. These points of understanding may be implicit, soon become clear, or are negotiated early in courses between tutors and their students. However, a student new to higher education would be wise to reference sources liberally at first, rather than frugally, until they have established the common knowledge 'rules of the game' on their particular course.

The big issue for students: time – and lack of it!

One of the main complaints from students in the 'Have your say' part of my research was about the large amount of time involved in referencing. This was aligned with the frustration of attending to the detail required by a particular referencing style.

> It's hugely time-consuming and a real pain, and that's because it takes so long to do it.
>
> (Undergraduate, English Literature)

> More time ends up being spent on checking the references than the work itself – which is ridiculous!
>
> (Foundation Studies student)

> I could not believe how long it took me to do the formatting of my references.
>
> (Postgraduate, Engineering)

There are two main issues to be addressed here. First, there is the issue of making thorough notes as you read; the second is about investing time to learn how to use referencing software – to save time in the longer term.

Saving time (1): the importance of making notes

At one of the research workshops a student complained bitterly of the time referencing had taken her. But it was clear that a large part of the problem was caused because by her own failure to record details of her sources as she encountered them.

It can be incredibly frustrating to discover halfway through writing an assignment that you have not taken a full note, or any note at all, of a particular source that you belatedly decide you need to use. It may be that you read something, thought 'that's useful', and meant to take note of it, but did not! You then have to start searching for the source, and if it is on the Internet, or buried in the depths of a book, it can be very time-consuming to track it down. One student commented on the frustration this causes:

> Sometimes I'm not organised enough, so lose references and spend a long time looking for a reference I found a week ago.
>
> (Undergraduate, Geography)

The moral is that if you think a source might be useful to a particular assignment or examination, then take an immediate note of it. This is a point made by a student who had organized her notes in a simple, but effective, way:

> I have learnt to have a notebook ready at the start of each assignment. I write a letter of the alphabet on each page and record each reference under the correct

letter as I go along. Although this is time consuming . . . it saves time at the end when I am trying to put the references list into alphabetical order.

(Undergraduate, Nursing Studies)

Note-taking and note-making serve a number of purposes. Notes act as a summary or reinforcement of the main points of what you saw, heard or read. They can also be a way of prompting you to think about your own response to the ideas of others.

However, for referencing purposes, notes are also an essential **record** of information sources. They also remind you of other things you should do, for example, other sources to check. You need to organize a system of note-making that suits you, although filing notes away by author, or topic, particularly for the name-date or author-page referencing styles, tend to be the best approaches.

Your notes can then be used both to remind you of the topic for revision purposes, and to help you compile a list of references or a bibliography. This can be done either manually, or with the help of bibliographic software (see later in this chapter).

The difference between taking and making notes is about the transition between a passive, to an active process, as described in Table 3.3.

Table 3.3 Note-taking and note-making

Note-*taking*	Note-*making*
A process that involves writing or recording what you hear or read in a descriptive way This is the first stage of the process of producing effective notes	An advanced process that involves reviewing, synthesizing, and connecting ideas from the lecture or reading; and presenting information in readable and creative ways, and in ways that will help you revise more effectively

Although electronic note-making is an important alternative to using manual notes, it is not always convenient to use a personal computer. Manual notes are still an important way of recording information, particularly in lectures and tutorials or in other situations when it is inconvenient to use electronic note-making systems.

Note-making, then, in addition to being an essential **record of sources**, has three main purposes:

1 A process for the **summarization** of main points
2 A process for **synthesizing ideas**, which involves looking for, and recording, the connections between ideas
3 A process for encouraging **critical analysis**: by adding your own observations and comments to the ideas summarized or paraphrased.

The example of note-making in Figure 3.2 illustrates how a student adds his or her own comments to the summary of the source, which can later help the student to plan and organize the critical discussion stage of the assignment. The topic or key words act as a form of subtitling to the main points, and the full details of the source are recorded at the top of the sheet. Notes can also serve as prompts for future action, as shown in Figure 3.2.

Topic & key words	Main points:
Management of change	Bridges identifies four stages of individual transition to change: disengagement, dis-identification, disorientation and disenchantment; individuals must pass through these to change.
Bridges 4 Stages of transition: Individual responses to change	Disengagement: breaking away from past activity; typical responses: loss of interest; unresponsive Disidentification: hanging on to the past; distorted view of future; typical responses: pessimism about new situation Disenchantment: anger at new changes; typical responses: self pity; sabotage; back-stabbing Disorientation: lost and confused; typical behaviours: continually asking questions/seeking reassurance.

Comments
Does this apply to everyone experiencing change? What about those who actively seek change in their lives? 'Must' individuals pass through **all** these stages? Does this apply to all cultures? How did Bridges arrive at this idea? The book was published 1980; how valid is the idea now?

To do: I need to check out to see if Bridges has revised the idea since 1980.

FIGURE 3.2 Example of a note-making sheet

Source:
Bridges, W. (1980). *Transitions: Making sense of life's changes*. Reading, MA: Addison-Wesley.

Saving time (2): using referencing management software

Referencing management software can help you to manage your referencing in a time-efficient way. Two students said this about it:

> Throughout the Masters and PhD I have used Endnote software to assist with organization of references and this has transformed the way I work. I can input and access references throughout my work with ease, which has taken away the negative aspects I used to complain about.
>
> (Doctoral student, Geography)

> The package in MS Word allows a simple method of recording any reference and producing a list of sources. This is extremely useful when writing an essay or report over a period of a few weeks.
>
> (Postgraduate, Management Studies)

In addition to the referencing management system built into more recent additions of MS Word, there is now a wide range of referencing management software systems designed to help students manage referencing; Endnote, as mentioned by the student quoted earlier, is just one of many packages available. Many universities provide these free for students to use within the institution, or enable students to purchase the software themselves, often at a discounted price. Features of this software include:

- Searching the Internet for references and importing to your database
- 'Cite while you write' features, which includes organizing information retrieved into a particular referencing style, including all the styles featured in this book
- Linking the citation in the text with the full reference, and a facility for ensuring that any citation featured in the text corresponds with a full reference entry
- Editing features: easy addition to references already entered
- Keyword sorting alphabetically of references.

There are obvious advantages for students in using this software, in both information retrieval and in organizing the citation and full referencing in an assignment. However, all software does have its limitations, and, arguably, no one system can offer completely all that students need for fully integrated information search and easy transfer of information into citation and full reference forms. With some systems, for example, the search facility may be limited; with others there may be particular problems, such as confusion in distinguishing between primary and secondary authors, or problems with referencing certain types of uncommon source (Shapland 1999).

The cost of these systems is also a factor, as site licences can be expensive and this is a major determinant of which system an institution finally adopts. Most institutions allow students to use the systems free when they are on site. However, the software can be expensive for a student to purchase and use privately, and students must decide if the cost is justified in terms of the use they will make of it. It also takes time, effort and practice before students can use the software proficiently.

However, there is no doubt that the effort to learn can be repaid by the consistent and detailed referencing entry that is given. Student user surveys of the referencing software, RefWorks (McGrath 2006; Stevens 2008), suggest that the majority of students surveyed found the software easy to use and saved them time by helping them to reference correctly and store their sources. Two users were quoted:

It saves me a tremendous amount of time. I don't have to spend any time on technical matters, such as referencing layout etc.

So much quicker to insert references [with the software] I don't know how to write references so this really helped. I would be lost without it.
(Both students quoted in Stevens 2008, App. 5)

Students should talk to the librarian at their institution and find out what referencing management software is available, and what training in its use is available.

4

Plagiarism

Plagiarism? ● Three main forms of plagiarism ● Levels of plagiarism ● Why do students plagiarize? ● International students ● Patchwork writing ● Discouraging plagiarism ● How to avoid plagiarism ● Plagiarism exercise

A fear of plagiarism now forces students to research any and every idea they might wish to include in a paper/assignment . . . I no longer understand when referencing is not necessary.

(Postgraduate, Health Studies)

I'm just scared about referencing wrongly and having marks deducted for it or accidentally being punished for plagiarism.

(Undergraduate, Economics)

When you start university referencing and plagiarism is completely hyped up to the point that I was really concerned that anything I wrote might be seen as plagiarism; after all, some things are difficult to say in other words.

(Undergraduate: Geography with Business)

Anxiety, about being accused of plagiarism, underpinned many of the frustrations and insecurities expressed by students in my research. Discussion about plagiarism has been a dominant concern in higher education over the past decade and it is clear that many students have 'got the message'. However, it has also made many anxious about expressing their own views in assignments, as they question if it really **is** their own view that they are expressing, which in turn raises the issue of where do 'our' own ideas come from? At what point can I take 'ownership' of them? And can I risk presenting them as my 'own', when these ideas may now be found, prolific and Internet-fresh, in the public domain?

There is no doubt that plagiarism continues to be a hot topic of discussion in higher education. But it is certainly not a new phenomenon. And you can find all colours of opinion among lecturers: from those who seize on plagiarism as a symptom of slipping academic standards, devaluation of higher education and an erosion of everything they believe higher education should be; to those who feel that there is more than a little intolerance, hypocrisy and inconsistency around the issue.

There are many academics, probably the majority, who oscillate between both positions, genuinely confused – about whether what they read in front of them in an assignment is plagiarism, carelessness, ignorance, misunderstanding, confusion or poor referencing practice. They can be driven to fury when they encounter blatant and wholesale copying, particularly if it comes during a particularly heavy and exhausting period of marking. Yet, when faced with the individual student explaining his or her case for apparently plagiarizing a text, they can understand why it has happened.

It is an issue that runs parallel to a debate with recurring questions about the purpose of higher education in the twenty-first century. Is an insistence on referencing about supporting a system and a process of learning that is a legacy of a different time and society? Are universities enforcing upon you an arcane practice of referencing that you will probably never use again outside of higher education? Or is there something deeper in the practice of referencing that connects with behaving ethically, properly, decently and respecting others – ageless societal values that universities should try to maintain? Plagiarism, from this latter perspective, can be viewed as an attack on these values.

Plagiarism?

But what is plagiarism? There is certainly no single universally agreed definition in Britain. Every institution develops its own definitions and even within these there can be a range of interpretations of what it is – and is not.

It can be argued that all imitative learning is plagiarism. We use ideas from other people all the time, weave them into our working and academic lives, gradually taking ownership of them until we eventually forget who influenced us in the first place; referencing becomes difficult, if not impossible, in some situations (see Angélil-Carter 2000; Lensmire and Beals 1994; Pennycook 1996). However, plagiarism, in an academic context, refers to an intentional decision not to acknowledge the work of others in assignments – or ignoring usually well-publicized obligations to do this.

In general, plagiarism is one of a number of practices deemed by universities to constitute cheating, or in university-speak: 'a lack of academic integrity'. These include:

- Collusion without official approval between two or more students, with the result that identical, or near identical work, is presented by all those involved
- Falsification: where content of assignments, e.g. statistics, has been invented or falsely presented by a student as their own work
- Replication: where a student submits the same, or very similar piece of work, on more than one occasion to gain academic credit
- Taking unauthorized notes into an examination
- Obtaining an unauthorized copy of an examination paper

- Communication with other students in an examination in order to help, or be helped, with answers.
- Impersonation of another person in an examination (Jones et al. 2005).

However, as stated earlier, plagiarism, specifically, is a term used to describe a practice that involves knowingly taking and using another person's **work** and claiming it, directly or indirectly, as your own.

This 'work' is usually something that has been produced by another person, 'published' in some tangible way, and presented formally into the public domain. It is not the ideas per se that are being plagiarized, as ideas can occur to people all the time; it is the **manifestation** of those ideas: in print, Internet, audio-visual, theatrical, cinematic, choreographic or other tangible form. It can also include assignments either ready written, or written to order, and sold from Internet sites, which are then presented to an institution by the buyer as his or her own original work.

Three main forms of plagiarism

As already stated, each institution develops its own interpretation of plagiarism, and it is likely your college or university has already made you aware of theirs. But in general, there are three main forms:

1 Copying another person's work, including the work of another student (with or without their consent), and claiming or pretending it to be your own
2 Presenting arguments that use a blend of your own and a significant percentage of copied words of the original author without acknowledging the source
3 Paraphrasing another person's work, but not giving due acknowledgement to the original writer or organization publishing the writing, including Internet sites. The exceptions to this would be in relation to common knowledge (see Chapter 3).

It sounds straightforward – and at its most blatant form of simply copying great chunks of someone else's work into your own work with or without any form of acknowledgement of the originator, it can be. As Angélil-Carter puts it, 'the true plagiarist writes to conceal the sources' (2000, p.22).

Levels of plagiarism

But life is not that simple, nor students so blatant, although a minority appear to be reckless enough to plagiarize regularly and deliberately in this way (see Carroll 2005). Howard (1995) has tried to unpick the forms of plagiarism that can occur: cheating, non-attribution and patchwork writing. The first is done deliberately, while the second usually results from the inexperience of the student with referencing, or from misunderstanding about academic conventions. The third results when a student tries to put together bits of assorted, copied text to make up an unsatisfactory whole; or what Barrett and Malcolm (2006) call 'omission paraphrasing', which is when a student copies in a single source and selectively changes words and sentences to make it fit the assignment. This latter practice moves them into a grey area betwixt paraphrasing and plagiarism and can lead to criticism, or worse, loss of marks.

The issue of non-attribution, Howard's second point, is a tricky one, as although misunderstanding can certainly be a cause, there is evidence that students do understand that they should cite their sources, but do not always do it, for a variety of reasons. A significant number of students, faced with a heavy workload, easy opportunity, plus pressure to succeed on degree courses, appear to be willing to copy from a printed source or paste from the Internet into their assignments in the hope they will not be noticed.

A study by Jones et al. (2005), for example, found one in five of 171 students from both Engineering and Psychology undergraduate degree courses admitting to copying and pasting material from a website into an assignment without crediting the source. Another study, by Dennis (2005), of 80 undergraduate and postgraduate students on Computer Science degree programmes produced a similar result with a quarter of respondents admitting to activities the institution regarded as plagiarism, which was largely about copying, or partial copying, from printed or web-based sources.

When students are asked what proportion of their peers are engaged in plagiarism, the estimates tend to be high. For example, a survey of 140 students and staff at Northumbria University suggested that 70.9 per cent of students believed that copying a few paragraphs from a book or Internet without citing the source was a common practice. Although this survey dealt with perception, this is important, as perception can transfer into discussion among students, and discussion into action. However, the same survey found only around 6 per cent of students who thought that downloading or buying whole essays from cheat sites or ghost writing services was common practice (Dordoy 2002).

Why do students plagiarize?

So why do students do it? One reason may be that they have always done it – maybe to the point when it becomes ritualized behaviour, and because it is easier and more tempting now than it ever has been to do it.

Hart and Friesner (2004) point out that studies of cheating behaviour in the USA date back to the 1940s. They cite studies from the early 1940s, which suggested that, even then, nearly a quarter of students admitted to some form of cheating behaviour. Twenty years later a study by Bowers in 1964 suggested that three-quarters of a sample group of 5000 students had admitted some form of academic cheating. They may have written on the palms of their hands then, or in dictionaries, prior to their examinations, but now there is the Internet and a vast, open orchard of ideas just waiting to be picked and downloaded.

You now invest a significant amount of your own or your parent's money into higher education and high grades are important to secure interviews at big companies. Higher education is now increasingly viewed by many students as a commodity, and the process of learning as part of a 'commercial transaction'. Dordoy (2002) quotes one student as saying: 'If the University sells itself as a business and people only come to get a bit of paper – then plagiarism will always be a problem' (p.5). The potential challenge and intellectual stimulation of learning at this level gives way to the more expedient business of getting the all-important bit of paper, so screw the rules! Politicians and corporations do it, best-selling authors do it, even Shakespeare is supposed to have done it, so why shouldn't I?

Some students blame the pressure of writing to strict word limits:

> We're expected to cite as many references as possible to gain maximum marks but keep our word limit to 1500. Well, it is almost impossible to use so many references as well as our own words, without it looking like a copy-and-paste job.
>
> (THES 2006)

Dordoy found the most common reasons cited by students for cheating were related to grades, poor time management and ease of opportunity:

* To get a better grade: 59 per cent
* Because of laziness or bad time management: 54 per cent
* Because of easy access to material via the Internet: 40 per cent
* Because they did not understand the rules: 29 per cent
* Because 'it happens unconsciously': 29 per cent (Dordoy 2002).

Dordoy also found that nearly 16 per cent of students felt that it happened because they did not think they would be caught. Students were aware of the pressure staff were under to teach large number of students and to mark hundreds of assignments and were simply taking the chance. Some were also disillusioned about the lacklustre approach to teaching and student support taken by hard-pressed staff and saw plagiarism as a form of retaliation: 'students are extremely proud when they "get one over" on lecturers' (2002, p.5). Other studies (Aggarwal et al. 2002; Culwin et al. 2002; Introna et al. 2003) suggest that students regard copying small amounts of material without citing the source as a trivial, or not particularly serious, breach of academic integrity.

Dennis (2005) also found a similar range of reasons given by students for why **others** cheated. The reasons given by 80 students were ranked as follows, with the most frequently cited at the top:

1 They started too late and ran out of time.
2 They simply could not do the coursework otherwise.
3 They did not think it was wrong.
4 They have to succeed. They got higher marks this way.
5 They did not need to learn that material, just pass the module.
6 They could not keep up with the work.
7 They wanted to see if they could get away with it.
8 They felt the tutor did not care, so why should they.
9 They thought paraphrasing would be disrespectful (Dennis 2005).

International students

This last point about 'disrespectful' paraphrasing is likely to be made by some international students. It is clear there are many different interpretations from one country to another on the practice of referencing in academic writing. What is unacceptable practice in Britain is quite legitimate, and even encouraged, elsewhere. What is regarded in Britain as plagiarism, for example, quoting from sources extensively without referencing them, can be regarded as perfectly normal in other countries, even within Europe (Sherman 1992). There may too, be differences in experience among students from the same country. Lake (2004) found differences among Chinese students studying in Britain, with more than half having no previous experience of referencing in academic writing, but with a third having had some previous experience of referencing in essays written in their own language.

Ha (2006), responding to suggestions that Asian culture contributes to acts of plagiarism, points out that in Vietnam simply copying other people's work is not acceptable and that it is usual practice for Vietnamese students to give a full bibliography at the end of essays, but not to cite individual authors in the main body of the assignment. Vietnamese universities do not regard this as plagiarism, as all the sources featured in the assignment are mentioned in the bibliography. Many teachers in Vietnam do not require students to cite and reference lecture notes given out in class, as there is an implicit understanding of where the notes came from between teacher and student. However, both these practices in Britain could result in the student being criticized, and probably penalized, for plagiarism.

Therefore, there are cultural differences in referencing practice for the international student to adjust to – and most do quickly if they are shown how, and it is explained why. A more significant issue for international students is how to cope with the pressure of writing six or more assignments in any semester, work with others in groups, read and take notes, listen to lectures, and contribute their ideas in tutorials – all in English – a language that many are still struggling to cope with.

They may have gained the requisite minimum English qualification to study in Britain, but these qualifications do not prepare many students for listening to a babble of regional British accents and in understanding all the subtle nuances and by-ways of the English language. It does not help either that they have to wade through baffling jargon, pomposity and the often ludicrous 'academic-speak' in textbooks on recommended reading lists that have been written by some authors more for their academic chums, than for students.

Add to this the small fortune they or their parents spend on paying for a British education, and the economic and social shame that flows from failure, then the pressure is really on them to succeed, and to succeed at any cost. Failure is not an option. They are told they should summarize or paraphrase in their own words, not copy text from books or paste in from the Internet. They may be given, if they are lucky, some practical instruction in referencing. But they are often faced with a task of paraphrasing something that they only half-understand. And they have to do it in a second language, in the best English they can muster, and by tomorrow. So it is no surprise some resort to copying text, and patching together copied ideas, rather than risk the shame of failure, and exposure of their still partial understanding of ideas and the meanings of words: 'taking a bit here and there helps with getting the meaning across. Paraphrasing, if you are not a native speaker, is difficult' (Greek student quoted in Introna et al. 2003, p.25).

Patchwork writing

Putting the issue of plagiarism aside, many academics discourage this form of patch-work writing by arguing that the process of summarization and paraphrasing helps students to gain a deeper level of understanding about a topic. By converting the ideas into a choice of one's own words, you have to think hard about them and thus gain a deeper level of knowledge. This may be true, but some of you may not see it like this.

Students, and not just those from overseas, argue that to put together an argument by patchwork copying does require an understanding of the topic. It requires the ability to select and connect ideas, and this cannot be done successfully if the student does not have a grip on the main arguments and counter-arguments around a topic:

> If you take all the sentences/paragraphs from other authors – then you have to do the work to put it together – you have learned and need a certain understanding of the topic, it is not just blatant copying.
>
> (UK student quoted in Introna et al. 2003, p.24)

This has found some sympathy among some academics. Some commentators, notably Howard (1999) and Introna et al. (2003), have argued that patchwork writing can be viewed as a transitional writing phase for inexperienced students as they struggle to come to terms with the demands and expectations of a subject, and particularly, but not exclusively, if they are trying to do this in a second language.

The entry standard for English language for international students to study in Britain tends to lie between score six and seven in the International English Language System (IELTS), which is somewhere between 'competent user' (band 6) and 'good user' (band 7) of English (Table 4.1).

So a score of 6.5 is somewhere between 'competent' and 'good'. Students in both bands can fall prone to 'misunderstandings', are still only at the stage of understanding 'fairly complex' to 'complex' language (of which there is much in education), and are in

Table 4.1 IELTS Scores 6 and 7

Band 6: Competent user	Band 7: Good user
Has generally effective command of the language despite some inaccuracies, inappropriacies and misunderstandings. Can use and understand fairly complex language, particularly in familiar situations.	Has operational command of the language, though with occasional inaccuracies, inappropriacies and misunderstandings in some situations. Generally handles complex language well and understands detailed reasoning.

(Source: British Council 2006)

a situation that is new, rather than 'familiar'. Given this, then, patchwork writing can be viewed as part of this transition of developing the skill to communicate using formal language and in a detached, third-person way acceptable to the expectations of academics. But is the style of third-person writing still a valid expectation, and if so why?

The convention of academic writing in higher education is still largely one where you are encouraged to step back from the assignment topic and look down at it, as if from afar, and to describe the scene in an objective way. In Britain, students are still largely discouraged from writing in the first person. 'I think' is discouraged, and 'It can be argued' encouraged instead (even though in reality it means the same thing). Teachers expect students to present an impression of objectivity (even though this is an illusion), where arguments can be selected to fit the chosen perspective: 'objective subjectivity', may be the best way to describe what is expected by tutors of students in academic writing.

The able, experienced student has learned the art of selecting material to suit his own viewpoint, but presenting it in a way that gives the veneer of objectivity to the reader – thus satisfying the conventions and traditions of academic writing. The postgraduate student, and certainly one with his or her first degree experience in the UK, has usually learned how to do this. However, the undergraduate and international postgraduate student can both struggle with this, not really knowing what is expected.

This reflects an apparent contradiction: on the one hand, the promise of higher education is that you will develop your own 'independent voice', while on the other, you are expected to conform to norms of writing that seem strangely out of tune with this aim. You are expected to imitate the style of writing of the commentators you read, but these commentators are likely to have a strong command of English and have learned to present their material in a sophisticated way.

Angélil-Carter (2000) argues that permitting the use of the first person 'I' in assignments is an important way of encouraging students to present openly their own words, supported with referenced evidence. Patchwork writing can occur because students feel discouraged about expressing their own views in their own words in the more analytical parts of the assignment. Yet they run the risk in this practice of being accused of plagiarism. The exercise later in this chapter shows examples of patchwork writing that can easily lead students into trouble with their institutions.

Writing in the third person can be an entirely appropriate way of presenting information in the more descriptive and background parts of an assignment. However, the more analytical parts – where the student is expected and encouraged to weigh up arguments – can be considerably more difficult to present when writing in the third person, even for the student with a strong command of English.

Discouraging the use of the 'first person' expression in writing, particularly when engaging with the more discursive parts of an assignment, arguably encourages students to patch together the words of others in the hope of appearing objective. But endorsing a change of writing style, from third to first person, could arguably encourage students to take ownership of the material they introduce into assignments and be more forward with their own ideas. Why not test this argument out on your tutors to see what their response to it is?

One response from them might be that writing in the first person encourages opinionated responses to set questions. But arguably, writing in the first person does not necessarily equate with polemic; one's own view can be presented formally and professionally, and supported with properly cited and referenced evidence. This would be an important way of helping students find their own voice in assignments. Students could be encouraged to seek relevant material that fits the direction they wish to take in an assignment (which happens now), but then to present ideas as their own, in the first person, and in the process take responsibility for them. 'With no authorial voice', writes Angélil-Carter, 'writing is inhibited' (2000, p.128). What do you think? You are part of this debate, too.

Discouraging plagiarism

Plagiarism prevention, rather than prosecution, tends to be the approach adopted by most British universities, although some have been driven to take action to discipline, and even expel students, for worst-scenario case plagiarism, which are usually cases involving repeated incidences of copying wholesale from texts without any attempt at acknowledgement of the original source. Attention has also turned to schools and colleges in an attempt to discourage pupils (and parents) from plagiarism, so that by the time students enter higher education they would have learned effective referencing and techniques of summary and paraphrasing.

Universities are also using software to detect where copied text has been slotted into assignments. Software, such as Turnitin and Ferret, can compare submitted assignments with a database of billions of web pages, and highlight passages that are directly copied. Some institutions are also encouraging students to check their assignments against the software, to highlight and change copied areas before they submit the work. This seems to be producing some positive results.

Barratt and Malcolm (2006), for example, report on a study involving 182 mainly postgraduate International Master's students on Computer Science, Automotive Engineering and Electronics courses. The students were asked to summarize a number of research papers in an essay, and their assignments were submitted to Turnitin and Ferret, with a view to giving feedback on how original their words appeared to be. A threshold of 15 per cent of matching text was used, as it is inevitable that some words and sentences will recur. It was found that 41 per cent of students had submitted work that exceeded this threshold, although on closer inspection a number of these, for a variety of reasons, could not be regarded as plagiarism. However, over a quarter (26 per cent) of assignments was above the threshold, and these students were shown their work with the copied passages highlighted and given an opportunity to resubmit it. On resubmission, the incidence of plagiarism had dropped to 3 per cent overall.

In a survey among Economics and Business Studies, Cohen (2007) found that a trial use of Turnitin had encouraged students to use their own words in assignments, discouraged copying and had helped students with their referencing.

Universities are also looking at the assessments they set, and making these more individual and project based, or written under supervised conditions. They are also looking more critically at the way referencing is taught, and reinforcing the message that good referencing is 'an indication of worthy membership of the academic community' (Hart and Friesner 2004, p.93). They are also regulating their own teaching, typically by peer evaluation, so that lecturers do not implicitly promote plagiarism by giving lectures accompanied by handouts and PowerPoint slides that do not cite the sources for the ideas presented or discussed with students.

They are doing this largely because they feel that they have to and want to. They have to, because the Quality Assurance Agency (QAA) – a watchdog of quality in higher education – seeks assurance from institutions that they are maintaining the quality of higher education, which will attract students, particularly those from overseas, in the first place. They want to, because most academics in higher education are interested in, and proud of, their work; they want students to be stretched intellectually and to gain careers where they can take responsibility and use their talents.

If higher education is devalued by a view from the outside that the degree is not worth the paper it is printed on, then this will do no good for either the morale of teachers or your morale – and career prospects. It is likely that you recognize the importance of this debate. If high standards of integrity are expected of you – and exemplified by the conduct of your tutors – it is likely you will respond positively to this. Who, after spending thousands on a degree programme, wants a qualification at which others will sneer?

How to avoid plagiarism

So, how to avoid plagiarism?

Applying, analysing, criticizing or quoting other people's work is perfectly reasonable and acceptable providing you always:

• Attempt to summarize or restate another person's work, theories or ideas and give acknowledgement to that person. This is usually done by citing your sources and presenting a list of references.

or

• By always **using quotation marks** (or indenting lengthy quotations in your text) to distinguish between the actual words of the writer and your own words. Once again, you should cite all sources and present full details of these in your list of references.

Summarizing and paraphrasing

The way to avoid accusations of plagiarism is to try to summarize or paraphrase what you read, choosing words that seem to do this best for you. You will need to ask your course tutor what style of writing is expected of you. Can you use the first person for the more analytical parts of it? If not, why not?

So what is the difference between paraphrasing and summarizing? Summarizing is about the general; paraphrasing is about the particular (Table 4.2).

Table 4.2 Summarizing and paraphrasing

Summarizing	Paraphrasing
Summarizing involves writing an account, in one's own words, of the main, broad and general meanings of a text	Paraphrasing involves close attention to a **particular section** of a text and attempting, in one's own words, to capture the essence of the original

It can be sometimes difficult, if not impossible, to avoid using some of the author's original words, particularly those that describe or label phenomena. However, you need to avoid simply copying out what the author said, word for word. Choose words that you feel give a true impression of the author's original ideas or action. There is an exercise later in the chapter that looks at the issue of paraphrasing and plagiarism. However, before you look at that, try the exercise on plagiarism awareness that follows.

Exercise

Remind yourself of the definition of plagiarism earlier in this chapter. Then look at the scenarios in Figure 4.1 and decide whether the situation described amounts to plagiarism. Tick the appropriate column.

See answers in Appendix 2

	Yes	No
1. You see a quotation in a book and copy the quotation out word for word into your assignment and do not cite the source.		
2. You see a quotation in a book or Internet site and copy some of the words and add some of your own words and do not cite the source.		
3. You see something on an Internet site, for example, an article from a named journal with a named author. You copy, or copy and paste, from the site into your assignment without citing the source.		
4. You see an interesting and different way of looking at a particular subject on an Internet website. No author's name is shown. You cut and paste the idea into your assignment and do not show the source, i.e. name of website, in your assignment.		
5. You find some interesting photos or other illustrations on a website. You copy the photos or illustrations and paste them into your assignment. You do not cite the artist, photographer or website.		
6. You read a range of interesting summaries of different approaches to a subject on a number of Internet websites. You do not copy and paste, but you paraphrase in your own words the summaries into your assignment. You do not mention the website sources in your assignment.		

	Yes	No
7. You are part of a study group of four or five and you all discuss an assignment that all are required to submit individually. You all agree on the approach and arguments to use in the assignment. One of the students, with a little help from another, writes the assignment that all the members of the group submit individually.		
8. You want to give a historical overview of something that has happened over a long period, for example, general employment trends. You read three or four general textbooks on the topic. They all say much the same thing so you summarize in your own words and do not cite the sources.		
9. You see some statistics in a magazine that are relevant to a report you are writing. There is no author cited. You use the statistics in your assignment and do not give a source, e.g. the magazine.		
10. You find an article summarizing a particular model, theory or practice associated with a particular theorist Mr X. It is a secondary source, which means the writer is summarizing him or herself what Mr X has said. You like this summary, as it says what you believe Mr X has accurately written. You can not think of a better way of summarizing Mr X yourself, so you copy out this summary without referring to the secondary source author.		
11. Your friend is better than you at writing assignments; your strengths are with statistics and mathematics and you have always find writing reports and essays difficult. You discuss a particular assignment together and you help your friend gain a better knowledge of the subject. Your friend is grateful for making things clearer and offers to write the assignment for you both. Your friend writes the assignment and you copy it. You both submit it as an individual assignment.		
12. You have an assignment to write and you do the research for it. In the process of writing the assignment, a new way of looking at the subject suddenly occurs to you, which you feel is unique. You put forward this 'unique' perspective on the subject and submit the assignment. However, you discover a day or two later that someone else has already published the same idea and perspective a few years earlier.		

FIGURE 4.1 Quiz 2

Plagiarism exercise

Is it plagiarism?

This exercise contains a number of examples of attempts to transfer the information from the original journal extract shown below into seven essay introductions. Read each example and decide whether the attempt amounts to plagiarism of the original journal article.

Original extract

For thousands of years, outsiders have regarded China as a xenophobic country. However, the stereotypes have been changing since China opened up its economy in 1979. Now, the encouragement of foreign direct investment (FDI) and international technology transfer (ITT) lies at the heart of economic relations between foreign countries and China. The international flows of capital, information and technology facilitate the economic growth of China and the influence of multinational enterprises (MNEs). The boom in FDI and ITT has brought to the fore the issue of intellectual property rights (IPRs) as a major topic in the economic development of China. Although a historical review shows that the germination of the concept of IPRs in China goes back more than 100 years, in reality no effective system of intellectual property protection (IPP) existed until very recent times.

(Source: Yang and Clarke 2004, p.12)

Now comment on the following extracts from student assignments. Do they amount to plagiarism – or not?

Example 4.1

This essay is about intellectual property (IP) in general and about the situation in China today, and about China's relationship with the West in relation to this issue. For thousands of years, outsiders have regarded China as a xenophobic country. However, the stereotypes have been changing since China opened up its economy in 1979. Now, the encouragement of foreign direct investment (FDI) and international technology transfer (ITT) lies at the heart of economic relations between foreign countries and China. The international flows of capital, information and technology facilitate the economic growth of China and the influence of multinational enterprises (MNEs). The boom in FDI and ITT has brought to the fore the issue of intellectual property rights (IPRs) as a major topic in the economic development of China. Although a historical review shows that the germination of the concept of IPRs in China goes back more than 100 years, in reality no effective system of intellectual property protection (IPP) existed until very recent times.

Plagiarism?   Yes   No   Not sure

Example 4.2

This essay is about intellectual property (IP) in general and about the situation in China today, and about China's relationship with the West in relation to this issue. For thousands of years, outsiders have regarded China as a xenophobic country.

However, the stereotypes have been changing since China opened up its economy in 1979. Now, the encouragement of foreign direct investment (FDI) and international technology transfer (ITT) lies at the heart of economic relations between foreign countries and China. The international flows of capital, information and technology facilitate the economic growth of China and the influence of multinational enterprises (MNEs). The boom in FDI and ITT has brought to the fore the issue of intellectual property rights (IPRs) as a major topic in the economic development of China. Although a historical review shows that the germination of the concept of IPRs in China goes back more than 100 years, in reality no effective system of intellectual property protection (IPP) existed until very recent times (Yang and Clarke 2004).

Plagiarism?   Yes   No   Not sure

Example 4.3

This essay is about intellectual property (IP) in general and about the situation in China today, and about China's relationship with the West in relation to this issue. For thousands of years, outsiders have regarded China as a xenophobic country. But since China opened up its economy in 1979, and with the encouragement of foreign direct investment (FDI) and international technology transfer (ITT), economic relations between foreign countries and China have improved. The international flows of capital, information and technology now facilitate the economic growth of China and the influence of multinational enterprises (MNEs). The boom in FDI and ITT has brought to the fore the issue of intellectual property rights (IPRs) as a major topic in the economic development of China. Although history shows that the germination of the concept of IPRs in China goes back more than 100 years, in reality no effective system of intellectual property protection (IPP) existed until very recent times.

Plagiarism?   Yes   No   Not sure

Example 4.4

This essay is about intellectual property (IP) in general and about the situation in China today, and about China's relationship with the West in relation to this issue. Outsiders have long regarded China as a xenophobic country. However, the stereotypes have been changing since China opened up its economy in 1979. Yang and Clarke (2004) argue that now the encouragement of foreign direct investment (FDI) and international technology transfer (ITT) lies at the heart of economic relations between foreign countries and China. They state

The international flows of capital, information and technology facilitate the economic growth of China and the influence of multinational enterprises

(MNEs). The boom in FDI and ITT has brought to the fore the issue of intellectual property rights (IPRs) as a major topic in the economic development of China (p.12).

Although a historical review shows that the germination of the concept of IPRs in China goes back more than 100 years, in reality no effective system of intellectual property protection (IPP) existed until very recent times.

Plagiarism?   Yes   No   Not sure

Example 4.5

This essay is about intellectual property (IP) in general and about the situation in China today, and about China's relationship with the West in relation to this issue. China has long been regarded as a closed and rather xenophobic country. But things have been changing fast since China opened up its economy in 1979. Some commentators, like Yang and Clarke (2004) argue that the encouragement of foreign direct investment (FDI) and international technology transfer (ITT) lie at the heart of economic relations between foreign countries and China. The flow of capital, information and technology between countries has pushed the economic growth of China forward. Also, the influence of multinational enterprises (MNEs) and boom in FDI and ITT has focused attention on the issue of intellectual property rights (IPRs), and this is now seen as a major topic in the economic development of China. Although the idea of IPRs in China goes back more than 100 years, in reality no effective system of intellectual property protection (IPP) existed until recently.

Plagiarism?   Yes   No   Not sure

Example 4.6

This essay is about intellectual property (IP) in general and about the situation in China today, and about China's relationship with the West in relation to this issue. For centuries China has been regarded by the outside world as a rather closed and insular country. However, Yang and Clarke (2004) argue that now things are changing, and particularly so since 1979, when China decided to open up its economy. Since then, foreign direct investment (FDI) and international technology transfer (ITT) are important connecting links between China and the rest of the world. Now the flows of capital, information, technology and the influence of multinational enterprises MNEs have stimulated the Chinese economy. But these developments have also caused attention to focus on the issue of intellectual property rights (IPR). Although the concept of IPR goes back more than a hundred years, there has been no effective system of intellectual property protection (IPP) until recently.

Plagiarism?   Yes   No   Not sure

Example 4.7

This essay is about intellectual property (IP) in general and about the situation in China today, and about China's relationship with the West in relation to this issue. For centuries China has been regarded by the outside world as a rather closed and xenophobic country. However things are changing. Since 1979, China has loosened and stimulated its economy by foreign direct investment (FDI), international technology transfer (ITT), and from the influence of multinational enterprises (MNEs). However, these developments have also focused attention on the issue of intellectual property rights (IPR) and until recently in China there has been no effective system of intellectual property protection (IPP).

Plagiarism?   **Yes**   **No**   **Not sure**

See Appendix 3 for comments.

5

Referencing styles

Why so many styles? • A confusion of styles? • Which referencing styles predominate in Britain? • In-text name-referencing styles • Numerical-referencing styles • Consecutive number, or 'Running notes', styles of referencing • Recurrent number styles of referencing

All referencing styles are built on the same idea of citing a source in the text of an assignment, either with a name or a number. The name or number connects with the full source details in a footnote, endnote or a bibliographic list. There are an estimated 14 referencing styles to be found within higher education in Britain, although they fall into three main groups (Table 5.1).

Table 5.1 Referencing styles

In-text name styles	Consecutive numbering	Recurrent numbering
These styles involves giving (or citing) the name(s) of author(s) or organization(s) in the text with the year of publication (or page number for MLA style)	This style uses superscript numbers in the text that connect with references in either footnotes or chapter/assignment endnotes (usually the former) **This system uses a different and consecutive number for each reference in the text**	This style uses bracketed (or superscript) numbers in the text that connect with a list of references at the end of the chapter/assignment **The same number can recur, e.g. if a source is mentioned more than once in the text**
All sources are listed alphabetically at the end of an assignment and labelled 'References', 'Reference list', 'Work cited, 'Works consulted' or 'Bibliography, according to the style	A list of sources is included at the end of the assignment, which lists all the works referred to in the notes ('References', 'Works cited') Some tutors may also require a list of all works consulted in preparation for the assignment (i.e. a 'Bibliography' or 'Works consulted')	Your tutors may also require you to include a bibliography, which could include additional sources consulted, but not directly referred to in the text

---

The three main groups divide into specific styles, each with their own guidelines (Table 5.2).

Table 5.2 Names of referencing styles

Name styles	Consecutive numbering	Recurrent numbering
• Name–date (Harvard) • APA • MLA • MHRA • Chicago (Turabian) • Council of Science Editors (CSE)	• British Standard (running notes) • MHRA • Chicago (Turabian) • Oxford: Oscola	• British Standard (numeric) • Vancouver • IEEE • Council of Science Editors (CSE)

The Chicago (Turabian) and Council for Science Editors (CSE) styles are more commonly used in the USA, but can be found within some UK institutions. These styles offer the choice between an in-text name–date referencing style or a running notes style, although the two styles must not be mixed within an assignment. Similarly, while the MHRA style is usually associated with a consecutive numbering approach, it offers a name–date style alternative to users.

Why so many styles?

Referencing styles can become adopted because of recommendations from the librarian at the institution, or because of departmental affiliations to style guides produced by an organization representing the interests of a professional group or discipline. Other reasons for the adoption of a particular style include departments imitating departments across institutions, an arbitrary past decision by someone in a department, probably now long gone; or because of an institutional or departmental decision to standardize practice.

Gibaldi has argued that referencing styles adopted by institutions and departments can be shaped by the kinds of research and scholarship undertaken. He suggested that, in the sciences (and business disciplines), the name–date referencing style is often used to give prominence to the year and general timeliness and currency of the research; whereas with the humanities it is often more important to guide the reader to exactly the right author and page, so a telling detail can more easily and speedily be found (Gibaldi 2003, p.143).

Related to this point, a survey in 2005 among learning support practitioners, suggested that the numerical related styles of referencing are often favoured by visual disciplines, such as art and design and architecture, because they are more subtle, less intrusive and pleasing aesthetically on the page, compared to the relative 'clutter' produced by the Harvard, APA and MLA styles (Neville 2007, p.47).

A confusion of styles?

Is there a confusion of referencing styles? Around one in ten students in my research survey certainly thought so. Two students commented:

> I wish there weren't so many styles of referencing and [there was] one standard referencing style for all courses.
>
> (Undergraduate, Applied Sciences)

> It would be better if there was just one style throughout all academic disciplines, as it is really confusing.
>
> (Postgraduate, Theology)

The issue was particularly significant for undergraduate students on combined studies courses who might encounter not only two or more referencing styles, but also differences in the ways styles were interpreted by their tutors:

> I am expected to use two different systems within my course. This can become somewhat confusing!
>
> (Undergraduate, Communication Studies)

> The different systems are confusing, and lecturers often have different preferences so that one essay may need to be referenced in one way, while another is almost completely different.
>
> (Undergraduate, Classics and Ancient History)

> Because my course is spread across many schools, they each have different ways that they like work referenced and they never specify which referencing style they want.
>
> (Undergraduate, Environmental Studies)

However, even within departments that had adopted one particular style, some students found that the way they had been taught or learned referencing conflicted with what some tutors expected:

> When seeking guidance from lecturers each uses a variation of the business school's recognised system . . . the core [referencing] guide . . . goes against what your lecturers say.
>
> (Undergraduate, Business Management and IT)

> I also find that different tutors want you to reference in different ways, even though we are informed to use Harvard referencing.
>
> (Undergraduate, Education)

> We are told to use the Harvard style of referencing and have had library seminars

on this. However . . . tutors have said that the way I have done it is not correct. The way they say it should be done is different to how I've understood I'm supposed to do it.

(Postgraduate, Dental Hygiene)

Learner support practitioners in higher education institutions are aware of the referencing style problems that students face, and often try to do something about it. In one study, support staff in UK institutions expressed their own concerns on this issue:

Different lecturers recommend different styles of Harvard to their students; it is difficult to get consistency across Schools, let alone the University!

The non-Harvard system used in one of our faculties is described as MLA, but uses numbered notes.

Students who take psychology and sociology modules, usually 1st and 2nd years, do get confused between the two systems (Harvard and APA) that they are asked to use. They are very similar but the psychologists get upset if their system (APA) is not used.

Some practitioners in this survey had tried to rationalise a confusion of referencing styles within their institution, but had found this difficult, if not impossible to achieve:

We tried to get the university to agree to just two systems but the academics concerned were unshiftable!

(All four extracts quoted in Neville 2007, p.45)

Can students do anything about this situation?

Yes. If students within an institution are concerned about the excessive number of referencing styles they are encountering, they can make their views known to senior managers. This is best done collectively through their Student Union, who could ask the institution to explain the rationale for the styles adopted by departments, and if there has been any institutional review of the situation. The head of library and information services is likely to be the best first point of contact for individuals or groups of students concerned about this issue.

Which referencing styles predominate in Britain?

Despite the apparent proliferation of referencing styles in higher education, and the difficulties this can cause to students, a survey of 25 institutions in Britain found that the name–date (Harvard) style of referencing had been adopted by nearly 80 per cent of schools and departments within the responding institutions. Two institutions had adopted name–date (Harvard) for all its courses, but in the majority of institutions, although name–date (Harvard) style was dominant, most of the other styles mentioned in this chapter were also being applied (Neville 2007, p.43).

In-text name-referencing styles

Pros and cons of this style

The **pros** are:

- Most useful when all sources are printed, and these have one or more designated authors
- Easy to follow the chronological progress of a particular debate
- Easy to add or subtract in-text citations and references (particularly useful for last minute assignments!)
- Relatively easy to learn; easy to teach
- Familiar: recognizable from many book and journal articles
- No distraction from the text to look at footnotes or endnotes.

The **cons** are:

- Less useful when citing and referencing sources without authors and/or dates, and particularly Internet references
- Can be awkward for citing television, radio and other audio-visual sources
- Long-winded for citing secondary sources
- In-text citations are normally counted in assignments on most degree courses, as the student takes 'ownership' of evidence cited. This can add significantly to the word count.

Features of the name-referencing styles

As the name–date (Harvard) style appears to be the style favoured by many higher education departments, this will be illustrated in its own chapter in this book (Chapter 6). However, the main characteristics of the other name-referencing styles are, as follows.

1 American Psychological Association (APA)

Many psychology departments, and psychology-related courses in the UK, require that referencing in assignments be prepared according to American Psychological Association style. This section will give you foundation information on the APA style, and Chapter 9 will present examples of references in this style, alongside other styles.

However, for more detailed guidance, and additional examples, you should consult the APA publications: *Concise Rules of APA style*, *APA Style Guide to Electronic References* or the latest edition of the APA *Publication manual*.

Examples of APA referencing

'Citation' means the partial reference in the main body of the assignment; 'Reference' means the full source details as they would appear in a list of references at the end of an assignment.

Book (one or more authors)
Citation:
(Murray, 2005)
Reference:
Murray, R. (2005). *Writing for academic journals*. Maidenhead: Open University Press.

Chapter from an edited book
Citation:
(Nicholls & Jarvis, 2002)
Reference:
Nicholls, G. & Jarvis, P. (2002). Teaching, learning – the changing landscape. In P. Jarvis (Ed.) *The Theory & Practice of Teaching*. London: Kogan Page.

Referencing journal articles
Citation:
(Torrance, Thomas & Robinson, 1993).
Reference:
Torrance, M., Thomas, M. & Robinson, E.J. (1993). Training in thesis writing: An evaluation of three conceptual orientations. *British Journal of Educational Psychology*, 61: 170–84.

There are, however, more noticeable differences between Harvard and APA in the way electronic sources are referenced (see Chapter 9 for more information and comparative examples).

2 Modern Language Association of America (MLA) style of referencing

The Modern Language Association of America was founded in 1883 at a time when modern languages were beginning to be established in the curriculum alongside classical languages. This referencing style is still widely used in Britain on language and related studies degree courses. The MLA has developed its own style of referencing and this is outlined in their guide: *The MLA Handbook for Writers of Research Papers*. Although this style of referencing also cites the name of the author or originator in the text, it differs from name–date (Harvard) and APA in the following ways.

Citations

- Although the author(s) name(s) are shown in the text, this is followed by **page number**(s) (instead of year of publication), e.g. (Handy 149) with no punctuation between author's name and page number(s). Where no page number is available, just give the author's name.
- If no author name is shown, the title, or shortened version of a **title**, can be used as a citation.
- If two authors have the same name, you can add initials to distinguish between them in the text, e.g. (K. Smith 53).
- When summarizing an author's ideas made over a number of different pages, this can be done within brackets, as follows: (Handy 29, 67, 113).
- If you cite two or more works by the same author, you can include a full, shortened or abbreviated title, depending on its length, e.g. (Handy, Beyond Certainty 44–45), or refer to the specific title in the text of your assignment, e.g. Handy, in 'Beyond Certainty', asserts that . . . (44).

References (or works cited)

- The full list of references at the end of the text is also labelled and presented in a different way to Harvard and APA. It is labelled **'Works cited'** (equivalent to 'References'), or **'Works consulted'** (equivalent to 'Bibliography'), and the second and subsequent lines of a reference entry are indented by five spaces (a hanging indent), with double spacing between lines. Sources in 'Works cited' are listed alphabetically, but with regards to 'Works consulted', MLA allows for either one list of sources in alphabetical order, or sources divided into sections and items alphabetized in each. For example, a 'Works consulted' list might be divided into primary and secondary sources, or arranged by subject matter, or different types of source, e.g. books, journals, websites.
- The last name of a single author, or lead author, is followed by his or her full first name(s), and not just the initial letters of these. However, this is reversed if two or three authors are listed. With second and third authors, the first names precede the last; see examples below:

  Gibaldi, Joseph. <u>MLA Handbook for Writers of Research Papers</u>, Sixth Edition. New York: MLA, 2003.

  Loach, Ken. (Director) and Sally Hibbin (Producer). <u>Raining Stones.</u> DVD. London: Channel Four Television (FilmFour), 1993.
- If the first name of the writer is not shown on the title pages of books or other sources, then just their initials can be used instead. Some writers deliberately use their initials in their writing, e.g. A.J. Cronin; T.S. Eliot. However, the MLA handbook (Gibaldi 2003, p.48) suggests that you may include first names if you feel the additional information would be helpful, in the following way: Rowling, J[oanne] K[athleen]; as the example shows, the remainder of name is enclosed in squared brackets.
- The same rules featured earlier in the Harvard style, applying to alphabetization of names, including treatment of non-English names, is applicable also to MLA style.
- After the first works cited entry for this author, the name can be replaced by three hyphens and a stop for other sources by the same author, for example,

Handy, Charles. <u>Beyond Certainty: the Changing Worlds of Organisations.</u> London: Hutchinson, 1995.

—— . <u>The Future of Work.</u> Oxford: Blackwell, 1985.

- The MLA handbook (2009) encourages students to 'avoid ambiguity' by underlining main source titles, rather than italicizing them (see earlier examples), and to use double quotation marks around titles of articles from the main source (see the 'Referencing a chapter from an edited book' example).
- In the title, the first letter in each word is capitalized.
- The publisher's name can be shortened, for example, W.W. Norton can be shortened to Norton. If the publisher's name is commonly abbreviated, or the abbreviations are likely to be familiar with the readership, they can be used instead of the full title, for example MLA, BBC, and so on.
- The year of publication usually comes last in the full reference, unless page numbers and essential additional bibliographic information is included, for example, supplementary information about a multivolume work, such as number of volumes, and the dates between which the volumes were published. Example:

Durant, Will, and Ariel Durant. <u>The Age of Voltaire</u>. New York: Simon, 1965. Vol. 9 of <u>The Story of Civilisation</u>. 11 vols. 1935–75. (Taken from Gibaldi 2003, p.169)

More examples of MLA style references

Referencing a chapter from an edited book
Citation:
(Segalen 51)
Works cited:
Segalen, Martine. "The Household at Work". <u>The Experience of Work.</u> Ed. Craig Littler. Aldershot: Gower, 1985. 50–71.

The title of the chapter is placed within double inverted commas; 'Ed.' is an abbreviation for 'Editor'; the reference ends with details of page numbers of the chapter in the book.

Referencing an article in a journal
Citation:
(Murray: 229)
Works cited:
Murray, Rowena. "Writing Development for Lecturers Moving from Further to Higher Education". <u>Journal of Further and Higher Education,</u> 26. 3 (2002): 229–39. The numbers refer to **volume** 26 of the journal, **issue** 3, the year (enclosed in brackets for a scholarly journal) and, finally, the page numbers are shown.

Electronic sources
Citation:
(Dixons)
If there is no page number to quote, just cite the name of the author or, as in this case, the name of an organization: the originator of the data concerned.

Works cited:

Dixons Group PLC. "Company Report: Profile". <u>Financial Analysis Made Easy (FAME)</u> online database, 13 Dec. 2005.

The item is presented within double inverted commas, while the main source (the FAME database) is underlined; the date the information is retrieved from the database completes the reference. In this online example, the URL address is not shown, as the FAME database is password restricted, and so there is no point in giving a URL address that cannot be publicly accessed. More examples of MLA references, including electronic sources, can be found in Chapter 9.

3 The Chicago (reference list) style

The benchmark for this referencing style, which is more commonly used in the USA than in Britain, is the current edition of *The Chicago Manual of Style*, although many users consult the latest edition of Kate Turabian's more student-oriented book: *A Manual for Writers of Term Papers, Theses and Dissertations*. This accounts for the alternative tag of the 'Turabian' style of referencing that can occasionally be presented to students. While the Chicago style is associated predominantly with footnote referencing, it does provide an in-text author-name option for writers who prefer to use this approach.

Citations

As with the name–date (Harvard) and APA styles, you give a shortened reference in the text of your work with the last name of the writer(s), or organizational name (or abbreviation), plus year, and if necessary, page number(s), e.g. (Goman 1989, 59) or (Fairbairn and Fairbairn 2001) or (MHRA 2004).

If a source has one to three authors, mention their last names in the citation. For four or more names, list the first name with 'et al.' replacing the others, e.g. (Brown et al. 2009).

Reference

At the end of the text, you include a 'Reference list' of all your sources, listed in alphabetical order. So, for the three citation examples shown above, these would be listed thus:

> Fairbairn, Gavin and Susan Fairbairn. 2001. *Reading at university: A guide for students*. Maidenhead: Open University Press.
> Goman, Carol Kinsey. 1989. *Creative thinking in business: A practical guide*. London: Kogan Page.
> MHRA: Modern Humanities Research Association. 2002. *MHRA style guide: A Handbook for authors, editors, and writers of theses*. London: MHRA.

- Use the full names of the authors. With the first author, start with his or her surname, followed by first name; for subsequent authors, list their first name(s) first (see the Fairbairn and Fairbairn example above).
- The year of publication follows the author(s) name(s), but is not placed in parenthesis.

- The book title is shown in italics.
- List **all** the author names in the full reference, regardless of how many there are.
- The second and subsequent lines of the full reference are not indented.
- For books, capitalize only the first letter of the first word, any proper noun, and first letter of first word of any subtitle.

Other Chicago (reference list) style examples

Journals

Murray, Rowena. 2002. Writing development for lecturers moving from Further to Higher Education. *Journal of Further and Higher Education* 26, no. 3: 229–39.
Bosworth, David and Deli Yang. 2000. Intellectual property law, technology flow and licensing opportunities in China. *International Business Review* 9, no. 4: 453–77.

- As with book titles, start with first author's surname, followed by first name; but for subsequent authors, list their first name(s) first, as shown in the second example, above.
- Capitalize all the words of the journal title, which should be shown in italics.

Electronic sources

E-Logistics 2003. *Call centres – an inexorable flight?* http://www.elogmag.com/ magazine/29/call-centres.shtml (accessed June 20, 2008).
Meredith, Sandra and Timothy Endicott, 2005. *The Oxford standard for citation of legal authorities* http://denning.law.ox.ac.uk/published/oscola.shtml (accessed April 26, 2006).

- Start with the named author(s), if shown; if not, start with the name of website.
- Show the title of item in italics.
- Show the URL in full – to take reader straight to the screen in question.
- Give the date of your access to the information: month, date, year.

4 MHRA style

The Modern Humanities Research Association (MHRA) is normally associated with the numerical-footnotes style of referencing (see later in this chapter), but it also allows for citation and referencing by the name–date system. For more information, consult the latest edition of the MHRA style guide: *A Handbook for Authors, Editors and Writers of Thesis,* What follows is a summary of the main points regarding MHRA name–date referencing.

MHRA in-text citations

The name(s) of authors, year of publication, and, if relevant, page number is located at an appropriate place in the text, e.g.:

'It has been argued (Brown, 2008) that . . .
'Brown has argued that . . . (Brown, 2008, p.201)

The MHRA style guide advises that if unpublished and unauthored documents are used as evidence, an abbreviated reference should be placed in brackets in the text and a separate list of these documents should be included at the end, but preceding the list of references (unpublished theses and dissertations, as they have named authors, can be included in the list of references). The MHRA style guide offers some examples as to how these unpublished documents should be listed: with the abbreviation in a left column, and full information on the right:

CRO, Probate	Cumberland Record Office, Carlisle Castle, Probate Records
PRO, HO 42/196	Public Record Office, Home Office, HO 42/196

(MHRA 2002, p.55)

MHRA references

Like other styles, MHRA requires an alphabetical list of references to be placed at the end of a text. The format recommended by MHRA is, using three books as examples, as follows:

> Fairbairn, G. & S. Fairbairn. 2001. *Reading at University: A Guide for Students* (Maidenhead: Open University Press)
> Goman, C. K. 1989. *Creative Thinking in Business: A Practical Guide* (London: Kogan Page)
> MHRA: Modern Humanities Research Association. 2002. *MHRA Style Guide: A Handbook for Authors, Editors, and Writers of Theses* (London: MHRA)

If a list includes more than one work published by an author, a long dash is substituted for second and subsequent entries, e.g.:

> Hampden-Turner, C. 1990. *Corporate Culture* (London: Hutchinson)
> —— 1990. *The Seven Cultures of Capitalism* (London: Piatkus Books)

Note the following:

- Use of last name first, followed by initial letter(s) of second names; this order is reversed for second and subsequent authors. (The MHRA style also allows for the full first name of an author to be used instead of initials, if preferred by the writer – or required by a tutor.)
- Use of ampersand (&) instead of using 'and' to separate author names.
- Second and subsequent lines indented by one tab space.
- Title in italics and the use of capital letters in title for all proper words.
- Location: town/city of publisher and name of publisher in brackets.
- No full stop at the end of the reference.

Other MHRA style examples

Journals

Murray, R. 2002. 'Writing development for lecturers moving from Further to Higher Education', *Journal of Further and Higher Education*, 26, (3): 229–39

- The title of the journal should be italicized.
- The title of the article is set within inverted commas.
- The example shown gives the volume number: 26, and item and page numbers: (3): 229–39.

Website

JISC Plagiarism Advisory Service. 2001. *Plagiarism – A Good Practice Guide*, <http://www.jiscpas.ac.uk/apppage.cgi?USERPAGE=6296> [accessed 23 August 2006]

- The main source item cited is italicized.
- The website address is shown within angle brackets.

5 Council of Science Editors (CSE) style

Some UK university science departments have adopted the Council of Science Editors (CSE) Style, although it is more commonly applied within the USA. Guidelines for referencing are shown in *Scientific Style and Format: The CSE Manual for Authors, Editors and Publishers*. The manual offers writers the choice of using either a name–year or recurrent number style of referencing. As with other name–date styles, the author(s) names(s) and year of origin are cited in parenthesis in the main text, e.g. (Brown 2008). The sources cited are listed alphabetically in a listed headed 'Works cited' at the end of the text.

Example

Citation
(Pines 1997)

Works cited

Pines J. 1997. Localization of cell cycle regulators by immuno-fluorescence. In: Dunphy W, vol. ed. Methods in enzymology, vol. 283: Cell cycle control. New York: Academic Press. p.109.

- Only the first word of book and article titles, along with their subtitles, and proper nouns, are capitalized.
- No commas are used to separate the author's last name from the initials of his or her first name.
- Use full stops to separate the elements of a source.
- Indent the second and subsequent lines of a 'Works cited' entry.

Comparison of five name–date styles

The examples in Tables 5.3–5.6 illustrate the differences between five name–date referencing styles. (The name–date (Harvard) style has a chapter on its own; to follow).

Table 5.3 Book: single author

APA	MLA
Kotre, J. (1984). *Outliving the self: Generativity and the interpretation of lives.* Baltimore: Johns Hopkins University Press, 1984.	Kotre, John. Outliving the Self: Generativity and the Interpretation of Lives. Baltimore: Hopkins, 1984.

Chicago	MHRA
Kotre, John. 1984. *Outliving the self: Generativity and the interpretation of lives.* Baltimore: Johns Hopkins University Press.	Kotre, J. 1984. Outliving the Self: Generativity and the Interpretation of Lives (Baltimore: Hopkins)

Council for Science Editors (CSE) style

Kotre J. 1984. Outliving the self: Generativity and the interpretation of lives. Baltimore: Hopkins.

Table 5.4 Edited book

APA	MLA
McGinty, J. & Williams, T. (Eds.) (2001). *Regional trends 36.* London: Stationery Office.	McGinty, Jon & Tricia Williams, Eds. Regional Trends 36. London: Stationery Office, 2001.

Chicago	MHRA
McGinty, Jon and Tricia Williams, eds. 2001. *Regional trends* 36. London: Stationery Office.	McGinty, Jon. & Tricia Williams, (eds.), 2001, *Regional Trends* 36 (London: Stationery Office)

Council for Science Editors (CSE) style

McGinty J, Williams T, editors. 2001. Regional trends 36. London: Stationery Office.

Table 5.5 Journal article

APA	MLA
Yang, D. (2005). Culture matters to multinationals' intellectual property business. *Journal of World Business, 40,* 281–301.	Yang, Deli. "Culture Matters to Multinationals' Intellectual Property Business". Journal of World Business, 40, (2005): 281–301.

Chicago	MHRA
Yang, Deli. 2005. Culture matters to multinationals' intellectual property business. *Journal of World Business,* 40: 281–301.	Yang, Deli. 2005. 'Culture Matters to Multinationals' Intellectual Property Business', *Journal of World Business,* 40, 281–301

Council for Science Editors (CSE) style

Deli Y. 2005. Culture matters to multinationals' intellectual property business. J World Bus: 40: 281–301.

Note: Journal titles must be abbreviated within the CSE style. You can gain access to a list of journal abbreviations through the *Web of Science*, which can be found within the *ISI Web of Knowledge*, accessible through your institution library.

Table 5.6 Website

APA	MLA
Meredith, S. & T. Endicott. (2005) *The Oxford Standard for citation of legal authorities.* Retrieved June 26, 2008 from http://denning.law.ox.ac.uk/published/oscola.shtml	Meredith, Sandra & Timothy Endicott (2005). The Oxford Standard for Citation of Legal Authorities. 26 June 2008 <http://denning.law.ox.ac.uk/published/oscola.shtml>

Chicago (Turabian)	MHRA
Meredith, Sandra and Timothy Endicott. 2005. The Oxford Standard for citation of legal http://denning.law.ox.ac.uk/published/oscola.shtml (accessed June 26, 2008).	Meredith, Sandra & Timothy Endicott. 2005. *The Oxford Standard for Citation of Legal Authorities.* <http://denning.law.ox.ac.uk/published/oscola.shtml> (accessed 26 June 2008)

Council for Science Editors (CSE) style
Meredith S, Endicott T. 2005. The Oxford Standard for citation of legal authorities [Internet]. [cited 2008 June 26]. Available from: http://denning.law.ox.ac.uk/published/oscola.shtml

Note the differences in the way the date the source was obtained from the Internet, e.g. terms used: 'accessed'; 'retrieved'; 'cited'. See Chapter 9, section S for full discussion on referencing electronic sources.

Numerical referencing styles

In Britain there are two main types of numerical referencing styles:

- **Consecutive** number referencing linked to footnotes, or end-of-chapter notes. British Standard refers to this as the 'Running-notes' style
- **Recurrent** number referencing, which is linked to a final list of sources. British Standard refers to this as the 'Numeric system' of referencing.

Consecutive number, or 'Running notes', styles of referencing

The Running-notes style of referencing, as illustrated in British Standard recommendations, uses a consecutive superscript (or bracketed) number in the text, for example, in superscript: [1] for the first source, [2] for the second source, and so on. This system, therefore, uses a different number for each note or reference in the text each time it is cited. One source may have many different numbers attached to it, depending on how often it is cited in the assignment.

These numbers connect with citations at the bottom of the page (footnotes), or at the end of the assignment, headed 'Endnotes' or 'Notes'. Both methods are usually acceptable and most university departments allow you to choose which to use, providing you are consistent and do not 'mix and match'. The full reference details of sources are shown against the numbers in the numerical order they appear in your assignment.

A full list of sources, in alphabetical order, usually titled 'Bibliography', normally appears at the end, as this is a way of bringing together all the sources referred to in the assignment.

The variants

However, as stated earlier there are three other UK referencing styles that use this consecutive number method, and each has its own subtle 'take' on the British Standard 'model' just described.

1 The Modern Humanities Research Association (MHRA)

Students who are asked specifically to follow MHRA style guidelines should consult the MHRA style guide: *A Handbook for Authors, Editors and Writers of Theses*.

2 The Chicago (Turabian) style

There are two recommended guides to this style; use the latest edition of either: University of Chicago, *The Chicago Manual of Style* (at time of writing the 15th edition, 2003 was the current edition); or the style guide for writers, written by Kate L. Turabian: *A Manual for Writers of Research Papers, Theses, and Dissertations: Chicago Style for Students and Researchers* (at the time of writing the 7th edition, 2007, was the most current edition).

3 OSCOLA

Students on law degree or related courses will learn a referencing style that is particular to this subject, which is usually the *Oxford Standard for Citation of Legal Authorities* (OSCOLA). This is the style used by the *Oxford University Commonwealth Law Journal*, which contributed to its development. Examples of legal referencing will be shown later in this book; see in Chapter 9.

More information on the OSCOLA style can be found at the following website: Oxford Standard for Citation of Legal Authorities at http://denning.law.ox.ac.uk/published/oscola.shtml

Pros and cons of the Running-notes style of referencing

The pros

There is a long tradition of using footnotes in essays, which, arguably, gives a dignified presence to their appearance in essays and imparts an air of authority, and credibility to the evidence presented. The long history and authority of footnotes can lead to a spirited defence of its continuation in the face of the slow march of the name–date (Harvard) style across higher education in Britain (see Grafton 1997).

The advantage of this referencing style is that it can be used for both authorial notes and to cite sources. Page numbers can be included in these footnotes or endnotes, so the text of your assignment remains uncluttered with source names, dates and page numbers. It is also particularly useful for referencing secondary sources, as details of both secondary and primary source can be given in the notes, rather than in the text.

The reader can also immediately identify the source on the same page it is mentioned without having to turn to the references or bibliography. Grafton (1997) argues that the use of footnotes enables writers: 'to make their texts not monologues but conversations, in which modern scholars, their predecessors, and the subjects all take part' (p.226).

They serve, therefore, as an opportunity for the writer to add authorial asides away from the main text. Although footnotes can be used within the name–date (Harvard) and related styles, their use within this style is not always encouraged by tutors, who, in the face of marking a hundred or more scripts, would prefer to zip through the text, without pausing to read too many footnote comments.

The cons

In mechanical terms, the main disadvantage of the style is that it can be awkward for a student to format last-minute additions and changes, although referencing management software has helped to reduce the problems this once caused. Some readers also find footnotes distracting from the text. Grafton, citing Hilbert 1989, quotes Noel Coward in his remark that 'having to read a footnote resembles having to go downstairs to answer the door in the midst of making love' (Grafton 1997, p.70, fn.16).

Students also need to take care when placing numbers in the text, to ensure it is clear to the reader what source is referred to. Thompson (2005) gives an example of how this type of referencing ambiguity can occur, with the following extract from a student assignment.

Example of referencing ambiguity

These factors (various health, alcohol and drug-related issues), among others, contribute to the lower life expectancy of Aboriginal people *(sic)* to non-Aboriginal people. For males it is 56.9 to 75, respectively. For females, 61.7 to 81.1. **10**

Other contributing factors include homicide/purposefully inflicted injury. Aboriginal people 677.1 per 100,000, compared to 28.8.

Health problems can also be linked to other social problems. The majority of the Indigenous community deemed their housing inappropriate by those living in them 'usually because the dwelling needed repair or did not have enough bedrooms'. **11**

10 COUNCIL FOR ABORIGINAL RECONCILIATION; Overcoming Disadvantage (2000). Pg. 1–18

11 1994 Aboriginal and Torres Strait Islander Survey, Year Book, Australia, 1996 (ABS Catalogue No. 1301.0).

(*Source*: Reproduced from Thompson (2005) with permission)

In the example shown it is not clear if the second paragraph is a continuation of the one preceding it, or whether an additional reference was necessary. If it was from the same source as shown in the footnote, item 10, the student could have given it a number, 11, and in the footnotes stated 'Ibid.' and given the page number (see 'Abbreviations' later in this chapter for an explanation of this).

Guidelines for Running-notes styles of referencing

The following extract from an essay demonstrates the Running-notes style of referencing, following British Standard recommendations, and how it is particularly useful for dealing with secondary sources – see reference numbered 12 in the footnote.

> This willingness to listen, negotiate, and respond to adult learners is, however, more related to empathy, than 'charisma', a term used by Jarvis[11] to describe the characteristics of inspirational teachers. However, the use of this term: 'charisma', because of the connotations of magnetism or aura that flow from it, may be an attribute hard for many teachers to attain. Empathy with the learner, on the other hand, is attainable by the majority of teachers and in the longer term is, arguably, more durable and appreciated by a wider range of students.
>
> As emphasised earlier, empathy involves listening, negotiation, treating others equally and attempting to equalise the power relationship that can exist between teachers and students. It also requires teachers to be honest with students and to give something of themselves to their students. They need to give this essence of self, paradoxically, in both a humble and bold way. Richard Hoggart asserts that all teachers should be wary of charismatic 'show off' displays, and compares the approach to a 'Pied Piper of Hamlet' teaching style. He points out that shiny-eyed devotion from a class, because of peacock teaching styles, can be addictive for the teacher. But this could also be perceived as an abuse of power, particularly when vulnerable and suggestible adults are involved. He encourages tutors to strive toward assisting students to stand on their own feet and *'be critical or . . . ironic about us and towards us.'*[12]

11 Jarvis, P. Teaching styles and teaching methods. In P. Jarvis (Ed.) *The theory & practice of teaching*. London: Kogan Page. 2002, pp.22–30.
12 Hoggart, R. The role of the teacher. Originally published in J. Rogers (Ed.), Teaching on equal terms, BBC Publications, 1969, and cited in Rogers, J. *Adults learning*. 3rd edition. Milton Keynes: Open University Press, 1989, p.81.

Bibliographies and references

As stated earlier, at the end of the essay some tutors may require you to submit either a Bibliography – which is an alphabetical list of all the works referred to in your notes, as **well as other works you consulted in preparation for the assignment** – or a list headed 'References' or 'Works cited' (for the Chicago (Turabian) style), which is an alphabetical list of all the evidence just cited in the text.

Abbreviations

As stated earlier, this referencing style uses a different number for each source in the text. So, the same source used in an assignment at a number of different points will have more than one number allocated to it. Therefore, to save you having to keep repeating the same full reference information in your footnotes or endnotes, abbreviations are used to link the references, as shown in Table 5.7. However, Turabian (2007) advises writers using the Chicago (Turabian) style of referencing to 'avoid all Latin citation terms except one – *ibid*' (p.155).

Table 5.7 Abbreviations

Ibid.	(*Ibidem*) Meaning: in the same book, chapter, passage etc. and in the **previous** reference. If used, you should always give the relevant page numbers
Op.cit.	(*Opere citato*) Meaning: in the work quoted. This is used for a further reference to a source previously cited, **but not the one immediately preceding it**. If you use it, give some means of identifying the previous reference, such as author's name and date of publication, and give a page number
Loc. cit.	(*Loco citato*) Meaning: in the same place in a work previously cited, i.e. a reference to the same work, the same volume, or same page. Loc. cit. is used in place of ibid. when the reference is not only to the work immediately preceding, but also refers to the **same page**. Loc. cit. is also used instead of op. cit. when reference is made to a work previously cited, and to the **same page** in that work

Examples of these abbreviations and how they might appear in a bibliography

1 ALI, L. and S. GRAHAM. *The counselling approach to careers guidance*. S. LENDRUM (Ed.). London: Routledge. 1996.
2 PARSLOE, E. and M. WRAY. *Coaching and mentoring*. London: Kogan Page, 2000.
3 Ibid. p.71.
4 ALI, L and S. GRAHAM. op. cit. p.85.
5 PARSLOE, E. and M. WRAY. loc. cit.

Some source examples

With both the MHRA and Chicago (Turabian) styles, there are differences between the way the source is shown in the footnote or endnote, and the way it is presented in the bibliography. The following examples illustrate the differences between British Standard Running-notes, MHRA, and Chicago (Turabian) styles (OSCOLA is treated separately and examples of referencing legal sources are shown in Chapter 9 of this book).

1 Example of a book written by a single author

Using British Standard (footnote and full reference entry)
GRAFTON, A. *The footnote: a curious history*. Cambridge (MA): Harvard University Press, 1997. p.71

• British Standard example shows name(s) of the author in upper case, but be guided by your own institution's guidelines, if any, on this point.

- The abbreviation 'MA' distinguishes Cambridge in Massachusetts, USA, from the Cambridge, UK.

Using MHRA
Footnote/endnote:

1. Anthony Grafton, *The Footnote: A Curious History*, (Cambridge, MA: Harvard University Press, 1997), p.71.

Bibliography:

Grafton, Anthony, *The Footnote: A Curious History*, (Cambridge, MA: Harvard University Press, 1997)

With MHRA style, the footnote or endnote form recommended is to show the full name of the author, with first name preceding the last, to indent the second line onward of the full reference by five points and to include the place, name of the publisher and year of publication in parenthesis, concluding with page number, if applicable. However, in the bibliography, if used, the order of author names is reversed, with the last name preceding the first. As the relevant page number was shown in the footnote/endnote, it does not need to be repeated in the bibliographic entry.

The MHRA style also tends to favour commas to separate parts of a reference, ending with a stop in the footnote/endnote entry (although not in the bibliography). For books in English, the first letter of principal words throughout the title is capitalized, plus the first letter of words after any colon in the title. For titles in other languages, follow the way the title is presented on the book, or conform to any known referencing guidelines for the language in question. In addition:

- The main source can be in italics or underlined in British Standard, although always italicized for MHRA.
- Unless page numbers are shown, the year of publication is the last item in the entry for both British Standard and MHRA styles.
- The second and subsequent lines of a full MHRA reference entry are indented by five points (a hanging indent).

Using Chicago (Turabian)
Footnote/endnote:

1. Anthony Grafton, *The Footnote: A Curious History*, (Cambridge, MA: Harvard University Press, 1997), 71.

Bibliography:

Grafton, Anthony. *The Footnote: A Curious History*. Cambridge, MA: Harvard University Press, 1997.

- Indent the first line of each footnote, but in the 'Bibliography', or 'Works cited', the second and subsequent lines are indented.
- If you are using endnotes instead of footnotes, they should be shown at the end of each chapter, or the text of a shorter assignment, and titled 'Notes'. Each source shown should, in both footnote/endnote and bibliographic entries, be single spaced, but with a double space between sources.
- In a footnote/endnote, the first name(s) in full, or initials, is presented first, followed by the last name; but in 'Works cited' or 'Bibliography', the last name is shown first.
- In a footnote/endnote, the publication information is placed within parenthesis, and the entry is finished with a page number, if relevant; but you do not need to use parenthesis with the 'Works cited' or 'Bibliography' entry. As the page number was shown in the footnote/endnote, it does not need to be repeated in the bibliography entry.
- The first time you cite a source in a footnote/endnote, you should give full information; but subsequent citations, in a relatively short list, require less detail, e.g. 7. Grafton, *The Footnote*, 85.
- In 'Works cited' or 'Bibliography' list, sources are listed alphabetically.
- Capitalize the first and last words in titles, along with other proper words and words that follow colons.
- Note the difference in punctuation between the footnote/endnote and bibliographic entries: commas are used in the former, while stops separate out items in the latter.

2 Edited book

Using British Standard (footnote and full reference entry)
COLLIN, A. Human resource management in Context. In *Human resource management: a contemporary perspective*. I. BEARDWELL and L. HOLDEN (Eds.). London: Pitman Publishing, 1994, pp. 29–68.

Using MHRA
Footnote/endnote:

2. Audrey Collin, 'Human Resource Management in Context', in *Human Resource Management: A Contemporary Perspective*, ed. by Ian Beardwell and Len Holden. (London: Pitman Publishing, 1994), pp. 29–68.

Bibliography

Collin, Audrey, Human Resource Management in Context', in *Human Resource Management: A Contemporary Perspective*, ed. by I. Beardwell and L. Holden. (London: Pitman Publishing, 1994)

Using Chicago (Turabian)
Footnote/endnote:

3. Audrey Collin, "Human Resource Management in Context", in *Human Resource Management: A Contemporary Perspective*, ed. Ian Beardwell and Len Holden. (London: Pitman Publishing, 1994), 29–68.

Bibliography:

> Collin, Audrey. "Human resource Management in Context". In *Human Resource Management: A Contemporary Perspective*. Edited by Ian Beardwell and Len Holden. London: Pitman Publishing, 1994.

- British Standard examples of numerical style show names of authors and editors in upper case.
- The term 'editor' can be shorted to 'ed', (except in the Chicago (Vancouver) bibliographic entry). However, to avoid confusing this abbreviation with 'edition', it is suggested the abbreviation is clarified by using an additional term, for example, 'ed. by . . .' (or edited by . . .).
- Note how the names are used in full in the MHRA and Chicago (Turabian) styles.
- The title of the article is also emphasized with inverted commas (single for MHRA, double for Chicago (Turabian)).
- Note that the main source, in both examples, is the **book** in which the chapter appeared, so the book title is italicized.

3 Example of journal article

Using British Standard (footnote and full reference entry)

> 3. DELLAVALLE, R.P. et al. Going, going, gone: lost Internet references. *Science*. vol. 302, no. 5646, Oct. 2003: pp.787–788.

Using MHRA
Footnote/endnote:

> 3. Robert Dellavalle and others, 'Going, Going, Gone: Lost Internet References', *Science*, 302, (October 2003), no. 5646: 787–788.

Bibliography:

> Dellavale, Robert, and others, 'Going, Going, Gone: Lost Internet References', *Science*, 302, no. 5646 (October 2003), 787–788.

Using Chicago (Turabian)
Footnote/endnote:

> 3. Robert Dellavalle et al., "Going, Going, Gone: Lost Internet References", *Science* 302, no. 5646 (October 2003): 787–788.

Bibliography:

> Dellavalle, Robert, Eric J. Hester, Lauren F. Heilig, Amanda L. Drake, Jeff W. Kuntzman, Maria Graber, and Lisa M. Schilling. "Going, Going, Gone: Lost Internet References". *Science* 302, no. 5646 (October 2003): 787–788.

- The article illustrated above has multiple authors; see how each style deals with this by the use, or otherwise, of the abbreviation 'et al.' (meaning 'and others'); but for more detailed information on the citation and referencing of multiple authors, see Chapter 7, 'Frequently asked questions', question 6.
- Note how the title of the article is punctuated in each example, with single quotation marks for the MHRA example, and double for Chicago (Turabian).
- The title of the journal (italicized) is followed by details of the volume and issue number, month (if applicable) and year, followed by page numbers.

4 Example of a website

British Standard (footnote and full reference entry)

MEREDITH, S. and T. ENDICOTT. *The Oxford Standard for citation of legal authorities*, 2005. p. 17. Available at http://denning.law.ox.ac.uk/published/oscola.shtml [Accessed 26/04/2006].

MHRA
Footnote/endnote:

4. Sandra Meredith and Timothy Endicott, *The Oxford Standard for Citation of Legal Authorities*, (2005), p.17, http://denning.law.ox.ac.uk/published/oscola.shtml [accessed 26 April 2006].

Bibliography:

Meredith, Sandra and Timothy Endicott, *The Oxford Standard for Citation of Legal Authorities*, (2005), p.17, http://denning.law.ox.ac.uk/published/oscola.shtml [accessed 26 April 2006]

Chicago (Turabian)
Footnote/endnote:

4. Sandra Meredith and Timothy Endicott, *The Oxford Standard for Citation of Legal Authorities*, (2005), 17, http://denning.law.ox.ac.uk/published/oscola.shtml [accessed 26 April 2006].

Bibliography:

Meredith, Sandra and Timothy Endicott, *The Oxford Standard for Citation of Legal Authorities*, (2005), 17, http://denning.law.ox.ac.uk/published/oscola.shtml [accessed 26 April 2006]

For more information on referencing electronic sources, read Chapter 9, section S.

Recurrent number styles of referencing

The recurrent number referencing styles uses a bracketed (or superscript) number in the text, which connects with list of references at the end of the text. If brackets are used to enclose numbers, you can use either square [ ] or curved ( ) brackets, providing you are consistent. What makes it different from the consecutive number styles of referencing is that the same number can be repeated, for example, if a source is mentioned more than once in the same assignment. A number in the text of your assignment will, therefore, connect with the same number in your final list of references. Your tutors may also require you to include a bibliography, which would list additional sources consulted, but not directly referred to in the text.

The advantage of this referencing style generally is that only one number is used per source or note, and therefore there is no need to use the abbreviations ibid. op. cit or loc. cit. as is the case with the consecutive number styles. If you want to refer to the same source on a number of occasions in the same assignment, but to different pages, you can add the relevant page numbers to the bracketed source reference numbers, e.g. (2: 47) or (2: 47–55).

The four recurrent numbering styles found within UK higher education are:

1 The bracketed numbered (or Numeric) referencing examples presented by **British Standard** (BS) in BS guides: (BS) BS1629:1989 (*References to published material*) and BS6505:1990 (*Citing and referencing published material*).
2 **Vancouver style**, as outlined by the International Committee of Medical Journal Editors (ICMJE), in their guide *International Committee of Medical Journal Editors Uniform requirements for Manuscripts Submitted to Biomedical Journals: Sample References*.
3 The **Institute of Electrical and Electronics Engineers** (IEEE) also make recommendations on referencing using this style of referencing. These recommendations are adopted by many electrical engineering and related disciplines in the UK. The IEEE produce an information sheet for authors: *IEEE Transactions, Journals, and Letters: Information for Authors* via their website, although many university libraries produce information sheets on IEEE for their engineering students.
4 The **Council of Science Editors (CSE) style**, while more commonly applied within the USA, is used by some UK science departments. As stated earlier, this style offers writer the choice of using either a name–year or the recurrent number style of referencing. Guidelines for CSE referencing are shown in the latest edition (at the time of writing, the seventh) of *Scientific Style and Format: The CSE Manual for Authors, Editors and Publishers*.

Examples

There are only small differences between the four variants of this referencing style in relation to printed material, although the differences with electronic sources are more marked. Nevertheless, students asked to adopt one of these variants need to be aware of the differences; see the examples in Tables 5.8–5.10.

Table 5.8 Book reference

British Standard	Vancouver
Torrieri, D. *Principles of secure communication systems*, 2nd ed. Dedham: MA: Artech House, 1992.	Torrieri D. Principles of secure communication systems, 2nd ed. Dedham: MA: Artech House; 1992.

IEEE	CSE
D. Torrieri, *Principles of secure communication systems*, 2nd ed. Dedham: MA: Artech House, 1992.	Torrieri D. 1992. Principles of secure communication systems, 2nd ed. Dedham: MA: Artech House.

Note minor differences in punctuation, lack of italicization of title in the Vancouver and CSE style examples, location of year element, and indentation of second and subsequent lines of the CSE style.

Table 5.9 Journal

British Standard	Vancouver
DEARING, K.F. and I. H. GOTLIB (2009). Interpretation of ambiguous information in girls at risk for depression. *Journal of Abnormal Child Psychology*, vol. 37, no. 1, Jan. 2009, pp: 79–91.	Dearing K,C, Gotlib, I,H. Interpretation of ambiguous information in girls at risk for depression. Journal of Abnormal Child Psychology, 2009; 37:1; Jan, 79–91.

IEEE	CSE
K.C. Dearing and I.H. Gotlib. "Interpretation of ambiguous information in girls at risk for depression", *Journal of Abnormal Child Psychology*, vol. 37, no. 1, pp:79–91, Jan. 2009.	Dearing K C, Gotlib, I H. 2009. Interpretation of ambiguous information in girls at risk for depression. J Abnorm Child Psych. 37:1, Jan: 79–91.

Note differences in punctuation, italicization of title in British Standard and IEEE styles, the quotation marks around the title of the article in the IEEE example, and the abbreviated title in the CSE example. A list of abbreviations can be found in the *Web of Science*, which can be found online within the *ISI Web of Knowledge*; you can access these through the library of your institution.

Table 5.10 Website

British Standard	Vancouver
IEEE. *IEEE Homepage*. Available: http://www.ieee.org/ portal/site [Accessed 16 Oct. 2006].	IFFF [homepage on the Internet]. New Jersey: The Institute. 2006. [cited 2006 Oct 16]. About the IEEE; Available from: http://www.ieee.org/portal/site

IEEE	CSE
IEEE (2006). *IEEE Homepage*. Available: http://www.ieee.org/portal/site	IEEE. 2006. IEEE Homepage [Internet]. [cited 2006 Oct 16]. Available from http://www.ieee.org/portal/site

Notes:
You will note with the **Vancouver** style reference that a wider range of information is included. It starts with the name of the Institute, which is followed by the title of the page and its location (homepage on the Internet). It then includes the place of 'publication' (New Jersey) and publishers name (The Institute). It gives the date the site was visited (cited 2006 Oct. 16), includes the screen title (About the IEEE), and finishes with the URL address.
Note the use of the words 'accessed' or 'cited' in relation to when the information was gained from the Internet, although this information is not required within the **IEEE** guidelines.

Example of an extract from an essay

The following brief extract from a student essay demonstrates how this referencing style works.

Transition and change: the terms are often used interchangeably, and indeed there is a sense of both movement and alteration conveyed in both meanings: from one state of existence to another, or transition. Hopson, Scally and Stafford highlight the movement element implicit in transition, and see it both as a 'passage' (journey) that will last a certain 'period' (of time) and within that time something happens: 'one style is developing into another' (1). So, common within these definitions, is an overall sense that a transition is a cognitive 'journey' of indeterminate length at the end of which change occurs.

However, Bridges (2) argues that 'change' refers to the context or situation itself, whereas 'transition' is aligned to the emotional processes associated with the situational or structural change. Bridges identifies three phases of transition, or emotional change: letting go; passing through 'the neutral zone' (when emotional realignments take place); and emergence into a new situation, when every ending is a beginning.

References

The references are entered at the end of the assignment in the numerical order they appeared (and not in alphabetical order). This is how they would appear in each of the four variants of this referencing style:

British Standard

1. HOPSON, B. M. SCALLY and K. STAFFORD. *Transitions: the challenge of change.* Didcot: Mercury, 1992. p.11.

Alternatively, you could also have put:

HOPSON, B. et al. *Transitions: the challenge of change.* Didcot: Mercury, 1992. p.11.

(See Chapter 7, 'Frequently asked questions', question 6, on how to reference multiple authors.)

2. BRIDGES, W. *Managing transitions: making the most of change.* London: Nicholas Brealey, 2003.

Vancouver

1. Hopson B, Scally M, Stafford K. Transitions: the challenge of change. Didcot: Mercury; 1992. p.11.
2. Bridges W. Managing transitions: making the most of change. London: Nicholas Brealey, 2003.

IEEE

1. B. Hobson, M. Scally and K. Stafford. *Managing transitions: making the most of change.* London: Nicholas Brealey, 2003.
2. W. Bridges. *Managing transitions: making the most of change.* London: Nicholas Brealey, 2003.

CSE

1. Hopson B, Scally M, Stafford K. 1992. Transitions: the challenge of change. Didcot: Mercury. 11 p.
2. Bridges W. 2003. Managing transitions: making the most of change. London: Nicholas Brealey.

6

Name–date (Harvard) style of referencing

Using citations in the text • Citations in the text • List references in full at the end of an assignment • Examples of the Harvard style of referencing • Harvard style in action

The name–date (Harvard) style does indeed appear to have its origins at Harvard University. Chernin (1988) argues that it grew from a referencing practice developed by Edward Laurens Mark, professor of anatomy and director of Harvard's zoological laboratory, who in turn appears to have been inspired by a cataloguing system in the Library of Harvard's Museum of Comparative Zoology.

For the sake of brevity this style, hereafter in the book, will be referred to as 'Harvard'.

Harvard style: basic idea

The basic idea of the Harvard style is to:

- Use citations (a partial reference) in the text, by citing the last or family name of the author(s), or organisational name, and the year of publication in the text of an assignment; and to
- list all references in full and in alphabetical order at the end of an assignment; and
- ensure that the name used in the citation connects with the name used to start the full reference entry.

Although British Standard recommendations are the benchmarks for the Harvard style in Britain, these are not prescriptive and so have been interpreted differently between higher education institutions.

This book has followed a now common practice of placing the year of a source in parenthesis and with the titles shown in italics. I have also presented the names of source originators in upper case letters, as this is in line with British Standard recommendations, as it distinguishes originator names from other elements in the source. However, students need to follow the recommendations on these stylistic matters given by their own institutions.

Using citations in the text

In the text of your assignment, you give a partial reference (called a **citation**). This is the last name of the originator, followed by the year of publication. An originator is an author or, if no named author(s), the name of an organization, newspaper, journal, etc. If there is no obvious name of an originator, the title or part of a title can be used instead.

Citing the source as you write involves giving a partial or shortened reference (last/family name of author(s) and year of publication) in the main body of your written assignment and then giving full details of the source in full at the end of the assignment in a 'References' or 'Bibliography' section. You can abbreviate lengthy organizational names in the citations providing you explain the citation in the full reference; see example that follows: (YHES 1998). (Citations are shown in bold, although there is no need to do this in an actual assignment.)

Although **Handy (1994)** has argued that education is the key to economic success for individuals, organisations and nations, a majority of adults in the UK have yet to be convinced or persuaded of this argument. In 1999 only forty per cent of adults had participated in any sort of formal learning in the previous three years. Of these, a significant majority was from social class groups A, B and C. Only a quarter of adults from semi-skilled or unskilled work backgrounds had involved themselves in formal education **(Tuckett 1999)**. The consequences for people without qualifications who lose their jobs are often serious. A study of long-term unemployed people in Yorkshire found that sixty-one per cent had no educational qualifications, and a significant number of these had special learning needs **(YHES 1998)**. There would appear to be a link too, between lack of qualifications, poor health and a disengagement from participation in political or civic life, and which could aggravate the situation of unemployment for the people concerned **(Hagen 2002)**.

The name used in the text **citation** connects with the full **reference entry**. The full list of references at the end of the assignment for just these four citations would look like this, and in this alphabetical order:

Section 1.01   References
HAGEN, J. (2002). *Basic skills for adults*. Birmingham: The Guidance Council.
HANDY, C. (1994). *The empty raincoat*. London: Hutchinson.
TUCKETT, A. (1999). Who's learning what? *The Guardian*, 18 May 1999, p. 13.
YHES: YORKSHIRE AND HUMBER EMPLOYMENT SERVICE (1998). *Survey of clients aged 25+* unemployed for two years or more. London: Department for Education and Employment.

Citations in the text

You can introduce citations into the text in a variety of ways, for example:

1. There would appear to have emerged by the end of the twentieth century two broad approaches to the management of people within organizations (Handy 1996).

This introduces a point of view, and the student points to Handy as a major proponent of this perspective. The citation in this example is at the end of a sentence. However, this is not the only way of citing the author. The student could have started with the citation, as follows:

2. Handy (1996) argues that by the end of the twentieth century two broad approaches to the management of people within organizations had emerged.

Or (if wanting to include Handy as an exemplar of this proposition):

3. Some commentators, for example, Handy (1996), have argued that by the end of the twentieth century two broad approaches to the management of people within organizations had emerged.

Or

4. It has been argued, (Handy 1996; see also Brown 1999 and Clark 2000), that two approaches to the management of people within organizations had emerged by the end of the twentieth century.

In the example above, a major source, Handy, has been advanced, with two (in this case, fictitious) supporting sources, which are presented in alphabetical order. Or

5. Charles Handy, amongst others, has argued that by the end of the twentieth century two broad approaches to the management of people within organizations could be observed (Handy 1996).

There is no one 'right' way of citing authors. It depends on the context of the sentence and the style of writing adopted at any particular point in the assignment.

The two key points are:

- The importance of giving credit to authors who have influenced your ideas and arguments
- The importance placing the citation in the sentence in a way that makes clear the authorship or origin of the source.

If there is no specific author name, or the term 'Anon.' is not shown in lieu of a name, look for the name of an 'originator', particularly an organizational name in the case of websites. In printed material, if no author's name is shown, you can cite the title of the work, or an abbreviated version of this.

List references in full at the end of an assignment

In the References or Bibliography section at the end of an assignment the **basic format** for listing references in the Harvard style is shown, as follows.

- All sources are listed in alphabetical order by last name or name of originator; as stated earlier, the citation connects with the alphabetical item in the reference.
- Where there is a named author, start with the surname/last name/family name, followed by the initials of the author's first names. Where there is more than one author, the initials of the first name of the second and subsequent writers precede the last name, for example:
  COLEMAN, A. and A. CHIVA (1991). *Coping with change- focus on retirement*. London: Health Education Authority.
- The forename(s) can be reduced to initials, as shown above, provided that the identity of the person is not obscured by doing this. It is common practice in the Harvard, APA and numerical styles to use initials only of forenames for printed material, although British Standard examples of Harvard and numerical referencing show the full forenames of originators of most audio visual material and public performances of creative work.
- Compound and hyphenated last names, such as Russell-Harris, should be alphabetized by the first part of the compound, e.g. Russell.
- Alphabetize the prefixes Mac, Mc, and M' in that order: MacDougall, comes before McAllister, which comes before M'Cardy. For guidelines on referencing foreign names, see Chapter 7, 'Frequently asked questions', question 16.
- If the name of author is shown as 'Anon.', this goes alphabetically into the list. If there is no author or originator's name shown, and 'Anon.' is not presented in lieu of an author's name, a title for printed material (as used as a citation) can be substituted. The first letter of the first proper title word can be the guide to placing it alphabetically in the list of references.
- If you are including several works by the same author, they are listed in chronological order, with the earliest work first; for example:

HUWS, U (1993). *Teleworking in Britain: a report to the Employment Department.* Research Series No 18, Oct 1993. London: Department of Employment.

HUWS, U (1996). *eWorking: an overview of the research.* London: Department of Trade and Industry.

HUWS, U (1999). *Virtually there: the evolution of call centres.* [Report]. London: Mitel Telecom Ltd.

- If you have references with the same first author, but different second and third authors, arrange these alphabetically by the surnames of these subsequent following authors.

- As stated earlier, if you do not have the name of an author, start with the name of the originator. This can be an organization name, e.g. BBC, or the name of a website, e.g. Bized.

- Author name is followed by the **year of publication**. Although British Standard does not show the year in brackets, as stated earlier, it has become common practice now in the Harvard style to do this to differentiate it from other similar name–date styles. The year of publication should be easy to find on printed documents; just look at the printer's imprint and copyright page, which usually follows immediately after the main title page. All the information you need should be there, including name of publisher, where published, when first published and edition. Always show the edition number for the source you looked at – although the edition is different from the impression or reprinted number. Look for the year of the edition and ignore the impression number years. So, 'Seventh edition by Oak Knoll in 1995. Reprinted 1997, 1998, 2000, 2002' would be shown as (1995) in your reference – you ignore the reprint years.

- However, in some older books the date of publication may be missing. In this event, put either (n.d.) or (no date). With Internet sources, look for the year the item was placed on the site or, in the absence of this, the year when the site was last updated, or if unsuccessful with either of these two, the year you looked at the information.

- This is followed by the title of the main source consulted. The main source is usually emphasized in some way, e.g. underlined or italics. The main source would be, for example, the title of a book, name of the magazine, journal or newspaper, item title from an Internet site, broadcast production source, title of video or CD-ROM, etc. Whichever mode of emphasis you choose – underlining or italics – keep it consistent throughout.

- If your source is a chapter from an edited book, you then give the name or names of the **editors** of the book, followed by the title of the edited book, underlined or in italics. To distinguish the name of the editor(s) from the writer, the initials of the editor(s) should precede the last name (see Example 2 that follows).

- In most printed items, you would give details of the publisher. You first give the name of the town or city where the source was published, followed by the name of the publisher.

- In the case of a journal article, you finish with the reference details of volume, edition/issue number (if shown) of the journal and the page number(s) of where the article can be located within the journal.

Examples of the Harvard style of referencing

1 Book (one or more authors)

- Start your full reference with the last name of the author(s) so it connects with the citation; then give initials or first name(s) of the author(s).
- Year of publication comes next.
- Next, give the title of book: in italics **or** underlined (but be consistent throughout your list of references).
- Finally, give the place of publication and name of publisher.

Example

In-text citation:
(Wilmore 2000)
(Just cite the last name(s) of writer(s) and the year the book was published).
Full reference:
WILMORE, G.T.D. (2000). *Alien plants of Yorkshire*. Kendall: Yorkshire Naturalists' Union.

2 Chapter from an edited book

- Start with the full reference entry with the last name of the chapter's author, followed by initials, then state year of publication.
- Then give name (s) of editor(s). The last name of an editor precedes his or her initials, to distinguish editor(s) from the name of the writer of the chapter. Indicate single editor by an abbreviation: (Ed.), or editors: (Eds.).
- State full title of book – in italics or underlined. It is helpful to then give a chapter number.
- Finally, give place of publication and name of publisher.

Example

Citation:
(Nicholls 2002)
(Cite the name of the writer of the chapter or section in the edited book).
Full reference:
NICHOLLS, G. (2002). Mentoring: the art of teaching and learning. In P. JARVIS (Ed.) *The theory and practice of teaching*, chap. 12. London: Kogan Page.

3 Referencing journal articles

- Start with the last name of the author of the article and initials of author.
- Year of publication.
- Title of article (this can go in inverted commas, if wished).

- Name of the journal or magazine (in italics or underlined).
- Volume number and part number (if applicable) and page numbers.

References to journal articles do not include the name of the publisher or place of publication, unless there is more than one journal with the same title, e.g. *International Affairs* (Moscow) and *International Affairs* (London).

Example

Citation:
(Bosworth and Yang 2000).
Reference:
BOSWORTH, D. and D. YANG (2000). Intellectual property law, technology flow and licensing opportunities in China. *International Business Review*, vol. 9, no. 4, pp.453–477.

The abbreviations, 'vol.' (for volume), 'no.' (for number) and 'pp' (for page numbers) can be omitted. However, for clarity and to avoid confusing the reader with a mass of consecutive numbers, they can be included, but be consistent. Note how, in the example above, the initials of the first author follows his last name (Bosworth, D.), but precede the second named (D. Yang). This is the practice illustrated by British Standard in their guidelines with Harvard and both numerical-referencing styles, although you may find the guidelines at your institution may differ on this point.

4 Example of referencing an electronic source

Example

Citation:
(Dixons Group 2004)
Reference:
DIXONS GROUP PLC (2004). *Company report: profile.* [Accessed online from Financial Analysis Made Easy (FAME) database at http://www.bvdep.com/en/FAME. html 13 Dec. 2005].

Harvard style in action

The following report illustrates the Harvard style of referencing in action. It is a report that contains a range of sources, including from the Internet. Note where, when and how references are used to support evidence.

CALL CENTRES IN THE UK: IS THERE A FUTURE FOR THEM?

Introduction

This report will examine the future for call centres in Britain. It will look at current call centre work trends and conditions generally in the UK, will use the Yorkshire region of Britain as an exemplar of trends and will discuss predicted work opportunities over the next decade.

Call centres are collective forms of teleworking, where a group of people work on non-domestic premises controlled by a third party. These premises may be called 'satellite offices', 'call centres', 'computer resources centres' and may use workers employed by the parent company or may use subcontracted workers for particular tasks (Huws 1999).

This detail contained in the last sentence of the introduction would not be generally known, so is outside of 'common knowledge'. The source, therefore, should be acknowledged, i.e. (Huws 1999).

The rise of call centres

The growth in call centres in the West was encouraged by economic and technological factors. From the late 1970s the growth of the service sector focused the attention of large organizations on communication with customers in more cost-effective and streamlined ways. This growth of a service sector economy connected with advances in telecommunications and changes in working practices in Western companies. The logic of call centres was that a centralized approach and rationalization of organizational operations would reduce costs, while producing a standard branded image to the world. The approach naturally lent itself to large companies with large, distributed customer bases.

The student presents a historical overview, drawn from a range of sources and where there is unlikely to be any dispute about the facts summarized. Referencing is not essential in this situation. However, if all the facts came from just one source, this should be cited and referenced.

Currently in Britain 800,000 people are employed in 4000 call centres, but it was predicted that, despite a loss of jobs to India and elsewhere, by 2005 this would have grown to a million workers (DTI 2004). As a result, there is still a future for the UK call centre sector.

Statistics are presented, so source must be cited, i.e. DTI.

Call centres in Yorkshire

The Yorkshire region of the UK is an example of how call centres can flourish. In South Yorkshire, there has been large investment in call centre development, encouraged by EU regional development. Around 6000 operators are already employed with companies such as Ventura (3750 staff), Selflex (1000) and One-2-One (300); in Doncaster, BT Cellnet employs 900 staff at its call centre (PSU 1996).

> Statistics presented, so source must be cited, i.e. PSU.

In West Yorkshire, 25 call centres had been established in Leeds by 2000, employing around 15,000 people and occupying 10 per cent of office space available in the city. Around a third of the Leeds call centres are within traditional single company financial services and the remainder offer a range of services to their clients, including retail sales, mobile phones services and road breakdown services (*Yorkshire Post* 24.9.98. p.3.). In Bradford, by 2004, around 7000 people were employed in call centres, and this is expected to rise to 10,000 by 2007 (Bradford *Telegraph and Argus* 21.06.04. p.4).

> Here an unattributed newspaper item is cited. If there is no named writer, an in-text citation with details of newspaper, date of publication and page number is usually enough; a full reference entry is not normally required by tutors.

Work opportunities and working conditions in call centres

Studies by Huws (1993; 1996; 1999) of teleworking in Britain have described and analysed the evolution of call centre operations. Types of calls are often divided into outbound and inbound. Inbound calls are calls that are initiated by the customer to obtain information, report a malfunction or ask for help. This is substantially different from outbound calls where the agent initiates the call to a customer, mostly with the aim to sell a product or a service to that customer.

> The beginning of this section makes it clear that a number of studies by Huws over a six-year period will be the main source of evidence for the information presented.

Call centre staff are often organized in tiers, with the first tier being largely unskilled workers who are trained to resolve issues using a simple script. If the first tier is unable to resolve an issue, the issue is escalated to a more highly skilled second tier. In some cases, there may be third or higher tiers of support.

A trend originally observed in the US is also becoming apparent in Britain: of a 'high' and a 'low' end to the services provided. The characteristics of employment at both ends of this spectrum can be summarized, as shown in Table 6.1.

Table 6.1 'High' and 'low' and call center

'High-end' call centre services	'Low-end' call centre services
• Usually involving detailed financial services advice, information and sales • Staff recruited for their knowledge and expertise in these areas • Training of staff a high priority • Emphasis on retaining staff • Staff reasonably well paid	• Operators require little technical knowledge • Generally perform a customer service role, typically within travel, retail and leisure industries • May involve 'cold selling' • Staff not particularly well paid • Turnover of staff as high as 80 per cent

(Source: Huws 1999)

We are reminded at the end of this boxed summary of the main source for the preceding section, i.e. Huws.

However, all is not well in call centres, particularly regarding working conditions. A report from Income Data Services (IDS 1998) found large variations in pay and work in UK call centres. This was emphasized in a 2004, report commissioned by the Health and Safety Executive that suggested some UK call centres should be compared to Victorian 'dark satanic mills'. The research found that employees at the worst call centres felt powerless and tied to their desks. Many complained that low wages, poor working conditions and repetitive tasks led to poor job satisfaction and high levels of depression (Management Issues 2005).

Evidence is presented to support the opening sentence, i.e. IDS.

Additional evidence is also cited to back-up the main point of the section, i.e. Management Issues.

It would seem, from the evidence cited so far, that where the dominant focus in any call centre is on answering calls as quickly as possible, the stress levels rise. The complaints by customers about call centre services include those of the length of time in queues, automated menu systems, premium rate lines, having to 'communicate' with staff confined to scripts and the lack of continuity of contact with operators between calls.

Note how the student starts this section by pulling together some key points from the evidence cited in the preceding paragraph.

According to a BBC website, these quality related problems appear to have risen for a number of reasons:

- The call centre industry is unregulated and no independent body exists to represent the views of consumers.
- Call centres often try to match the number of available operators with the volume of calls coming in, but often the number of calls exceeds this, which results in long queues.
- Some call centres judge operators on the number of calls they take, and set unrealistic targets so customer service suffers.
- Call centre operators are often given a script, which is meant to cover all possible scenarios, so are unable to give an answer to an unscripted query.
- Operators at offshore call centres do not necessarily have the knowledge of UK culture and language to answer every customer query (BBC 2004).

> Important information is presented in bullet point form to enable the reader to understand why problems have occurred. The source is introduced at the start of the section and cited at the end of the list, i.e. BBC.

However, there appears, from the evidence cited so far in this section of the report, to be an increasing recognition of the need for UK call centres to improve the quality of customer experiences. For many businesses the call centres become the yardstick by which they are judged. In a competitive situation, a customer who has had a poor experience is likely to take his or her business elsewhere.

> The student takes the opportunity to summarise some key points from the sources previously cited. Therefore, there is no need to repeat the citations.

The future for call centres

At one time in the recent past, the call centre industry in Europe was dubbed a 'bubble market' after a study into the future of call centres by the London-based economic consultants, Business Strategies, warned that the growth of Internet and automatic voice response technology would make call centre operators redundant (Business Strategies 2000). Another communications company, the OTR Group, suggested around the same time that one in five jobs in all call centres in Europe would disappear over the next decade (Financial Times 1999). The increasing use of automatic voice response technology (AVR) was thought to reduce the need for direct operator interventions, and that the growth of Internet sales would reduce the number of operator–customer contacts.

> **Source of the study mentioned is cited, i.e. Business Strategies, and other evidence cited to back up the opening points.**

However, in recent years this prediction has been revised (Huws 1999; Business Strategies 2000). AVR technology is currently unpopular with many callers, who often prefer more human interaction. In Britain, the Yorkshire and Tyneside accents are popular with callers from within the UK and from other countries, and call centres report that customers from other countries, particularly the USA, are noticeably inclined to lengthen their call times in order to engage Northern British operators in friendly discussion. British Asian call centre operators are particularly in demand to communicate with customers who speak no English. The relative low cost of commercial property and lower wages, compared to the South of England, is also cited as attractive factor with employers, and particularly with the public sector.

> **The student makes it clear who has revised the prediction, i.e. Huws 1999, and Business Strategies 2000.**

As mentioned earlier, another more serious potential threat to many UK call centre jobs comes with the increasing 'globalization' of work and where multinational companies have subcontracted work to English-speaking countries in South East Asia. In July 2003, the market intelligence company, Key Note, predicted that by 2008 the UK would lose 97,000 call centre jobs to the Indian sub continent (E-Logistics 2003). British Telecom currently has much of its data entry work done in India, and British Airways has established a call centre in Bombay to handle its bookings (Observer 2003).

> **Sources of the statistics (E-Logistics) and the example (Observer), are cited**

It is certainly true that UK call centre jobs have been lost as employers look to cut costs and relocate overseas. However, USDAW, one of the main trade unions in the call centre industry, has drawn attention to differences in the levels of service between UK and overseas call centres. Referring to studies conducted by a research firm, Contact-Babel, of 290 UK call centre directors and managers, and of 44 Indian call centre operations, they highlighted that:

> **Our attention is drawn to the source for the data and information to be presented, i.e. USDAW**

- On average, UK agents answer 25 per cent more calls each hour than their Indian counterparts, and resolve 17 per cent more of these calls first time.
- UK call centre workers tend to stay with their company for well over three years, while the 'burn out' rates in this £1 billion a year industry in India are extremely high, with an estimated one in three workers quitting within a year.
- more than a third of callers to India have to ring back at least a second time (UK has a first-time resolution rate of over 90 per cent);
- almost a third of Indian call centres do not measure customer satisfaction, while very few perform any proactive quality checking (USDAW 2004).

The source (USDAW), was introduced at the start of the section is cited at the end.

It does appear then, that the call centre industry in India appears now to be encountering some of the same problems that emerged in the West and the sector is finding it harder to retain workers as the Indian economy strengthens and career options for well-qualified workers increase. Operators working at a distance from customers are also likely to feel remote from them, physically, socially and culturally. There is no shared understanding of place and society that often underpins discussion between people from similar geographical backgrounds (Observer 2003).

A reputable UK Sunday newspaper, i.e. the Observer, is cited. The specific page number is given in the full reference.

The recent DTI report suggests that the expansion of call centre services in the UK is likely to be in the realm of more specialisation, with UK call centre operators offering a more informed advisory and information services. UK operators are also likely to be expected to use, at least in the short to medium terms, a wider range of communication technology than operators in other countries (DTI 2004).

Cites a UK government report (DTI). The abbreviation is explained in the full reference.

We can conclude from the evidence cited and discussed in this report that a likely scenario for the future of call centres globally is one where call centres use a mixture of Internet and operator services. The DTI estimates by 2010 that 900 million people worldwide will be using the Internet and already a quarter of UK call centres have staff dealing with email communications from customers (DTI 2004). Developments, such as computer telephony integration (CTI) and Internet provision enable call centres to diversify their products and services. Computer telephony integration enables call centres to offer support services to the online retail market. Although only a small percentage of sales in the UK are currently conducted through the Internet, this market is growing rapidly. Call centre staff will need to develop more advanced computer skills in the future, and are likely to communicate both by email and verbally with customers.

The student attempts to pull together points emerging from the sources cited, but is careful to cite any new statistical information that is presented, i.e. DTI.

Conclusion

The future for call centres in Britain is certainly not as gloomy as predicted in the late 1990s, provided that call centres respond to the need for more personal, more responsive and bilingual modes of contact with customers. There is a particularly need in Britain to offer more specialist bilingual services to customers and particularly Asian language services in multi-ethnic areas.

It is uncommon for citations to appear in conclusions. An exception to this rule might be if a quotation is used for final effect.

Bibliography

ASIA BUSINESS TODAY (2006). *Outsourcing: is India to be blamed? http://www.asiabusinesstoday.org/ briefings/* [Accessed 11/01/2006].

BBC (2004). Brassed-off Britain: call centres. *http://www.bbc.co.uk/bob/callcentres/* [Accessed 09/08/ 2004].

BUSINESS STRATEGIES (2000). Tomorrow's call centres: a research study. *www.business-strategies.co.uk* [Accessed 02/01/2001].

DTI. DEPARTMENT FOR TRADE AND INDUSTRY (2004) *The UK contact centre industry: a study'*. London: Department for Trade and Industry.

E-LOGISTICS (2003). Call centres – an inexorable flight? *http://www.elogmag.com/magazine/29/call-centres.shtml* [Accessed 20/6/04].

FINANCIAL TIMES 23 Aug. 1999 p.3.

HEALTH AND SAFETY EXECUTIVE (2004). *Psychosocial working conditions in Great Britain in 2004*. London: Health and Safety Executive.

HUWS, U (1993). *Teleworking in Britain: a report to the Employment Department*. Research Series No 18, Oct 1993. London: Department of Employment.

HUWS, U (1996). *eWorking: an overview of the research*. London: Department of Trade and Industry.

HUWS, U (1999). *Virtually there: the evolution of call centres*. Report: Mitel Telecom Ltd.

IDS: INCOME DATA SERVICES (1998). *www.incomesdata.co.uk/index.html* [Accessed 20/06/2004].

MANAGEMENT ISSUES (2005). Call centres are modern day satanic mills. *http://www.management-issues.com/display_page.asp?section=*researchandid=1063 [Accessed 20/07/2005].

OBSERVER. *Bombay calling . . .* 07/12/2003, p.19.

PSU: POLICY RESEARCH UNIT (1996) *Shaping the future: an economic and labour market assessment of Yorkshire and Humberside.* Leeds Metropolitan University/ Leeds Training and Enterprise Council.

USDAW (2004). Indian vs UK call centres: new reports find faults in both. *www.publictechnology.net/modules.php?op*=modloadandname=Newsandfile=articleandsid=442 [Accessed 20/06/2004].

A **bibliography** has been presented, as not all the sources listed were cited in the report. The student, however, wants to present to the tutor the totality of reading done in preparation for writing the report.

See Chapter 8 for an example of an essay written using the Harvard style.

And for those interested . . .

A benchmark for the Harvard referencing style in Britain

A benchmark for using the Harvard style of referencing in Britain is British Standard (BS), and the recommendations in the following BS publications: *Recommendations for references to published materials*: BS 1629:1989; *Recommendations for citing and referencing published material*: BS 5605:1990; *Copy preparation and proof correction – part 1: Design and layout of documents*: BS 5261-1:2000, and BSO ISO-690-2: 1997: *Information and documentation – Guidelines for bibliographic references and citations to information resources.*

7

Frequently asked questions

1 What is the difference between references and a bibliography? • 2 When should I use page numbers in my in-text citations? • 3 The author of the book I read mentions another author. I want to refer to this other author. How do I reference this? • 4 How do I cite work from an author that has published more than once in the same year? • 5 How do I cite in my assignment where an author has written different books, but has made similar points in each? • 6 How do I cite and reference works written and edited by more than one author? • 7 I read a book in my own (non-English) language. Do I give you an English translation of the title in the full reference? • 8 What punctuation and capitalization style should I use in referencing? • 9 The source has no date. How can I reference this? • 10 Can I use abbreviations in references? • 11 I have noticed that some writers cite more than one author occasionally in support of a particular argument or point of view. When and why should I do this? • 12 Are quotations and citations in the text counted in the assignment word count? • 13 How do I cite sources where no author's name is shown? • 14 How do I cite sources recorded on microfiche/microfilm/microform? • 15 I have noticed that both parenthesis ( ) and squared brackets [ ] are sometimes used in full references. Why is this? • 16 How do I reference foreign author names? • 17 When I am writing an assignment, I want sometimes to respond to a writer's point of view from what I have learned in the past – but I cannot always remember the source of my inspiration. What can I do in this situation? • 18 How can I present and distinguish my own ideas and opinions from those in published sources?

This chapter presents a range of questions that students most frequently ask about referencing. The questions are, as follows:

1 What is the difference between references and a bibliography?
2 When should I use page numbers in my in-text citations?
3 Secondary referencing: the author of the book I read mentions another author. I want to refer to this other author. How do I reference this?
4 How do I cite work from an author that has been published more than once in the same year?
5 How do I cite in my assignment where an author has written different books, but has made similar points in each?
6 Referencing multiple sources: how do I cite and reference works written and edited by more than one author?
7 I read a book in my own (non-English) language. Do I give you an English translation of the title in the full reference?
8 What punctuation and capitalization style should I use in referencing?
9 The source has no date. How can I reference this?
10 Can I use abbreviations in references?
11 I have noticed that some writers cite more than one author occasionally in support of a particular argument or point of view. When and why should I do this?
12 Are quotations and citations in the text counted in the assignment word count?
13 How do I cite sources where no author's name is shown?
14 How do I cite sources that are recorded on microfiche/microfilm/microform?
15 I have noticed that both parentheses ( ) and squared brackets [ ] are sometimes used in references. Why is this?
16 How do I reference foreign author names?
17 When I am writing an assignment, I want sometimes to respond to a writer's point of view from what I have learned in the past – but I cannot always remember the source of my inspiration. What can I do in this situation?
18 How can I present and distinguish my own ideas and opinions in an assignment from those in published sources?

1 What is the difference between references and a bibliography?

This issue was also discussed in chapter three, but here is a summary of the differences. **References** (or 'Works cited' in the MLA, CSE and Chicago styles) are the items you have read and specifically referred to (or cited) in your assignment.

A **bibliography** (or 'Works consulted' in the MLA, CSE and Chicago styles style) is a list of everything you consulted in preparation for writing an assignment, whether or not you referred specifically to it in the assignment. A bibliography will, therefore, normally contain sources that you have cited in the assignment **and** those you found to be influential, but decided not to cite. A bibliography can give a tutor an overview of

which authors have influenced your ideas and arguments, even if you do not specifically refer to them. You would normally only have one listed, headed 'References'
(Works cited) **or** 'Bibliography' (Works consulted), unless your tutor has asked you to
provide both.

2 When should I use page numbers in my in-text citations?

Only the MLA style of referencing shows page numbers as an integral part of the
citation. With the other referencing systems, the following comments apply.

Single topic books

Many single subject books often have a main or dominant message, perspective
or argument that forms the essential core or essence of the book. Authors build their
arguments around these cores by presenting evidence and examples to back up their
perspectives or by challenging counter-arguments. If you wish to offer evidence in
your assignment that summarizes these essential core perspectives, then a page number
is not necessary. You could, though, include a chapter number if you wanted to isolate
a particular feature of the core perspective.

However, if you use and include a quotation from the book, you will need to include
a page number in the citation, as shown here using the Harvard style:

> Ron Todd of the Transport and General Workers' Union commented, 'we've got
> three million on the dole and another 23 million scared to death' (quoted by
> Bratton 1992, p.70).

You can also include a page number in the citation, if you are referring to some specific
detail that is secondary or incidental to the book's core point or perspective and which
would be hard to find without a page number. These might include, for example:

- Statistics
- Illustrative examples
- Author comments not directly related to the main topic
- Definitions.

You would also give a page number if you are using the book as a **secondary source**
– see question 3 below.

Other books and sources

The same comments for books on a single topic apply for other sources. If the reader
will struggle to find precisely what you looked at without the benefit of page numbers

in the citation, then include them. If it is an electronic online source, your full reference will include the digital object identifier (DOI) or uniform/universal resource locator (URL) to enable the reader to go straight to the text that you looked at, or will include search terms to lead the reader from an opening page to the source. You may need, however, to include a section or paragraph sub-heading if the section that encompasses the evidence is a lengthy one.

3 The author of the book I read mentions another author. I want to refer to this other author. How do I reference this?

This is called secondary referencing. Typically, you will be reading a chapter in a book and the author will mention an interesting piece of research done by someone else, or provide a useful fact for your assignment, then give a citation, naming another writer or writers.

You have two choices in this situation. You can find and read the source mentioned yourself and check out the accuracy of the summary given by the secondary source author – this is the recommended option. You can refer directly to this author, as you have then read the source yourself.

However, there are circumstances when it would be appropriate to use the secondary source:

- If you find it difficult to find or gain access to the primary source
- If you are confident the secondary source author is reliable and accurate in the way he or she has summarized, paraphrased or quoted the original author
- If you do not need to go into any great depth of analysis on what the primary author has written.

For example, in the book *Licensed to Work* by Barrie Sherman and Phil Judkins (1995), there is a reference to another writer, Ivan Illich, who refers to 'shadow work': tasks in society that were once the responsibility of extended families and close communities.

If the Sherman and Judkins book was used as a secondary source, your **citation** must make this clear. So, within the name–date (Harvard) referencing systems you could write:

Ivan Illich (1981), as summarized by Sherman and Judkins (1995, p.121), has suggested that 'shadow work', a term he coined, which means . . .

or

Illich (1981) has coined the term 'shadow work', meaning the tasks in society that were once the responsibility of extended families and close communities (in Sherman and Judkins 1995 p.121).

or

Sherman and Judkins in their book (1995, p.121) refer to the work of Ivan Illich (1981), who coined the term 'shadow work' as being . . .

Within the **Harvard and APA** styles, it is only necessary to give details of the source you looked at. So your full reference would be for the item you looked at:

SHERMAN, B. and P. JUDKINS, (1995). *Licensed to Work*. London: Cassell.

If anyone wanted to read Ivan Illich's book to pursue in more depth the point he makes, they could look at *Licensed to Work* and find the full reference details there.

However, with the **MLA** style, you can use the term 'qtd. in' (for 'quoted in'), followed by the author or originator name of the source you looked at, e.g. (qtd. in Raimes 78). But like the Harvard and APA styles, you would only reference the source you looked at in your list of works cited.

However, with both the numerical styles of referencing, your tutors may want you to present full information about both sources, as footnotes and endnotes are useful for containing this additional information. For example, with the running-notes referencing style, your footnote on a secondary source, as shown earlier, could look like this:

Footnotes

Hoggart, R. 'The role of the teacher'. Originally published in J. Rogers (Ed.), *Teaching on equal terms*, BBC Publications, 1969, and cited in J. Rogers, *Adults learning*. 3rd edition. Milton Keynes: Open University Press, 1989, p.81.

---

4 How do I cite work from an author that has published more than once in the same year?

Within the name–date **Harvard and APA** styles you use letters a, b, c and onward in your citations to differentiate between the different sources, for example:

The term 'communication apprehension' was coined by James McCroskey (1976a) and is defined as . . .

Later in the assignment you might want to refer to the same author, writing in a different source published in the same year, e.g.:

Studies suggest that high CA can impact on a person's behaviour, relationships, the perceptions of others, occupational choice and employment opportunities and education (McCroskey 1976b; McCroskey and Richmond 1979 . . .

In the references/bibliography, you would then link the two different sources to the citation (as shown here in the Harvard style):

McCROSKEY, J. C. (1976a). The effects of communication apprehension on non-verbal behavior. *Communication quarterly*, vol. 24, pp: 39–44.
McCROSKEY, J. C. (1976b). The problems of communication apprehension in the classroom. *Speech communication journal*, vol. 4, pp: 1–12,

Within the author–page **MLA** style, you can (a) either make it clear in your text which book or other source you are referring to, or (b) give a shortened version of the title in a parenthetical citation, e.g.:

(a) McCroskey, in his book 'Problems of Communication Apprehension in the Classroom', argued that . . . (45)

or

(b) (McCroskey, Problems 45)

With both numerical styles of referencing, there is less of a problem. With the **Running-notes** referencing styles you allocate a different number to each source cited and link these with footnotes and endnotes. With the **Numeric** styles of referencing, you allocate a number to the source in question, repeat this number in the text each time you refer to the source, and link the number with the full reference detail at the end of the assignment.

5 How do I cite in my assignment where an author has written different books, but has made similar points in each?

With the name–date **Harvard and APA** styles you might on occasions want to refer to two or more books that an author has written in a single citation – as the author may have presented the same argument on more than one occasion. You can cite the author with the earlier works listed first, e.g. (Handy 1984; 1994; 1997). These are then listed in chronological order in your full list of references, each separated with a semicolon.

With the author–page **MLA** style, if the points made by the author are at the core of the book, i.e. a central recurring theme, it might be easier to refer to the author and years in the text, e.g.:

Handy has argued over nearly twenty years that . . .

You could then list the sources you have in mind, along with the sources you specific-ally cite, in a list at the end labelled 'Works consulted', which, like 'Bibliography', indicates that the list of sources is not confined to just those specifically cited in the text. If you did need to refer to specific page numbers, these could be linked to a title or shortened version of book titles concerned, e.g.:

Handy has argued for over nearly twenty years that . . . (see Future of Work: 34; Empty Raincoat: 45; Hungry Spirit: 55).

With the numerical styles of referencing, a specific number can be allocated to each of the sources, e.g.:

Running notes: 'Handy has argued over nearly twenty years **13, 14, 15,** that . . .' The footnotes would show the respective sources:

---

13. HANDY, C. *The future of work.* Oxford: Blackwell, 1984.
14. ibid. *The empty raincoat: making sense of the future.* London: Hutchinson. 1994.
15. ibid. *The hungry spirit: beyond capitalism; a quest for purpose in the modern world.* London: Hutchinson, 1997.

A **bibliography**, at the end of the assignment, would also list all sources consulted, including the sources shown in the footnotes.

Numeric styles: 'Handy has argued over nearly twenty years **(1, 2, 3)** that . . .' The same sources, as shown in the running-notes example, would appear in the **References** at the end of the assignment:

1. HANDY, C. *The future of work.* Oxford: Blackwell, 1984.
2. HANDY, C. *The empty raincoat: making sense of the future.* London: Hutchinson. 1994.
3. HANDY, C. *The hungry spirit: beyond capitalism; a quest for purpose in the modern world.* London: Hutchinson, 1997.

Your tutor may also want you to include a bibliography, which will include all sources consulted in preparation for the assignment, included those cited in the text.

6 How do I cite and reference works written and edited by more than one author?

This depends on the style of referencing. A distinction also needs to be made about what happens in the in-text citation, and in the full reference.

Harvard and British Standard numerical styles

In the citation: if a document has one to three authors, their names should be given in the citation. If there are **more than three**, the name of the first should always be given, but the names of the others may be omitted and replaced by the term 'et al.' (meaning, 'and others'), e.g. (Burchell et al. 1999).

In the full reference: in British Standard ISO-690-3: the recommendation is that when a publication is by two or three authors, the surnames of all should be shown in the reference list or bibliography. When there are more than three authors, the names of all may be given, or the name of the first author only, followed by et al., or by writing 'and others'.

So although the first three names should be cited in the text of your assignment, in the full reference it is discretionary whether you add names beyond the first. However, you need to follow your institutional guidelines, as some may vary from this.

If you use more than one author's name in the full reference, British Standard examples of full references show the initials or full first names of second or more authors preceding their last names; see the example below:

MERRITT, F.S., M.K. LOFTIN, and J.T. RICKETTS (1995). *Merritt's standard handbook of civil engineering*. 4th edn. [CD-ROM]. New York: McGraw Hill.

Vancouver numeric and IEEE

In the full reference the first six authors are listed, thereafter you can add et al. after the sixth author.

MHRA

In the reference the names of up to three authors should be given in full. For works by more than three authors, the name of only the first should be given, followed by 'and others' (and not et al.).

APA style

In the APA citations

- When a work has two authors, both names should be cited each time the source is mentioned in the text.
- When a work has three to five authors, all of them should be cited the first time the source is mentioned. In subsequent citations only the last name of the first (lead) author is mentioned, followed by et al. (not italicized), plus the year of publication, e.g. Saunders et al. (2003).
- If the citation is used again in the same assignment, the year can be omitted, e.g. Saunders et al.
- If you have two or more different sources, but with the same lead author, cite the last names of as many of the subsequent authors to distinguish the sources from each other, followed by a comma and et al.

- If a work has six or more authors, you should cite only the last name of the first author followed by et al. and the year.

In the full APA reference

- The full name information of the first six authors should be given, but then use et al. for the remaining names.

MLA style

In the MLA citation

- For a work with up to three authors, include all the names in the in-text citation. For a work with **four** or more authors, use only the first author's name followed by et al.

In the full MLA reference

- Give names of the three authors in the order in which they appear on the title page, but put the last name first for the first named author only, e.g. Brown, Jim, Timothy Edwards and Mary Lacy.
- When the work has more than three authors, you can use et al. to replace all the author names, except the first.

Chicago

In the Chicago citation

- For a work with up to three authors, include all the names in the in-text citation. For a work with **four** or more authors, use only the first author's name followed by et al.

In the full Chicago reference

- List all the authors' names; do not use et al. Put the last name first for the first named author only, e.g. Brown, Jim, Mary Clarke, Alice Edwards, Thomas Evans.

See Table 7.1 for a summary of the above.

Table 7.1 Summary

Harvard and British Standard numerical styles	**Citations:** Cite first three names in full; you can substitute four or more authors for et al. **Full reference:** If more than three authors, you can substitute names beyond the first with et al. (but abide by institutional guidelines that differ on this)
Vancouver Numeric and IEEE	First six authors are listed, thereafter you can add et al. after the sixth author
MHRA	Names of up to three authors should be given in full. Over three authors, the name of only the first should be given, followed by 'and others' (and not 'et al.').
APA	**Citations:** • **One or two authors:** always give names for one or both throughout the assignment • **Three to five authors:** give their names the first time mentioned; thereafter use et al. to substitute • **Six or more authors:** just use the first named and substitute 'et al.' for remainder **Full reference:** First six names are listed; et al. to represent the others
MLA	**Citations:** Cite first three names in full; if more than three, use first name and substitute et al. for rest **Full reference:** If more than three authors, you can substitute et al. after the first
Chicago	**Citations** Cite first three names in full; if more than three, use first name and substitute et al. for rest **Full reference:** Do not use et al; all the authors' names should be included

7 I read a book in my own (non-English) language. Do I give you an English translation of the title in the full reference?

You should give details of the source you looked at, which will include the title and author, in the language concerned. However, it is accepted practice to add an English translation [in square brackets] immediately after the title, particularly if the book was originally published in non-European characters, e.g. Chinese, Arabic, and Japanese.

In addition, if the book has also been translated from the original language, the name of the translator should be shown.

British Standard (1989: 6.2) gives an example of this:

GORKI, Maxim. *Delo Artamonovykh* [The Artamonovs]. Translated from the Russian by Alec Brown. London: Folio Society, 1955.

8 What punctuation and capitalization style should I use in referencing?

Punctuation

In all referencing styles, except IEEE and MHRA, stops are usually shown after each integral part of the full reference. In relation to Harvard and both numerical styles of referencing, the British Standard recommendations presents examples that show sentence stops or commas after each distinct part of the reference, e.g.:

HANDY, C. (1994). *The empty raincoat: making sense of the future.* London: Hutchinson.

Capitalization

All referencing styles except MHRA and MLA show all words in the titles of full references, in lower case, apart from the first letters of titles and names of people, organizations and places. British Standard illustrative examples confine capitals to proper names, e.g. Victoria, Essex, Britain; this would include the names of journals, magazines, newspapers, films, and works of art referenced in the text.

However, you may find institutional variations on this and it is important that you adhere to the referencing style guidelines issued by your institution. Students on science and technology related courses, for instance, are often required to start the main source title in a reference with a capital letter, but then to use lower case for remaining words, as this tends to be in line with referencing styles found in professional journals; for example (in the Harvard style):

ASHBY, M.F. and K. JOHNSON. (2002). *Materials and design: the art and science of material selection in mechanical design.* Oxford: Butterworth Heinemann.

However, students on other courses, and using the Harvard style referencing, may be advised to start each proper word in the title with a capital letter. This tends to reflect referencing styles in journals for disciplines in these areas, and is an example of how British Standard guidelines merge with other practices to produce hybrids.

As mentioned earlier, the APA style guide shows the capitalization of the first letter of a book or article title in the first word, and the word following a colon in the title; e.g.:

Torrance, M., Thomas, G. & Robinson, E.J. (1991). Strategies for answering examination essay questions: Is it helpful to write a plan? *British Journal of Educational Psychology*, vol. 61, pp. 46–54.

The exception to this first rule would be when naming organisations within a book title, e.g.:

American Psychological Association. (2001). *Publication manual of the American Psychological Association* (5th edn.). Washington, DC: APA.

9 The source has no date. How can I reference this?

Older books may not show a date of publication. In that event, state 'no date' in your citation and in the reference, or use an abbreviation, 'n.d.'. You may find other sources, e.g. videos, without apparent production dates, so 'no date' or the same abbreviation can be used with other undated sources.

10 Can I use abbreviations in references?

Abbreviations in the text of assignments are not generally encouraged by tutors, except in scientific and technical writing, in tables, graphs and charts, and in relation to the terms 'ibid', 'op cit.' and 'loc cit.', discussed previously in Chapter 5 (see 'Consecutive number, or running notes styles of referencing'). However, in footnotes and in lists of references or bibliographies they can be used, although clarity always takes precedence over brevity in references. You should use a full word if the abbreviation might confuse readers.

British Standard guidelines, the MLA *Handbook for Writers of Research Papers* and the APA style guide all give advice on abbreviations commonly found and acceptable within full references.

However, Table 7.2 shows a common list of abbreviations found in most styles of referencing; MLA referencing style exceptions are shown.

Table 7.2 Abbreviations

Term	Abbreviation
abbreviated/abbreviation	abbr.
abstract	abs.
adapted	adapt.
bibliography	bibliogr. (MLA: bibliog.)
compact disc read-only	CD-ROM
cassette	cas.
chapter	ch. or chap.
circa	c. or ca.
Department of . . .	Dept. of. .
diagram	diagr.
disk	dk.
edition	edn.
(Revised edition)	Rev. edn.
Second edition, etc.	2nd edn.
Editor (s)	ed/s.
electronic mail	email
figure	fig.
folio	fol.

from	fr.
index	ind.
Number/number	No./no.
no date	n.d.
opus (work)	op.
page	p.
pages	pp.
paragraph	par.
part	pt. or part (in music)
plate (as in photographic) or plural	pl.
record(ed)	rec.
series	ser.
summary	sum.
supplement	suppl. (MLA: supp.)
table	tab.
Technical Report	Tech. Rep.
track	tr.
tome	t.
variant	var.
volume	vol.

Abbreviating months

For Harvard, MLA, Chicago, and British Standard numerical styles, the months of the year in full reference can be abbreviated, except May, June and July. The APA style shows all the months of the year spelt in full.

11 I have noticed that some writers cite more than one author occasionally in support of a particular argument or point of view. When and why should I do this?

A number of authors can be cited in support of particularly key or important points that you want to make, or to support contentious statements or arguments presented by others. An example to illustrate this:

> As the behavioural response of communication apprehension (CA) is to avoid or discourage interaction with others it is not surprising that CA has been linked to feelings of loneliness, isolation, low self-esteem and the inability to discuss personal problems with managers or others (Daly and Stafford 1984; Mc Croskey et al. 1977; Mc Croskey and Richmond 1987; Richmond 1984; Scott and Rockwell 1997).

Multiple sources can add emphasis to a specific point – particularly if it is a central one for your assignment, or is the subject of ongoing debate. As stated earlier, you should be careful not to take this practice to ludicrous proportions, and citing five or six authors is a suggested maximum for this practice; see also the next question, number 12, for other reasons to discourage overuse of multiple citations.

12 Are quotations and citations in the text counted in the assignment word count?

Normally, yes, although check with your institution on this, as some courses may have decided differently. The general view is that, if you include quotations in your assignment, you take 'ownership' of them. You have decided to include quotations for emphasis or to make a particular point, so normally you must include them in your word count, unless your tutor indicates otherwise.

In addition, name–date or author–page citations in the text, e.g. (Handy 1994), are also usually included in the word count on most courses, although footnotes, endnotes, and the references, bibliography or works cited lists are normally excluded from the word count (but again, there can be institutional variations on this point!).

13 How do I cite sources where no author's name is shown?

Books

If a book has no author or editor name shown on the title page, you can cite and reference by starting with the title and list the source alphabetically, but ignore any prefix article words: 'The', 'An', 'A'. 'The Hobbit', for example, would be listed under 'H'. However, if the book shows 'Anonymous' or 'Anon.' on the title page, against the author, this can be cited and referenced as such, but only in these circumstances.

Magazine/journals/newspapers

If no author's name is shown, British Standard recommends citing and starting the reference within the Harvard and British Standard numerical styles with the 'originator's' name, e.g. the name of the newspaper. With MLA and APA styles, cite the title, and start the full references or bibliography by letter of alphabet of first significant starting word in the title, again ignoring any article word, e.g. 'The', 'An', 'A'.

Internet sources

- Do not put a www address as a citation in the text, unless there is no other way of identifying the originator of the site/source.
- Do not put the name of a search tool or engine, e.g. 'Google'.

If no author's name is shown, look for the name of an organization that produced the source, or, failing that, the name of the host site, e.g. (Business World 2006), to cite, and this title will connect with your full reference entry.

The **MLA** recommend, however, within this style, to cite and begin the 'Works cited' entry with the **title** of the document if the author's name is absent. This could be shortened if it is lengthy. For more information and examples on referencing electronic sources, see Chapter 9.

14 How do I cite sources recorded on microfiche/microfilm/microform?

Sources that have been photographed and stored on microfilm are referenced as for the original item, e.g. book, journal, map, etc. (see examples in Chapter 9).

15 I have noticed that both parentheses (   ) and squared brackets [   ] are sometimes used in full references. Why is this?

Although British Standard does not show the year in brackets, it has become an accepted hybrid practice in Harvard style referencing to enclose the year of publication within round brackets in line with the APA style, e.g. Hardy, T. (1887). *The Woodlanders*. This appears to be to distinguish these styles from others. However, whenever you add information that does not appear in the original source, and which is necessary for identification purposes, this should be enclosed in square brackets.

Example (Harvard)

HARDY, T. (1887). *The Woodlanders*. [Online]. (Ed.) M. MONCUR. The Literature Page. Available at http://www.literaturepage.com/read/the-woodlanders.html [Accessed 25 July 2006].

The information about the type of source [Online] and the date when the student found it on the Internet [Accessed] is additional information to help the reader understand the type of source and currency of the information, so is contained within square brackets.

16 How do I reference foreign author names?

When alphabetizing names for citations and reference lists in languages other than English, you should treat the last name in accordance with the conventions that apply in the country of origin. For instance, when the name of an author consists of several words, the choice of entry word is determined as far as possible by agreed usage in the country concerned.

In parts of Asia, for example, a father's personal name is commonly combined with the son's name, so that in two-worded names the **second** is the father's personal name, and not the family name. You may need, therefore, if you are unfamiliar with these conventions, to seek advice from the librarian at your institution or the help of a fellow student from the country in question.

However, here are some recommendations for some specific countries or global regions.

European names

- **French:** The *de* following a first name is not normally used with the last name for referencing purposes. However, there are some exceptions, as follows: when *De* is normally used or associated with the name, e.g. De Quincy; or when the last name has only one syllable, e.g. *de Gaulle*; or when the name begins with a vowel, *d'Arcy*; or when the prefixes *Du* and *Des* are applied.
- **German:** the prefix *von* is usually not used with the last name in references, unless it has become associated by tradition and convention with a particular person.
- **Italian:** Renaissance or pre-Renaissance names are cited and alphabetized by first name, e.g. Leonardo da Vinci. Post-Renaissance and modern Italian family names are often prefixed with *da, de, del, della, di or d'*, which should be included in the reference, although the alphabetization should be with the last name, e.g. *De Sica*, placed in the alphabet under 'S'.
- **Spanish:** last names should be shown in full, e.g. García Márquez; García Lorca. The prefix *Del* is capitalized and used with the last name for referencing purposes.

Arabic names

Arabic last names that begin with 'al-' or 'el-' should be alphabetized against the name that follows, e.g. al-Hakim, would be listed under 'H'. Arabic names that that begin with 'Abu', 'Abd' and 'Ibn' are similar to Scottish names beginning with 'Mac', so they should be alphabetized accordingly, e.g. 'Abd' would precede 'Abu'.

Asian names

In some countries, e.g. China, Korea, and Japan, the family name is followed by a given or personal name. So the male Chinese name 'Mao Zedong', consists of the family name: 'Mao', and his given or personal name: 'Zedong'. However, full names often consist of three parts, e.g. 'Kim Yong-il'. In this example, 'Kim' would be treated as the surname, while 'Yong' indicates the generation of the person, and 'il' the personal name (Akhtar 2007). In a reference entry under the Harvard style this would appear as 'Kim, Yong-il'.

However, some people who live or work frequently outside their home countries adopt a Westernized name by simply reversing the order of their names, and/or by adopting a Westernised personal name, e.g. Deli Yang. You need, therefore, to establish the family name, because some referencing styles, e.g. Harvard, require you to use this as the citation in your text and to start the main reference entry.

If an author's name does not easily conform to APA or any other European or North American referencing style guides – where it is relatively easy to establish what is the 'surname', 'last name' or 'family' name – then it is reasonable, and culturally respectful, to give the name in full in the citation, which is repeated in the same order in the full reference; for example: (Jamaludin Mohd. Jahi, and Abd Rahim Mohd. Nor 2000).

If an author has adopted a Christian-European name, which they place first in their full name, this should be reversed in the reference, so that, with the example, James Kim Jun-Orr, the citation would present the full Korean name, i.e. (Kim Jun-Onn), and the full reference entry would start Kim Jun-Onn, J.

17. When I am writing an assignment, I want sometimes to respond to a writer's point of view from what I have learned in the past – but I cannot always remember the source of my inspiration. What can I do in this situation?

What is behind a question like this is often a worry or concern about plagiarism. You may be concerned that you will be accused of plagiarism if you advance your own interpretation or response to a topic – and find that someone has published an identical or similar response.

For your peace of mind, it is a good idea to get into the habit of always noting and recording the sources of all your reading for academic purposes (see Chapter 3 on note-making and using referencing management software).

However, we are influenced by ideas all the time; this is how we learn, and it can sometimes be difficult, if not impossible, to remember the sources that have influenced us. A student in my research made this point well:

> As a mature student, I have been reading around my subject for the last 30 years. I can't always remember where I read a particular fact – just that I 'know' it. How much research do I need to do to find a 'source' for something I've absorbed over the years?
>
> (Postgraduate: Italian Cinema)

If you find yourself in this situation, you can present a personal interpretation – but make it clear it is your own view (see question 18 below). In an otherwise well-referenced essay, most tutors will appreciate that such an unreferenced statement is a genuine attempt by a student to express his or her own ideas, or to interpret events in their own ways, drawn from their past experiences – and will not accuse them of plagiarism. Most experienced tutors can spot plagiarists and plagiarism very easily (see Chapter 4). Now read the next frequently asked question!

18 How can I present and distinguish my own ideas and opinions from those in published sources?

Students often want to include their own view on an assignment topic, but are not sure how to do this, particularly in essays where their tutors have advised them to write in the third person and avoid using the first person term 'I'. Tutors often have mixed views about students using the term 'I', and this often depends on the subject, the tutor's own academic background, and their views on academic writing. However, if you have been advised to avoid using the term 'I' in assignments, it is important to be aware of conventions in academic writing on how to distinguish the ideas of others from your own.

Table 7.3 shows some phrases that could be used.

Table 7.3 Phrases

When citing the work of others	When suggesting that the idea is your own
• It has been argued . . . (state by whom, e.g. Devlin 2005; and Hague 2007) • XYZ has argued/asserted/implied • XYZ has suggested/stated/claimed • Recent evidence suggests . . . (state who has suggested it) • It has been shown by (state by whom) that . . . • Strong evidence was found by (state by whom) that . . . • A positive correlation was found by (state by whom) between . . . • The relationship between X and Y has been explored by (state by whom)	• It may be argued that . . . • It can be argued that . . . • Arguably, . . . • The problem with this perspective is, however, that . . . • Another perspective on this topic is that . . . • It may/might/could be that . . . • One question that needs to be asked, is . . . • However, a contradiction to this argument could/might/may be/is that . . .

The phrases in the right-hand column of Table 7.3, if presented unreferenced, would suggest to the tutor that the ideas and views were your own (albeit based on a wide reading of the topic). These personal comments could also be linked with evidence from sources that connect with, and reinforce, your own perspective. So you could start a sentence **with your own view**, and then use supporting evidence to back-up these up, e.g. 'It can be argued that . . .' (and later) 'The work of Smith (2008) supports this (perception/view/argument) to a large extent, as her work suggests . . .'.

Another thing you can do in answer to this question is . . . read the next chapter!

8

How to express your own ideas in assignments

So what does such an essay look like? • Comments on the exercise • Your own voice

A number of students in my research surveyed felt constrained from expressing personal opinion in their work, for fear of being accused of plagiarism. This resulted in their assignment becoming like raggedy-patched things, made up of other people's words and ideas, and where their own identities were lost. Two students wrote:

> The need to reference every proposition or idea diminishes the opportunity to develop my own ideas for fear of not having properly referenced all knowledge in the assignment.
>
> (Postgraduate, European and International Business Law)

> Sometimes I have my own idea, but I am not sure whether it is similar to any author and then whether lecturers will consider my work is plagiarism or not.
>
> (Postgraduate, Human Resources Management)

The most successful academic writing is often a blend of objectivity and subjectivity; both the 'big picture' and the telling detail. It has the structure of a good story, with a beginning, a middle and an end, and like any good story it has something of the writer in it. The real person behind the keyboard is not lost in a forest of jargon, interminable sentences, multiple references, endless footnotes and mind-numbing statistics. But is this easier said than done? The problem for many students is that they simply do not know what such an effective essay **looks** like.

So what does such an essay look like?

The following essay was submitted in 2009 by a student, **Jonas Juenger**, for an essay-writing competition sponsored by the *LearnHigher* Centre of Excellence in Teaching and Learning (CETL) network. The set title was 'What is the point of referencing?', and there was a maximum word limit of 1500 words.

Jonas's essay is a good example of an essay that:

- Uses sources to develop, and not just reflect, arguments
- Demonstrates accurate referencing within the Harvard style
- Is well structured and well written
- Blends Jonas's own experiences with other evidence, so is a good example of a student 'finding their own voice' in assignments
- Above all, answers the essay question.

Exercise

- As you read, I suggest you underline or mark any section you feel is a particular example of Jonas writing in his own voice. How does he assert his own identity into the text at these points?
- Look at the sections in the essay **when** Jonas references sources of evidence – ask yourself **why** is he referencing on these occasions? You may like to reread Chapter 3 to remind yourself of when to reference.
- Look for examples of critical analysis – this is where the writer moves away from just describing phenomena to being more analytical of it. What does Jonas do at these points in the essay?

The paragraphs are numbered to help with the commentary that follows, but normally assignments would not be numbered in this way.

Now read the essay.

What is the point of referencing?

1. The reasons why accurate referencing is essential for academic work are not immediately apparent, particularly for students new to higher education. This essay will, therefore, examine why referencing is an integral part of academic writing and in the process address the question: 'What is the point of referencing?'

2. There have been countless times when I finished an assignment and then spent another day on referencing. At the start of my university studies this seemed like a useless exercise without any additional value, since my assignment was already written. In the first year of my studies I knew only one reason for it: if I don't reference properly, I'll be marked down. But with a few more years of academic experience I now appreciate why referencing is

essential – and the main reason is not because tutors punish deviation from the guidelines.

3. There are three main reasons for referencing. Firstly, referencing helps student writers to construct, structure, support and communicate arguments. Secondly, references link the writer's work to the existing body of knowledge. Thirdly, only through referencing can academic work gain credibility.

4. This essay will discuss these three aspects of referencing in detail, examine their validity, identify how referencing affects a writer's writing style, and show how referencing helps students to present their own ideas and opinions in assignments.

Constructing, supporting and communicating the argument

5. Becker (1986) believes the construction of arguments is the most important function of referencing systems. There are four dimensions to this. Firstly, drawing on existing literature, authors can construct their own arguments – and adopting a referencing system supports this process. Secondly, it helps to structure the existing information and arguments by linking published authors to their respective works. Third, referencing helps writers identify sources, gather evidence, as well as show the relationships between existing knowledge. Finally, referencing also provide a framework to enable writers to structure their arguments effectively by assessing, comparing, contrasting or evaluating different sources.

6. However, merely reiterating existing research, rather than producing innovative contributions, is inadequate for most academics. It is important for every academic writer to avoid this narrow-minded argumentation trap; academic works are not only about compiling existing arguments, but adding new perspectives, finding new arguments, or new ways of combining existing knowledge. For example, Barrow and Mosley (2005) combined the fields Human Resources and Brand Management to develop the 'Employer Brand' concept.

7. When the argument has been constructed, it needs academic support – and only references can provide this required support. We all know that academic works are not about stating opinions, as that would be akin to journalistic comment, but arguments are supported by evidence, and only arguments with sufficient and valid support are credible. Hence arguments are only as strong as the underlying evidence: arguments relying on questionable sources are – well, questionable.

8. Referencing also enables writers to communicate their arguments efficiently. The referencing framework allows them to produce a holistic work with different perspectives, whilst still emphasising their own positions; quotations, for example, help the reader to differentiate the writer's opinions from others. Again, if arguments are badly referenced, readers might not be able to distinguish the writers' own opinions from their sources. Especially for academic beginners, referencing helps them to adapt to the precise and accurate academic writing style required for degree level study. Neville (2007, p.10) emphasises this issue of writing style, and identifies the quest to 'find your own voice' as one of the main reasons for referencing. In academic writing, this requires developing an individual style that is neither convoluted nor convivial

in tone, but which is clear, open but measured, and is about identifying and using evidence selectively to build and support one's own arguments.

Science as network of knowledge, interlinked by referencing

9. Immanuel Kant said 'Science is organized knowledge.' This short quote brilliantly captures my next point: the primary mission of science and other disciplines is not to promote individual achievements, but to establish a connected, collective, and recognised body of knowledge. This is the most fundamental reason for referencing from a theoretical point of view. Hence some authors identify this as the principal reason for referencing: 'The primary reason for citation [. . .] is that it encourages and supports the collective construction of academic knowledge' (Walker & Taylor, 2006, pp.29–30).

10. The writer's references are links to this network of knowledge. Without these links an academic work would operate within an academic vacuum, unrelated to existing academic knowledge. A writer needs to contextualise his or her work to show how it relates to current research and debates. References also indicate in which particular knowledge network the writer operates. And these links to existing knowledge enable the reader to follow the writer's link to the existing knowledge network to gain a more in-depth insight.

11. Referencing not only connects a student writer's work to existing research, but clearly distinguishes the writer's own contributions from established arguments. Failing to indicate that ideas are taken from the existing body of knowledge would be plagiarism. This is one of the five principles of referencing identified by Walker and Taylor (2006). Neville also identifies the link to existing knowledge as one of the main reasons for adopting a referencing style; he highlights 'tracing the origin of ideas', 'spreading knowledge' and 'indicating appreciation' (2007, pp.9–10), which is my next point.

12. Referencing a work indicates that the writer finds the referenced material important: hence references create 'academic clout' in an assignment. In the global academic community a more-cited article will find more recognition. However, this practice is not without its critics. Thody, for example, calls this the 'sycophantic' use of referencing – and it can certainly be used to 'flatter your mentors' (2006, p.186). And Thompson calls this 'ritualized obedience to the reigning authorities' (2003, p.27). So the important issue here is not about selecting references for their expediency value, but for their enduring quality. Writers have to link their work to a recognised and credible knowledge network – and this becomes increasingly important in contemporary society, with vast amounts of information readily available. References indicate in which knowledge network the writer operates – if the references are untrustworthy, changeable sources, the writer's work can only be seen as untrustworthy and changeable. This brings us to the next point, credibility.

Credibility

13. Martin Joseph Routh said in 1878: 'You will find it a very good practice always to verify your references, sir!' Correct referencing enables the reader to do exactly that: check sources and verify conclusions. The issue of credibility is identified by commentators as a key issue in referencing. Nygaard, for example,

identifies credibility as the main reason for referencing: 'The goal of referencing is to enhance [. . .] your credibility as an author' (2008, p.177). Neville came to the same conclusion that "to be taken seriously, [a writer] needs to make a transparent presentation of valid evidence" (2007, p.10). Also the Academic Learning Support from Central Queensland University (2007) sees the credibility of arguments as primary motive for correct referencing.

14. References allow the reader to trace the source of the writer's arguments, consult the original independently and verify whether the writer's usage of the sources is valid. Some readers, for example, interested in a point in question, might want to verify the writer's interpretation of a referenced work. The quality of references is, therefore, extremely important for the credibility of an academic work. Arguments are only as good as the underlying references – untrustworthy and unreliable sources can even invalidate an argument, while reliable and dependable sources strengthen the writer's argument.

15. Finally, the writer's selection of sources also demonstrates whether the writer has evaluated all important arguments and has a thorough understanding of the subject. Only a credible work that takes all important arguments into account will find acceptance in the academic world.

Conclusion

16. So what is the point of referencing? I have argued that there are three main aspects why academic writers have to adopt a referencing system: Firstly, it helps to structure, support and communicate arguments. Secondly, it links the work to the existing body of knowledge, although it is also important for writers not merely to present the ideas of others, but to contribute where possible with innovative ideas of their own. Thirdly, only referencing can give the argument credibility – and this is a particularly significant element for success in the academic world.

References:

ACADEMIC LEARNING SUPPORT (2007). Division of Teaching & Learning Services, Central Queensland University. *Harvard (author-date) referencing guide*. 2007 edn. Rockhampton, Queensland: Central Queensland University.

BARROW, S. & R. MOSLEY (2005). *The employer brand*. Chichester: John Wiley & Sons.

BECKER, H.S. (1986). *Writing for social scientists*. Chicago: The University of Chicago Press.

NEVILLE, C. (2007). *The complete guide to referencing and avoiding plagiarism*. Maidenhead: McGraw-Hill/Open University Press.

NYGAARD, L.P. (2008). *Writing for scholars*. Universitetforlaget.

THODY, A. (2006). *Writing and presenting research*. London: Sage Publications.

THOMPSON, A. (2003). Tiffany, friend of people of colour. *International Journal of Qualitative Studies in Education*, 16(1), pp.7–30.

WALKER, J.R. & T. TAYLOR (2006). *The Columbia guide to online style*. 2nd edn. New York: Columbia University Press.

Comments on the exercise

1 Examples of student's own voice in the essay

Paragraph 2 is an example of Jonas talking directly to us. He tells us about his early experiences of referencing – experiences that will be shared by many students – and how his perceptions changed as he gained more experience of academic writing. He uses the first person term 'I' at this point, so we are left in no doubt that this is his authentic voice speaking directly to us.

But how acceptable is this form of personalized writing in an academic assignment? It is impossible to generalize, as it depends on the subject and the attitude of the tutor marking the assignment. Some tutors will not accept this type of personal engagement within an essay; but others will, particularly if, for the most part, the essay is presented in a traditional way, using the third person style of writing.

The use of personal experiences, if done discreetly, can add a lighter style to an academic essay and make a vivid connection between theory and everyday reality. However, your own comments, when included in an essay, will need to make direct connections between your own experiences, and the theories, ideas and practices that you are discussing. You need to ask yourself: 'What do my experiences add to this discussion?' In this case, Jonas uses his own experiences as a bridge to the points he makes in paragraph 3 and onwards. It also encourages us to identify with the writer and gain a sense of the person behind the keyboard.

Jonas's own voice emerges briefly again at the beginning of paragraph 9, when he writes: 'Immanuel Kant said "Science is organized knowledge." This short quote brilliantly captures my next point . . .' He reminds us here, that the points being made are **his**; he has selected them, and has taken ownership of them. Jonas also uses this technique again at the end of paragraph 11, as a bridge to paragraph 12. And in the conclusion we are again reminded, with the opening to the second sentence: 'I have argued', that it has been **this** particular student, Jonas Juenger, who has selected and presented the evidence in the essay.

The **selection** of evidence is, in fact, one of the main ways that you can assert your own voice in an assignment: you look for evidence that supports your arguments, and the viewpoints you feel are relevant and important; referencing thus becomes your servant, rather than your master.

A writer's own unique **style** of writing is another way of adding individuality to an academic essay. In this essay Jonas uses the repetition of words effectively to reinforce and make points; for example:

> Paragraph 7: 'Hence arguments are only as strong as the underlying evidence: argu-
> ments relying on questionable sources are – well, questionable'.
> Paragraph 12: 'if the references are untrustworthy, changeable sources, the writer's
> work can only be seen as untrustworthy and changeable'.

He also uses a number of quotations to add authority to the points that he wants to make (see paragraph 9), and to add some stylistic 'colour' to his text (see paragraph 13).

2 When to reference

Jonas uses evidence:

- When describing and discussing theories associated with particular writers (see examples in paragraphs 5 and 11)
- When presenting an illustrative example (see example in paragraph 6)
- In support of points made (see examples in paragraphs 8, 11, and 13)
- To cite the source of quotations (see examples in paragraphs 9, 12, and 13).

You may have noticed that Jonas includes two unreferenced quotes in paragraphs 9 and 13. However, as was mentioned in Chapter 3, if the quotation is by a well-known person, and is included to add stylistic 'colour', credibility, a way into an idea or for general interest, the name of the source should be cited, but it does not need to be given a full reference entry. However, if in doubt, always supply a full reference entry.

3 Example of critical analysis

Critical analysis is about looking at a subject from a range of perspectives, and following or creating logical arguments. There is a choice of six directions you could take (adapted from Taylor 1989):

(a) **Agreeing** with a particular point of view, and giving good reasons to support it
(b) **Rejecting** a particular point of view, but again using reliable evidence to do this
(c) **Conceding** that an existing point of view has merits, but that it needs to be qualified in certain respects, and stating what these are
(d) **Proposing** a new point of view, or reformulating an existing one, backed with supporting evidence
(e) **Reconciling** two positions, which may seem at variance, by bringing new perspectives to bear on the topic
(f) **Connecting or synthesizing** different ideas, so that new approaches and points of view can be advanced.

In the essay, we find examples of critical analysis that connect with the above items (a), (c) and (d). We can find an example of **agreement** with a particular point of view in paragraph 5: 'Becker (1986) believes the construction of arguments is the most important function of referencing systems.' Jonas then presents four reasons in support of this argument. But then, in the following paragraph, he **proposes** another fifth dimension to the discussion:

> It is important for every academic writer to avoid this narrow-minded argumentation trap; academic works are not only about compiling existing arguments, but adding new perspectives, finding new arguments, or new ways of combining existing knowledge.
>
> (Paragraph 6)

He comes back to this key point in paragraph 9, and reinforces the idea of combining knowledge for the greater good: 'the primary mission of science and other disciplines is not to promote individual achievements, but to establish a connected, collective, and recognised body of knowledge'.

In paragraph 12, Jonas writes:

> Referencing a work indicates that the writer finds the referenced material important: hence references create 'academic clout' in an assignment. In the global academic community a more-cited article will find more recognition.

He partially **concedes** the point, but then moves on to qualify it:

> However, this practice is not without its critics. Thody, for example, calls this the 'sycophantic' use of referencing – and it can certainly be used to 'flatter your mentors' (2006, p.186). And Thompson calls this 'ritualized obedience to the reigning authorities' (2003, p.27). So the important issue here is not about selecting references for their expediency value, but for their enduring quality.
>
> (Paragraph 12)

Your own voice

We have seen in this chapter an example of how a student combined his own experiences with referenced evidence to engage with an essay question. Our experiences are drawn from many sources and it can sometimes be difficult, if not impossible, to reference all that have influenced us. We cannot always remember where we read, heard or discussed a particular idea. And sometimes our statements in assignments may be a fusion of our own instincts or viewpoint and what someone has written or said.

In an assignment tutors want evidence of your general ability to research a topic, develop ideas critically, and correctly reference your sources when this is needed. And in an otherwise well-referenced essay most tutors will appreciate that the occasional unreferenced statement is a genuine attempt by you to express your ideas or interpret events in your own way.

9

Referencing in action: example references

A Books • B Pamphlets, booklets, brochures and leaflet • C Journals, magazines and newspapers • D Occasional papers and reports • E Government publications (non-parliamentary) • F Parliamentary publications • G Legal documents • H Standards and patents • I Course manuals and lecture notes • J Unpublished work • K Cartographic material: maps and atlases • L Graphs and charts • M Visual art and graphics • N Audio-visual sources • O Public performances and events (including theatre, dance, music, talks) • P Referencing course lectures (see also section S1 'Online teaching material') • Q Interviews and discussions, including telephone conversations • R Miscellaneous sources • S Referencing electronic sources

In this chapter comparative reference examples of the four most common referencing styles in Britain will be presented. These styles are Harvard, APA, MLA, and the two British Standard Numerical styles, which can be combined in the full reference.

- **Sections A–R** give examples of how to reference printed, audio-visual and other non-Internet sources.
- **Section S** is the largest in this chapter, and contains many examples of **website and data base** related sources, including the same type of sources found in sections A–R.

Section	Type of source
A	Books
B	Pamphlets, booklets, brochures, leaflets.
C	Journals, magazines and newspapers
D	Occasional papers and reports

E UK government publications (non-parliamentary)
F UK parliamentary publications
G Legal documents
H Standards and patents
I Course manuals and lecture notes
J Unpublished work: dissertations, conference papers, archived material, proceedings of meetings
K Cartographic material: maps and atlases
L Graphs and charts
M Visual art and graphics (including posters)
N Audio-visual sources
O Public performances and events (including theatre, dance, music, talks)
P Course lectures
Q Interviews and discussions, including telephone conversations
R Miscellaneous sources: music scores; posters and wall charts; advertisements: printed, radio and television; postal items; postcards; display and information panels; sacred or classical texts.
S Referencing web-based and database sources. This is the largest section and contains examples of the following:
   S1 Online teaching material
   S2–3 Books online
   S4 Online reference sources
   S5 Academic journals
   S6 Preprints: journal articles
   S7 Online magazines
   S8 Online newspapers
   S9–10 Online reports
   S11 Online dissertations
   S12 Online conference papers
   S13 Government and other statistics online
   S14 Public/archival records
   S15 Personal communications
   S16 Networking and public communication sites
   S17 Audio and visual downloads, including phonecasts
   S18 Visual materials online: maps, photographs, paintings, three-dimensional art, graphics, and so on)
   S19 Portable databases.

Essential information in a reference entry

What to include:

- **Originator or creator of the source:** this should be the starting point for the reference. The originator or creator can be the name, nickname or nomenclature of the author, writer, editor; or name of a government or government body, an organization, institution, group, or website/website host.

Then include:

- **Date:** the **year** of origin of the information, and other **specific dates**, if relevant, e.g. in the case of newspapers, journals, etc.
- **Title:** title and subtitle of source in question. If the creator/originator of the source is unknown, the reference can be started with the source title.
- **Specific identifiers:** for example, the nature of the source, e.g. [DVD], volume and edition numbers and page numbers.
- **Where to locate the source:** this can be the location and name of the publisher/originator; or in the case of the Internet, a web 'address'.

The 'golden rule' of referencing

The 'Golden Rule' of referencing is to give an interested reader enough information to help them easily and quickly find the source you have cited. If they wanted to look at your source and check it for themselves, could they find it easily with the information you have supplied?

A Books

A book can be a hardback or paperback (or 'soft cover') publication on any subject, with one or more authors and/or editors. Despite the proliferation of the Internet, books are still very important to students and their tutors for their research. The order in which bibliographic elements appear depends on the referencing style, but the following should be included, if applicable.

- **Name(s) of author(s) or originator(s).** If 'Anon.' (anonymous) is shown specifically on the title page, then this should be stated in the full reference entry, but only when this happens. If no author name is given (and 'Anon.' is not shown), you can start with the first proper word of the title. If the book has been written under an assumed name, this is the one that should be referenced, although the creator's real name, if known, may be included in brackets following the pseudonym.
- **The year of publication.** If no year shown, state 'no date' or 'n.d.', and it may be appropriate to give an approximate indication of when the book was published. This can be done by stating 'circa', or 'c', and an idea of the period, e.g. 'circa 1920', or 'c.1920'.
- **Main title of the book,** in italics or underlined.
- **Title of a chapter** in an edited collection. This may be contained within single or double inverted commas, depending on referencing style.
- **Name (s) of editor(s),** if applicable, and indicated as 'Ed.' or 'Eds.'.
- **State edition,** but only if it is **not** the first edition. With Harvard and Numerical styles this can be abbreviated to 'edn.' to avoid confusion with 'Ed.' for 'editor'.
- **Place of publication and publisher.** The place of publication is the town or city where the publisher is located. If the publisher is outside the UK, state the country, then the town or city, unless this is obvious from the name of the city.

- **Page number or other numeration**, if applicable. The abbreviation 'p.' or 'pp.' can be used for all styles, except MLA.

A1 Book: single author

Table 9.A1 Book: single author

Harvard	APA
KOTRE, J. (1984). *Outliving the self: generativity and the interpretation of lives*. Baltimore: Johns Hopkins University Press.	Kotre, J. (1984). *Outliving the self: Generativity and the interpretation of lives*. Baltimore: Johns Hopkins University Press, 1984.
MLA	**Numerical**
Kotre, John. Outliving the Self: Generativity and the Interpretation of Lives. Baltimore: Hopkins, 1984.	KOTRE, J. *Outliving the self: generativity and the interpretation of lives*. Baltimore: Johns Hopkins University Press, 1984.

A2 Book: two or more authors

(Also see Chapter 7, 'Frequently asked questions', question 6.)

Table 9.A2 Book: two or more authors

Harvard	APA
SAUNDERS, M., P. LEWIS, and A. THORNHILL. (2003). *Research methods for business students*. Harlow: Prentice Hall.	Saunders, M., Lewis, P. & Thornhill, A. (2003). *Research methods for business students*. Harlow: Prentice Hall.
MLA	**Numerical**
Saunders, Mark, Philip Lewis and Adrian Thornhill. Research Methods for Business Students. Harlow: Prentice Hall, 2003.	SAUNDERS, M., P. LEWIS, and A. THORNHILL. (2003). *Research methods for business students*. Harlow: Prentice Hall.

A3 Edited book

Table 9.A3 Edited book

Harvard	APA
MCGINTY, J. and T. WILLIAMS (Eds.) (2001). *Regional trends 36*. London: The Stationery Office.	McGinty, J. & Williams, T. (Eds.) (2001). *Regional trends 36*. London: The Stationery Office.
MLA	**Numerical**
McGinty, Jon & Tricia Williams, Eds. Regional Trends 36. London: TSO, 2001.	MCGINTY, J. and T. WILLIAMS (Eds.) *Regional trends 36*. London: The Stationery Office, 2001.

A4 Edited collections of articles (sometimes called 'readers')

It is the title of the book that is underlined or set in italics, not the chapter.

Table 9.A4 Edited collections of articles

Harvard
NORTH, D., R. LEIGH and J. GOUGH (1983). Monitoring industrial change at the local level: some comments on methods and data sources. In M. HEALEY (Ed.) *Urban and regional industrial research: the changing UK data base.* Norwich: Geo Books, pp.111–29.

APA
North, D., Leigh, R. & Gough, J. (1983). Monitoring industrial change at the local level: Some comments on methods and data sources. In M. Healey (Ed.) *Urban and regional industrial research: The changing UK data base,* pp. 111–29. Norwich: Geo Books.

MLA
North, David, Roger Leigh and Jamie. Gough. "Monitoring Industrial Change at the Local level: Some Comments on Methods and Data Sources". Urban and Regional Industrial Research: The Changing UK Data Base, Ed. M. Healey Norwich: Geo Books, 1983. 111–29.

Numerical
NORTH, D., R. LEIGH and J. GOUGH. Monitoring industrial change at the local level: some comments on methods and data sources. In M. HEALEY (Ed.) *Urban and regional industrial research: the changing UK data base.* Norwich: Geo Books, pp.111–29.

A5 Book published by an agency or organisation (no specific named author)

The group that produced the book is the originator, so this takes first position in the reference.

Table 9.A5 Book published by an agency or organization (no specific named author)

Harvard
AMERICAN PSYCHOLOGICAL ASSOCIATION (2005). *Concise rules of APA style.* Washington, DC: American Psychological Association.

APA
American Psychological Association (2005). *Concise rules of APA style.* Washington, DC: as author.
(If publisher same as author, put 'as author')

MLA
American Psychological Association. Concise Rules of APA Style. Washington, DC: APA, 2005.

Numerical
AMERICAN PSYCHOLOGICAL ASSOCIATION. *Concise rules of APA style.* Washington, DC: American Psychological Association, 2005.

A6 Translated book

Include name of translator, date of publication of source and date of publication of original work.

Table 9.A6 Translated book

Harvard
TURGENEV, I. (1972). *Spring torrents.* (L. Schapiro. Trans.). London: Eyre Methuen. (Original work published 1873).

APA
Turgenev, I. (1972). *Spring torrents.* (L. Schapiro. Trans.). London: Eyre Methuen. (Original work published 1873).

(Cont.)

MLA	Numerical
Turgenev, Ivan. <u>Spring Torrents</u>. Trans. L. Schapiro. London: Methuen. 1972. Trans. of original work publ. 1873.	TURGENEV, I. *Spring torrents*. (L. Schapiro. Trans.). London: Eyre Methuen 1972. (Original work published 1873).

A7 Book in a series

Show both the author(s) and editor(s) names. State if the editor is the series editor (Series Ed.) or volume editor: (Vol. Ed.). If both are shown, list the series editor first, and the volume editor second. Note how the initials (or first name with MLA) precede the last name of the editor.

Table 9.A7 Book in a series

Harvard	APA
PINES, J. (1997). Localization of cell cycle regulators by immuno-fluorescence. In W. D. DUNPHY (Vol. Ed.) *Methods in Enzymology, vol. 283: cell cycle control*. New York: Academic Press, pp.99–113.	Pines, J. (1997). Localization of cell cycle regulators by immuno-fluorescence. In W. D. Dunphy (Vol. Ed.) *Methods in Enzymology*, (Vol. 283): *Cell cycle control* (pp. 99–113). New York: Academic Press.

MLA	Numerical
Pines, Jonathan. "Localization of Cell Cycle Regulators by Immuno-Fluorescence". <u>Methods in Enzymology: vol. 283, Cell Cycle Control</u>. Vol. ed. William D. Dunphy. New York: Acad. Press, 1997. 99–113.	PINES, J. Localization of cell cycle regulators by immuno-fluorescence. In W. D. DUNPHY (Vol. Ed.) *Methods in Enzymology: vol. 283, cell cycle control*. New York: Academic Press, pp.99–113, 1997.

A8 Multivolume work

Give full information on the name(s) of writers of the chapters cited or editor(s) names, plus full information of the main title and volume title of the work concerned. You may also need to add page numbers to isolate a particular section of the chapter.

Table 9.A8 Multivolume work

Harvard	APA
Tsien, T.H. (1985). Paper and printing. Vol. V (1). J. Needham (Ser. Ed.) (1954–1998). *Science and civilisation in China*. Cambridge: Cambridge Univ. Press, pp. 32–39.	Tsien, T.H. (1985). [Paper and printing]. Vol. (1). In J. Needham (Ser. Ed.) (1954–1998). *Science & civilisation in China*. (pp.32–39). Cambridge: Cambridge Univ. Press.
	(If the volume has its own title, as shown above, put this in brackets before the main title of the work)

(Cont.)

MLA	Numerical
Tsien, Tsuen-Hsuin. "Paper and Printing". Vol. V (1) (1954–1998). Joseph Needham (Ser. Ed.). Science and Civilisation in China. Cambridge UP, 1985. 32–39.	Tsien, T.H. Paper and printing. Vol. V (1). J. Needham (Ser. Ed.) (1954–1998). *Science and civilisation in China*. Cambridge: Cambridge Univ. Press, pp. 32–39, 1985.

A9 Encyclopedia

It is unlikely that the name of an individual writer or contributor will be shown, but if a name is given, then start with this: last name first, then the initials of the writer. However, if no writer's name is shown, start with the title of entry. For well-known general encyclopedias, you can omit the place of publication and name of publisher, but if in doubt, include it.

Table 9.A9 Encyclopedia

Harvard	APA
Goshen. (1975). *New Encyclopaedia Britannica*. Vol. 4. p.642.	Goshen (1975) in *New Encyclopaedia Britannica*. Vol. 4, p. 642.
MLA	**Numerical**
"Goshen". New Encyclopaedia Britannica. Vol. 4. 1975. 642.	Goshen. *New Encyclopaedia Britannica*. Vol. 4, p.642, 1975.

A10 Other reference books

If no author is shown for an individual entry, or for the book as a whole, start with:

- The title of the reference book, if referring generally to the book (see example i)
- Or the title of entry, if that is more relevant to the particular evidence presented in your assignment (see example ii).

Do not cite or reference the name of an editor for a reference work.

Table 9.A10i Directory

Harvard	APA
Directory of management consultants and professional service firms in the UK (2004), 15th ed. Centre for Management Creativity. Peterborough: Kennedy Information Inc. p.220.	*Directory of management consultants & professional service firms in the UK*, 2004 (15th ed.), (p.220). Centre for Management Creativity. Peterborough: Kennedy Information Inc.
MLA	**Numerical**
Directory of Management Consultants and Professional Service Firms in the UK. 15th ed. Ctr. for Mgt. Creativity. Peterborough: Kennedy, 2004.	*Directory of management consultants and professional service firms in the UK* 15th ed. Centre for Management Creativity. Peterborough: Kennedy Information Inc. p.220, 2004.

Table 9.A10ii Reference work

Harvard	APA
'Everything has an end'. (1992). *The concise Oxford dictionary of proverbs*. 2nd ed. Oxford: Oxford University Press, p.82.	'Everything has an end'. (1992). *The concise Oxford dictionary of proverbs* (2nd ed.). (p.82). Oxford: Oxford University Press.
MLA	**Numerical**
"Everything has an end". The Concise Oxford Dictionary of Proverbs. 2nd ed. Oxford UP, 1992.	'Everything has an end'. *The concise Oxford dictionary of proverbs*. 2nd ed. Oxford: Oxford University Press, 1992, p.82.

A11 Dictionary

If the author (not editor) is shown on the title page, start with this, if not start with the title of the dictionary. If the dictionary has been revised by another writer, then name this person, as shown in the example below.

Table 9.A11 Dictionary

Harvard	APA
BLOM, E. (1988) *The new Everyman dictionary of Music* 6th ed. Revised by D. CUMMINS. London: J.M. Dent.	Blom, E. (1988) *The new Everyman dictionary of music* (6th ed.) Revised by D. Cummins. London: J.M. Dent.
MLA	**Numerical**
Blom, Eric. The New Everyman Dictionary of Music. 6th ed. rev. by David Cummins. London: Dent, 1988.	BLOM, E. *The new Everyman dictionary of Music* 6th ed. Revised by D. CUMMINS, London: J.M. Dent, 1988.

A12 Republished book, including book-club or paperback reprint

State both the year and publisher information of the republished book, and the publication year and publisher of the original version.

Table 9.A12 Republished book

Harvard	APA
MASTERS, J. (1970). *Fourteen Eighteen*. London: Corgi (originally published by Michael Joseph 1965).	Masters, J. (1970). *Fourteen eighteen*. London: Corgi (originally published by Michael Joseph 1965).
MLA	**Numerical**
Masters, John. Fourteen Eighteen. London: Joseph: 1965. London: Corgi, 1970.	MASTERS, J. *Fourteen Eighteen*. London: 1970 Corgi (originally published by Michael Joseph 1965).

If the book you are looking at was originally issued under a different title, give the new title first and publication details, and then state 'Reprint of . . .', followed by the original title and original year of publication.

B Pamphlets, booklets, brochures and leaflet

Pamphlet: a short essay, composition or treatise on a subject, usually printed in paperback

Booklet: a non-fiction paperback publication with a limited number of pages

Brochure: a non-fiction publication promoting or advertising a product or service, or produced for public information purposes

Leaflet: a very short non-fiction publication promoting or advertising a product or service, or produced for public information purposes.

What to include in the reference:

- Name(s) of author(s) or originator(s). if no author's name is shown, either start with the name of the organisation producing the booklet, or if that is not obvious, the title of it (see example 9.B3).
- Year of publication, and edition, if applicable.
- State the medium, if not obvious, e.g. [Leaflet].
- Title, in italics or underlined.
- Editor(s), if applicable: (indicated Ed./Eds.).
- Place of publication and publisher.
- Page number or other numeration, if applicable.

B1 Pamphlet

Table 9.B1 Pamphlet

Harvard	APA
STEFF, B. (1977). *My dearest acquaintance: a biographical sketch of Mary and Henry Webb.* Ludlow: The King's Bookshop.	Steff, B. (1977). *My dearest acquaintance: A biographical sketch of Mary & Henry Webb.* Ludlow: The King's Bookshop.
MLA	**Numerical**
Steff, Bernard. <u>My Dearest Acquaintance: A Biographical Sketch of Mary and Henry Webb</u>. Ludlow: King's Bookshop, 1977.	STEFF, B. *My dearest acquaintance: a biographical sketch of Mary and Henry Webb.* Ludlow: The King's Bookshop, 1977.

B2 Booklet

Table 9.B2 Booklet

Harvard	APA
HANDS, T. (1992). *Thomas Hardy and Stinsford Church: a brief companion for the visitor.* Stinsford Parochial Church Council.	Hands, T. (1992). *Thomas Hardy & Stinsford Church: A brief companion for the Visitor.* Stinsford Parochial Church Council.

(Cont.)

MLA	Numerical
Hands, Timothy. <u>Thomas Hardy and Stinsford Church: A Brief Companion for the Visitor.</u> Stinsford Parochial Church Council, 1992.	HANDS, T. *Thomas Hardy and Stinsford Church: a brief companion for the visitor.* Stinsford Parochial Church Council, 1992.

B3 Brochure

Brochures may contain statistical or other information that you might want to include in your assignment. You may need, therefore, to refer to a particular page number so the reader can go straight to this. If no author's name is shown, start with the name of the organization and name the publisher as 'author', or 'as author'. If no date is shown, put 'n.d.', or 'no date', in place of the year. With MLA style, if no author's name is shown, start with the title of the brochure.

Table 9.B3 Brochure

Harvard	APA
UNIVERSITY OF BRADFORD (2006). *Lifelong Education Prospectus 05/06.* Bradford: as author.	University of Bradford (2006). *Lifelong Education Prospectus 05/06.* Bradford: as author.
MLA	**Numerical**
<u>Lifelong Education Prospectus 05/06</u>. U of Bradford, 2006.	UNIVERSITY OF BRADFORD. *Lifelong Education Prospectus 05/06*, p.6. Bradford: as author, 2006.

Table 9.B4 Leaflet

Harvard	APA
NHS: NATIONAL HEALTH SERVICE (2009). [Leaflet] *Important information about Swine Flu.* United Kingdom.	NHS: National Health Service (2009). [Leaflet]. *Important information about Swine Flu.* United Kingdom.
MLA	**Numerical**
<u>NHS</u> Leaflet: "Important Information about Swine Flu". UK. 2009.	NHS: NATIONAL HEALTH SERVICE. [Leaflet] *Important information about Swine Flu.* United Kingdom.

C Journals, magazines and newspapers

C1 Journals

You will need to include details of:

- Name of writer
- Title of article

- Name of journal, in italics or underlined
- Volume and issue number (if applicable) and page numbers. If it is a special edition or supplement to a journal, you need to indicate this, e.g. (Suppl.).

With the Harvard and Numeric styles the abbreviations 'vol.', 'no.' (number) and 'pp.' can be omitted. However, for clarity, and to avoid confusing the reader with a mass of consecutive numbers, they can be included.

Journals and the APA style of referencing

- Do not enclose titles of articles within quotation marks.
- Both the title of journal and volume number should be shown in italics.
- The issue number should be enclosed in brackets.
- Do not use pp. before page numbers for academic journals, but this abbreviation should be used with newspaper references.

Journals and the MLA style of referencing

- Enclose the titles of articles within journals within double quotation marks.
- Put the volume number after title of the journal.
- If there is an issue number, put this after the volume number, as shown in example 2 that follows, e.g. 220:C3.
- For academic journals, put the year in brackets and do not use the pp. (page numbers) abbreviation.

Table 9.C1i Journal

Harvard	APA
YANG, D. (2005). Culture matters to multinationals' intellectual property business. *Journal of World Business*. No. 40, pp.281–301.	Yang, D. (2005). Culture matters to multinationals' intellectual property business. *Journal of World Business, 40,* 281–301.
MLA	**Numerical**
Yang, Deli. "Culture Matters to Multinationals' Intellectual Property Business". <u>Journal of World Business</u>, 40, (2005): 281–301.	YANG, D. Culture matters to multinationals' intellectual property business. *Journal of World Business.* 2005, No. 40, pp.281–301.

References to journal articles do not usually include the name of the publisher or place of publication, unless there is more than one journal with the same title, e.g. *Banking Weekly* (New York) and *Banking Weekly* (London).

Table 9.C1ii Journal (special issue)

Harvard	APA
TRENDAFILOVA, I. (2006). Vibration-based damage detection in structures using time series analysis. *Journal of Mechanical Engineering Science* (Special Issue on Chaos in Science and Engineering), vol. 220, no.C3, pp. 361–272.	Trendafilova, I. (2006) Vibration-based damage detection in structures using time series analysis. *Journal of Mechanical Engineering Science* (Special Issue on Chaos in Science and Engineering): *220*: (C3), 361–272.

(Cont.)

MLA	Numerical
Trendafilova, Irena. "Vibration-based Damage Detection in Structures Using Time Series Analysis". Journal of Mechanical Engineering Science, special issue: Chaos in Science and Engineering 220: C3 (2006): 361–272.	TRENDAFILOVA, I. Vibration-based damage detection in structures using time series analysis. *Journal of Mechanical Engineering Science* (Special Issue on Chaos in Science and Engineering), 2006, vol. 220, no. C3, pp.361–272.

C2 Magazines

The same sequence of referencing academic journals applies to magazines with a general readership. However, if an author's name is shown, start with this.

MLA

For articles in a monthly magazine with a general circulation, show the month and the year. If there is an issue number show this too, and also show the page number(s). Unlike references for academic journals, the year does not need to go in brackets for a magazine with a general readership.

APA

The month of the edition follows after the year for magazines published monthly. For weekly magazines, add the month and the day, e.g. 2006, July 28.

Table 9.C2 Magazine

Harvard	APA
COOPER, S. (2006). Almost tomorrow: the speculative fiction of Edmund Cooper. *Book and Magazine Collector*, July, no.270, pp.51–61.	Cooper, S. (2006, July) Almost tomorrow: The speculative fiction of Edmund Cooper. *Book & Magazine Collector*, 270, 51–61.
MLA	**Numerical**
Cooper, Shaun. "Almost Tomorrow: The Speculative Fiction of Edmund Cooper". Book and Magazine Collector July 2006. 270: 51–61.	COOPER, S. Almost tomorrow: the speculative fiction of Edmund Cooper. *Book and Magazine Collector*, July 2006, no.270, pp.51–61.

C3 Newspapers

Include the following information:

- Name of writer, if shown
- Name of the newspaper, in italics or underlined
- Day, month and year of publication. For Harvard, MLA and Numerical styles, the months of the year can be abbreviated, except May, June and July. For the APA style write the month in full

- Title of article
- Details of any special identifying feature, e.g. late edition, review sections, supplements. If a particular edition is involved, e.g. late edition, this can be shown next to the date, e.g. 4 June 2006 (late edn.)
- Page number(s).

Table 9.C3i Newspaper article (with an author's name shown)

Harvard	APA
MARTIN, L. Top women cheated by pay gap. *The Observer*, 4 June 2006, p.18.	Martin, L. Top women cheated by pay gap. (2006, June 6). *The Observer*, p.18.
MLA	**Numerical**
Martin, Lorna. "Top Women Cheated By Pay Gap." <u>Observer</u> 4 June 2006.	MARTIN, L. Top women cheated by pay gap. *The Observer*, 4 June 2006, p.18.

Newspaper item (no author's name shown)

Short, snippet-type items in newspapers, without author's name given, can be cited just by giving full details in the text of your assignment (citation only). If it is a local paper, it is helpful to include the city of origin, e.g. (Bradford *Telegraph and Argus* 21 June 2004, p.4). If the item is in a supplement, give information of this after the name of the newspaper, e.g. *Financial Times: FTfm (Fund Management)* 12 Dec. 2005, p.3; or *Financial Times (FT Companies and Markets supplement)* 12 Dec. 2005, p.24.

However, if the article is particularly significant, in terms of data provided or for other evidential purposes in the assignment, it should also included in the references or bibliography list, as follows.

Table 9.C3ii Newspaper item (no writer name shown)

Harvard	APA
FINANCIAL TIMES. Duke does u-turn over spin-off sale, 12 Dec. 2005, p.14.	Duke does U-turn over spin-off sale (2005, December 12). *Financial Times*, p.14.
MLA	**Numerical**
"Duke Does U-turn Over Spin-off Sale". <u>Financial Times</u> 12 Dec. 2005.	*FINANCIAL TIMES*. Duke does u-turn over spin-off sale, 12 Dec. 2005, p.14.

D Occasional papers and reports

For all discussion, occasional or working papers, and all types of report, you should include:

- Author's name (if given)
- If no name of author, start with name of organization
- Year of publication

- Full title of report, in italics or underlined
- Subsection or subtitle information and edition number
- Place of publication
- Name of publisher or originating organization
- Volume, sections, page number(s) if not cited in the text. abbreviations 'p.', or 'pp.' can be used, if required, for all styles, except MLA.

D1 Discussion paper (named authors)

Table 9.D1 Discussion paper (named authors)

Harvard	APA
ANAND, S. and A.K. SEN (1996). *Sustainable human development: concepts and priorities.* United Nations Development Programme (UNDP), Discussion Paper Series. New York: UNDP: Office of Development Studies, p.23.	Anand, S. & Sen, A.K. (1996). *Sustainable human development: Concepts & priorities.* United Nations Development Programme (UNDP): (Discussion Paper Series). New York: UNDP: Office of Development Studies, p.23.

MLA	Numerical
Anand, Sudhir and Amartya Sen. <u>Sustainable Human Development: Concepts and Priorities</u>. United Nations Dev. Programme. (UNDP), Discussion Paper Series. New York: UNDP: Off. Dev. Studies, 1996.	ANAND, S. and A.K. SEN. *Sustainable human development: concepts and priorities.* United Nations Development Programme (UNDP), Discussion Paper Series. New York: UNDP: Office of Development Studies, 1996. p.23.

D2 Occasional paper (with a named author)

Table 9.D2 Occasional paper (with a named author)

Harvard	APA
SYMONDS, M. (1994). *The culture of anxiety: the middle class in crisis*, Occasional Paper No.9. London: Social Market Foundation,	Symonds, M. (1994). *The culture of anxiety: The middle class in crisis* (Occasional Paper No.9). London: Social Market Foundation.

MLA	Numerical
Symonds, Matthew. <u>The Culture of Anxiety: The Middle Class in Crisis</u>, Occ. Paper No.9. London: SMF, 1994.	SYMONDS, M. *The culture of anxiety: the middle class in crisis*, Occasional Paper No.9. London: Social Market Foundation, 1994.

D3 Annual report: non-commercial organization (no named author)

If no named author, start with the name of the organization. Give full details of the report, plus any information on relevant subsections and pages, if applicable.

Table 9.D3 Annual report: non-commercial organization

Harvard	APA
OVERSEAS DEVELOPMENT INSTITUTE (2003). *Annual report 2002/03*: finance: balance sheet summary, pp.30–33. London: as author.	Overseas Development Institute (2003). *Annual report 2002/03*: Finance: balance sheet summary, pp.30–33. London: as author.
MLA	**Numerical**
Overseas Development Institute. <u>Annual Report 2002/03</u>: "Finance: Balance Sheet Summary". London: as author, 2003, 30–33.	OVERSEAS DEVELOPMENT INSTITUTE. *Annual report 2002/03*: finance: balance sheet summary, pp.30–33. London: as author, 2003.

D4 Annual report: commercial organization (no named author)

Company annual reports often involve multiple authors and rarely show the name or names of the compilers or editors; but if they do then start with these. If not, start with the company or organizational name, then give the year, full title of report, details of any relevant chapter or section. You can also include page numbers, if applicable, and details of publisher – which is often the organisation concerned.

Table 9.D4 Annual report: commercial organization

Harvard	APA
CABLE AND WIRELESS Plc (2005). *Annual report 2005*: cash flow, p.80. Bracknell: as author.	Cable & Wireless Plc (2005). *Annual report 2005*: Cash flow, 80. Bracknell: as author.
MLA	**Numerical**
Cable and Wireless Plc. <u>Annual Report 2005</u>: "Cash Flow". Bracknell: as author, 2005.	CABLE AND WIRELESS Plc. *Annual report 2005*: cash flow, p.80. Bracknell: as author, 2005.

D5 Other reports (no named author)

Give as much information as is necessary to identify title, subsection and page numbers of the report concerned.

Table 9.D5 Report (no named author)

Harvard	APA
BUSINESS RATIO REPORTS (2004). *Security industry*, edn. 26, section 4: performance league tables: sales: 4–2. Hampton: Keynote.	Business Ratio Reports (2004). *Security industry* (ed. 26, section 4): Performance league tables: Sales: 4–2. Hampton: Keynote.
MLA	**Numerical**
Business Ratio Reports. <u>Security Industry</u>, ed. 26, section 4: "Performance League Tables": Sales: 4–2. Hampton: Keynote, 2004.	BUSINESS RATIO REPORTS. *Security industry*, edn. 26, section 4: performance league tables: sales: 4–2. Hampton: Keynote, 2004.

(See also E: Government publications, next entry, for other examples of reports.)

E Government publications (non-parliamentary)

The publishers for many UK government publications is The Stationery Office (TSO), although documents published before 1996 are usually shown as published by HMSO (Her Majesty's Stationery Office). The Stationery Office was privatized from the HMSO (now the Office of Public Sector Information) in 1996. However, other government departments and agencies also produce their own publications, e.g. Office of the Deputy Prime Minister (ODPM), Department for Transport (DfT), and Health and Safety Executive (HSE). Government-sponsored research may also be published by other bodies or organizations; see example E3.

What to include

You need to include the following information:

- Name of author(s) or name of government department or agency. You may also need to mention the country of origin, if it is not obvious from the place of publication
- Year of publication
- Title of article or the title of publication, in italics or underlined
- Place of publication and name of official publisher
- Volume or edition date number, table or page number, if applicable.

E1 Government publication (no named author)

Table 9.E1 Government publication (no named author)

Harvard	APA
OFFICE FOR NATIONAL STATISTICS (2000). *Standard occupational classification: vol. 2: the coding index*. London: The Stationery Office.	Office for National Statistics (2000). *Standard occupational classification: Vol. 2: The coding index*. London: The Stationery Office.
MLA	**Numerical**
Office for National Statistics. Standard Occupational Classification: Vol. 2: The Coding Index. London: TSO. 2000.	OFFICE FOR NATIONAL STATISTICS. *Standard occupational classification: vol. 2: the coding index*. London: The Stationery Office, 2000.

E2 Government publication (named author)

Table 9.E2 Government publication (named author)	
Harvard SUDLOW, D. (2003). *Scoping study on motorcycle training.* Great Britain. Department for Transport: Road Safety Research Report no. 36. Wetherby: DfT Publications.	**APA** Sudlow, D. (2003). *Scoping study on motorcycle training.* Great Britain. Department for Transport (Road Safety Research Report no. 36). Wetherby: DfT Publications.
MLA Sudlow, Diane. <u>Scoping Study on Motorcycle Training</u>. Great Britain. Department for Transport: Road Safety Research Report no. 36. Wetherby: DfT Pub, 2003.	**Numerical** SUDLOW, D. *Scoping study on motorcycle training.* Great Britain. Department for Transport: Road Safety Research Report no. 36. Wetherby: DfT Publications, 2003.

E3 Government-sponsored publications

Government-sponsored reports often have long titles, but become commonly known by the name of the chairman/chairwoman of the committee responsible. You should always give the full official title of the report in a reference, but you can also give the popular title, if you wish. An abbreviated title can be shown in citations in the text, but the full title must always be explained in the reference, as shown in the example that follows.

Table 9.E3 Government-sponsored publications	
Harvard UNWCED: UNITED NATIONS WORLD COMMISSION ON ENVIRONMENT AND DEVELOPMENT (1987). *Our common future* (Brundtland Report). Oxford: Oxford University Press.	**APA** UNWCED: United Nations World Commission on Environment & Development (1987). *Our common future* (Brundtland Report). Oxford: Oxford University Press.
MLA UNWCED: United Nations World Commission on Environment and Development. <u>Our Common Future</u> (Brundtland Report). Oxford UP, 1987.	**Numerical** UNWCED: UNITED NATIONS WORLD COMMISSION ON ENVIRONMENT AND DEVELOPMENT. *Our common future* (Brundtland Report). Oxford: Oxford University Press, 1987.

F Parliamentary publications

UK parliamentary publications can be grouped into four main categories:

Table 9.FO Parliamentary publications categories

Parliamentary business	Records of debates
• Weekly information bulletins • Sessional information digest • Votes and proceedings (House of Commons: HC) • Minutes of proceedings (House of Lords: HL) • Journals (HC and HL)	• Parliamentary debates (Hansard, abbreviated House of Commons or Lords: HC and HL) • Standing Committees Debates (HC)
Parliamentary papers	**Acts of Parliament**
• House of Commons Bills • House of Commons Papers • Command Papers • House of Lords Bills • House of Lords Papers	• Public General Acts • Local and Personal Acts

(Source: Butcher 1991)

What to include:

• United Kingdom Parliament: The House of . . . (Commons or Lords)
• Year of publication
• Title of publication, in italics or underlined
• Place of publication and name of publisher
• Other identifying features, e.g. details of Paper, Bill, Series, numbers.

F1 Minutes of proceedings

Table 9.F1 Order of business

Harvard	APU
UNITED KINGDOM PARLIAMENT. House of Commons (1999). *Order of business, Wed. 11 Nov. 1998*. Oral questions to the Secretary of State for International Development. Norwich: Office of Public Sector Information.	United Kingdom Parliament. House of Commons (1999). *Order of business, Wed. 11 Nov. 1998*. Oral questions to the Secretary of State for International Development. Norwich: Office of Public Sector Information.
MLA	**Numerical**
United Kingdom Parliament. House of Commons. Order of Business, Wed. 11 Nov. 1998. Oral questions to the Secretary of State for International Development, Norwich: OIPC,1999.	UNITED KINGDOM PARLIAMENT. House of Commons. *Order of business, Wed. 11 Nov. 1998*. Oral questions to the Secretary of State for International Development. Norwich: Office of Public Sector Information, 1999.

F2 Parliamentary debates

Hansard is the collective name of the independent record of debates and speeches in the Chamber of the House of Commons, sub-chamber in Westminster Hall and in Standing Committees of the House of Lords. The impartial recording of parliamentary proceedings dates from the early nineteenth century, but the term 'Hansard' derives from Thomas Curson Hansard, the son of Luke Hansard, a printer in the House of Commons. Thomas Hansard employed reporters to record verbatim parliamentary procedure, and their reports rapidly gained public respect for their accuracy and attention to detail.

Today much the same procedure applies, with Hansard reporters in the Press Gallery recording by shorthand, or by sub-editors recording the proceedings of Westminster Hall and the Standing Committees.

Hansard is produced in daily, weekly and bound volume versions of proceedings in the Chamber of the House of Commons. In Select Committees there is no Hansard record published, but instead 'minutes of evidence' are published by the Committee and form part of their report.

There is a fact sheet (ref. G17) that can be obtained from The House of Commons Information Office, London SW1A 2TT, and this give examples of how to reference Hansard entries.

For all styles of referencing the following abbreviations should be used:

HC Deb: House of Commons Debate
W: Written Answers
WH: Westminster Hall
WS: Written Statements
SC: Standing Committee
c: column numbers.

Harvard, APA and MLA citations in the text can show 'United Kingdom Parliament' (or UK Parliament) and the date, e.g. (United Kingdom Parliament 13 Nov 2001), and these can then link to the full references.

Full reference examples:

- United Kingdom Parliament HC Deb 13 November 2001 c345; or cc345 6 or c134W or c101WH or 1WS.

For the older versions of Hansard, the volume and series numbers can be quoted.

Examples

- UNITED KINGDOM PARLIAMENT HC Deb 3 February 1977 vol 389 c973
- UNITED KINGDOM PARLIAMENT HC Deb 17 December 1996 vol 596 cc18–19
- UNITED KINGDOM PARLIAMENT HC Deb 4 July 1996 vol 280 c505W
- UNITED KINGDOM PARLIAMENT HC Deb (5th series) 13 January 1907 vol 878 cc 69–70.

In Standing Committees, the citations are, as follows:

- UNITED KINGDOM PARLIAMENT SC Deb (A) 13 May 1998 c345.

Note: the term 'United Kingdom Parliament' has been added to the above references.

This term is used on the office website for parliamentary sources in Britain, so has been used here to make it clear which country is referred to.

However, British Standard BS 1629: 1989 offers an alternative version of citing Hansard, as follows:

- GREAT BRITAIN. House of Commons. *Official Report. Parliamentary debates (Hansard)* ... (then details, as above examples) (see BS 1999 p.18)

Check with your tutor which version is preferred.

F3 Command papers

Command papers are those 'commanded' by the sovereign to be presented to Parliament, including 'White' or 'Green' Papers: policy proposals or consultation documents, or reports of committees of inquiry, responses to Select Committee reports and other important departmental reports or reviews.

References to Command papers should include name of originating department, title, Command paper number and year of publication.

Table 9.F3 Command paper	
Harvard SCOTLAND OFFICE (2006). *Departmental report.* CM 6834. London: The Stationery Office.	**APA** Scotland Office (2006) *Departmental report.* CM 6834. London: The Stationery Office, 2006.
MLA Scotland Office. <u>Departmental Report</u>. CM 6834. London: TSO, 2006.	**Numerical** SCOTLAND OFFICE. *Departmental report.* CM 6834. London: The Stationery Office, 2006.

F4 Select Committee reports

Select Committees examine particular and selected subjects. In the House of Commons they review the running of each of the main government departments and associated public bodies and have the power to take evidence and issue reports.

In the House of Lords, Select Committees examine broader issues, such as the European Union, and Science and Technology.

You should include the name of the Select Committee, title of the report, and HC or HL to indicate House of Commons or House of Lords respectively, and the serial number of the report.

Table 9.F4 Select Committee report	
Harvard UNITED KINGDOM PARLIAMENT (2005). *The Select Committee on BBC charter review.* HL50–1 [75]. London: The Stationery Office.	**APA** United Kingdom Parliament (2005). *The select committee on BBC charter review.* HL50–1 [75]. London: The Stationery Office.

(*cont.*)

MLA	Numerical
United Kingdom Parliament. The Select Committee on BBC Charter Review. HL50–1 [75]. London: TSO, 2005.	UNITED KINGDOM PARLIAMENT. *The Select Committee on BBC charter review.* HL50–1 [75]. London: The Stationery Office, 2005.

The numbers in squared brackets indicate paragraph numbers. If you wanted to refer to sequential paragraphs, this can be done by linking them, e.g. [75]–[80].

See also 'Legal documents', next section.

G Legal documents

Students on law degree or related courses will learn a referencing style that is particular to this subject, which is usually the *Oxford Standard for Citation of Legal Authorities* (OSCOLA). This is the style used by the *Oxford University Commonwealth Law Journal*, which contributed to its development. However, students on other courses, who occasionally have to cite legal cases, may also find this section helpful.

OSCOLA style of referencing

More detailed information on the OSCOLA Style of referencing can be obtained from the website of Faculty of Law, University of Oxford, and most institutions of higher education that offer law degrees will offer students summary versions of the OSCOLA guide. Briefly, the OSCOLA referencing style links with the running-notes style of referencing in that it uses a raised or superscript numbers in the text, combined with footnotes. OSCOLA style is, however, different to the four main referencing styles in the way it is presented.

With books, for example, the first name or initials of the author(s) is presented before the author's last name, without a stop or comma between them. The title is always in italics and the edition, publisher, place of publication and date(s) are all enclosed within brackets. Page numbers can be included, if relevant, as the last items in the reference. When there are more than three authors, just state the first, followed by 'and others'.

OSCOLA examples:

- D French, *How to Cite Legal Authorities* (London: Blackstone, London 1996) 33–35.
- P Loose and others, *The Company Director* (9th rev edn Jordans, Bristol 2006).

(*Note*: the book mentioned above, *How to Cite Legal Authorities*, is recommended reading regarding citations and referencing for any student studying for a law degree.)

Cite essays and chapters in edited journals, as follows:

- D Cullen, 'Adoption – a (Fairly) New Approach', Child and Family Law Quarterly (Oct 2005) 17 475, 486.

A minimum of punctuation is used, and commas should be used only to stop words running into each other. All words in the title should be capitalized, except prepositions ('of', 'by', 'which'), articles ('the', 'an', 'a') and conjunctions ('and', 'or').

G1 Case citation

Case citation is a frequent occurrence in law course assignments. You need to include:

- Names of the parties
- Year, in square or round brackets (see below discussion for when to do this)
- Volume number
- Abbreviated name of the law report series
- First page of the reference.

Case names should be italicized in assignments, e.g.:

Murphy v Brentwood District Council [1990] 2 All ER 908.

When referring to a case for the first time, give its full name exactly as it appears in the report. In subsequent references a case can be referred to by a shortened name, e.g. *Murphy v Brentwood District Council*, and can be referred to as the *Murphy* case.

If you give the full details of the case in the text, you do not need to repeat the information in a list of references.

Examples:

1 Campbell v Mirror Group Newspapers Ltd [2004] 2 All ER 995.
2 Rees v United Kingdom (1987) 9 EHRR 56.

You could, however, refer to part of the citation in the text, e.g. *Campbell v Mirror Group Newspapers*, and give the full reference details in footnotes.

Square or round brackets?

Square brackets are used when the date is essential for finding the report. Round brackets are used when the date is merely of assistance in giving an idea of when a case was featured in law reports that have cumulative volume numbers.

Abbreviations?

The abbreviations in the examples shown above refer to All England Law Reports (All ER) and European Human Rights Reports (EHRR). A full list of abbreviations in the names of law reports and journals can be found at the Cardiff University 'Cardiff Index to Legal Abbreviations' website at http://www.legalabbrevs.cardiff.ac.uk/searchabbreviation/ or from OSCOLA.

Punctuation?

Use open punctuation – no stops after parts of the abbreviation, e.g. *All ER* (and not All. E.R.)

Specific page references?

When a particular passage is being quoted or referred to, the specific page references must be included, e.g.:

Jones v Tower Boot Co Ltd [1997] 2 All ER 406 at 411.

Judge's name?

When the judge's name is being quoted or referred to in a particular passage, the judge's name should be provided as part of the citation, e.g.:

That was the opinion of Lord Mackay LC in *Pepper v Hart [1993] 1 All ER 42 at 47.*

G2 UK Acts of Parliament (Statutes)

These are Acts passed by Parliament, which eventually receive royal assent and become law. You would normally list the source in the full reference, as follows:

* Title of Act and year
* The part: pt, and section: s, and/or
* The schedule: sch, and section: s.

Example:

Citation: (Data Protection Act 1998)
Reference: Data Protection Act 1998. pt 1, s2.

Note: the year, 1998, does not appear in brackets in the reference, as the date is part of the title.

For older statutes, the *Oxford Standard* suggests it can be helpful to give the appropriate year of reign and chapter number, e.g. Crown Debts Act 1801 (14 Geo 3 c 90), meaning that the Act was given Royal Assent in the fourteenth year of the reign of George the Third, and was the ninetieth Act given Royal Assent in that Parliament, hence c 90).

G3 UK bills

A bill is proposed legislation before Parliament. Bills are cited by their name, the Parliamentary Session, the House of Parliament in which it originated and the running order assigned to it, and any relevant sections or subsections. HC = House of Commons; HL = House of Lords.

Example:

Citation: (Identity Cards Bill 2004–5)
Reference: Identity Cards Bill 2004–5 HC-8, s 9(4).

G4 UK statutory instruments

These are orders and regulations linked to particular Acts and should be referenced by name, date and serial number (where available).

Subsidiary words in long titles within the in-text citation may be abbreviated (see example below), but the full title must be given in the reference.

Example:

Citation: (Telecommunications (LBP) (IC) Regulations 2000)
Reference: The Telecommunications (Lawful Business Practice) (Interception of Communications) Regulations 2000.

G5 EC legislation

European Community (EC) legislation (Regulations, Directives and Decisions), and other instruments (including Recommendations and Opinions) should be referenced by providing the legislation type, number and title, then publication details from the *Official Journal (OJ)* of the European Communities. Be warned, these references can be lengthy!

Example:

Citation: (Commission Regulation 1475/95)
Reference: Commission Regulation (EC) No 1475/95 of 28 June 1995 on the application of Article 85 (3) [*now 81 (3)*] of the Treaty to certain categories of motor vehicle distribution and servicing agreements *Official Journal L 145*, 29/06/1995 pp. 0025–0034.

The capital letter 'L' in the example, i.e. '*Official Journal L*', indicates the series stands for Legislation; the C series contains EU information and notices, and the S series contains invitations to tender (see *Oxford Standard* p.18).

H Standards and patents

Standards

The full reference should include:

- The number and year of standard, e.g. BS 5605:1990
- Year of republishing, if applicable; see example below (shown in brackets for APA and Harvard)
- Title of Standard, in italics or underlined
- Place of publication, and name of publisher.

H1 British Standard

Table 9.H1 British Standard recommendations

Harvard	APA
BS 5605:1990 (1999). *Citing and referencing published material*. London: British Standard Institution.	BS5605:1990 (1999). *Citing & referencing published material*. London: British Standard Institution.
MLA	**Numerical**
BS4821:1990. <u>Citing and Referencing Published Material</u>. London: BS, 1999.	BS 5605:1990. *Citing and referencing published material*. London: British Standard Institution, 1999.

H2 International Organization for Standardization (ISO)

Table 9.H2 ISO recommendations

Harvard	APA
ISO 14001:2004. *Environmental management systems*. Geneva: International Organization for Standardization.	ISO 14001:2004. *Environmental management systems*. Geneva: International Organization for Standardization.
MLA	**Numerical**
ISO 14001:2004. <u>Environmental Management Systems</u>. Geneva: ISO.	ISO 14001:2004. *Environmental management systems*. Geneva: International Organization for Standardization.

H3 Patents

The full reference should include:

- Name(s) of inventor(s) or patentee(s)
- Year of publication
- Title of patent, in italics or underlined, with the exception of MLA style, which does not show a title underline for this particular type of source
- Country of origin and serial number
- Date of application and date of acceptance.

Table 9.H3 Patent

Harvard	APA
LUND-ANDERSON, B. (2001). *Device for the damping of vibrators between objects*. US Patent 6296238. Appl. 24 June1999. Acc. 2 Oct. 2001.	Lund-Anderson, B. (2001). *Device for the damping of vibrators between objects*. US Patent 6296238. Appl. 24 June 1999. Acc. 2 Oct. 2001.

(Cont.)

MLA	Numerical
Lund-Anderson, Bernard. Device for the Damping of Vibrators Between Objects. US Patent 6296238. Appl. 24 June 1999. Acc. 2 Oct. 2001.	LUND-ANDERSON, B. *Device for the damping of vibrators between objects*. US Patent 6296238. Appl. 24 June1999. Acc. 2 Oct. 2001.

I Course manuals and lecture notes

You can also reference printed course material given to you by teaching staff. You should include:

- Name of the lecturer
- Year of lecture
- Title of lecture or course notes. These can be in italics or underlined, although this is not strictly necessary unless the notes have been made more widely and publicly available
- Title of course or module
- Level (undergraduate or postgraduate)
- Name of institution, department or school.

These notes may be a **primary source**, e.g. a summary or explanation written by a lecturer, or a **secondary source**, where a lecturer is quoting what someone else has said, or referring directly to a third person.

To illustrate the difference between primary and secondary sources, the following extracts from two student essays illustrate the use of a course manual as both a primary and secondary source. Harvard style referencing has been used to illustrate both examples.

Primary (extract 1)

When choosing from the mix of promotional activities available to market a product, the market objectives should be the main driving force. Low (2004) has suggested four main questions: who is your target group? What do you want them to do? When do you want them to act? And how much are you prepared to spend to communicate with them?

Secondary (Extract 2)

Marketing Communications has been defined by Fill as a process *'through which an organisation enters into a dialogue with its various audiences'*. The objective is to influence in a positive way a particular target audience in its awareness, understanding and actions towards that organisation and its products or services' (Fill 2002, as cited in Lowe, 2004, p.2).

The secondary reference for the extract above, in the four main referencing formats, would be presented, as follows:

Table 9.11 Course notes	
Harvard	**APA**
LOWE, C. (2004). *Marketing communications.* MA course manual, 2004/5, p.2, University of Bradford, School of Management.	Lowe, C. (2004). *Marketing communications.* MA course manual, 2004/5, p.2, University of Bradford, School of Management.
MLA	**Numerical**
Lowe, Chris. Marketing Communications. MA Course Manual, 2004/5. U of Bradford Sch. of Mgt., 2004.	LOWE, C. *Marketing communications.* MA Course Manual, 2004/5, p.2, University of Bradford, School of Management, 2004.

However, you might want to go to the original source, i.e. Fill 2002, to enable you to expand on the definition presented, or to be critical of it. If you did this, you could then treat it as a primary source and cite and reference Fill, instead of Lowe.

J Unpublished work

You can reference work of scholarly interest that is unpublished, providing it is still publicly accessible in some way. 'Unpublished', in this sense, means that the source has not featured in any publication produced for large-scale public consumption, although it may be available as a limited circulation document, e.g. to delegates, members of a group, internal circulation within an organization, or available for inspection in a collection. Despite the limited circulation, it is often possible to obtain copies of these documents, although you should be wary of their validity as evidence unless the work has been subject to critical scrutiny in some way; for example, by the delegates at a conference or seminar.

Unpublished work you might want to use could include:

- Dissertations
- Papers presented at conferences and seminars
- Manuscripts and other documents in libraries and archives
- Personal correspondence, if relevant to make particular points
- Minutes of meetings.

The same basic format referencing published work applies for referencing unpublished sources. You should include:

- Author name(s)
- Year
- Title or name of work/conference/seminar, in italics or underlined

- Name of any host institution
- Location of archive material, if applicable
- Any other information to help locate the material.

J1 Dissertation

Table 9.J1 Postgraduate dissertation

Harvard	APA
COOPER, T. (2003). *Implementing strategic change in the recruitment advertising/ employment communication industry.* Unpublished MBA project report, 2002/3. Bradford: University of Bradford, School of Management Library.	Cooper, T. (2003). *Implementing strategic change in the recruitment advertising/ employment communication industry.* Unpublished MBA project report, 2002/3. Bradford: University of Bradford, School of Management Library.
MLA	**Numerical**
Cooper, Thomas. <u>Implementing Strategic Change in the Recruitment Advertising/Employment Communication Industry.</u> Unpublished MBA project report, 2002/3. U of Bradford, Sch. of Mgt. Libr. 2003.	COOPER, T. *Implementing Strategic Change in the Recruitment Advertising/Employment Communication Industry.* Unpublished MBA project report, 2002/3. Bradford: University of Bradford, School of Management Library, 2003.

J2 Unpublished conference papers

Table 9.J2 Unpublished conference papers

Harvard	APA
BROADBENT, M. (2005). *Tackling plagiarism: a teaching and learning perspective.* Unpublished paper presented at 'Tackling Plagiarism' Conference. University of Hertfordshire, Business School, 22 Mar. 2005.	Broadbent, M. (2005, March 22). *Tackling plagiarism: a teaching and learning perspective.* Unpublished paper presented at 'Tackling Plagiarism' Conference. University of Hertfordshire, Business School.
MLA	**Numerical**
Broadbent, Mick. (2005). <u>Tackling Plagiarism: a Teaching and Learning Perspective</u>. Unpublished paper presented at 'Tackling Plagiarism' Conf. U of Hertfordshire, Bus. Sch. 22 Mar. 2005.	BROADBENT, M. *Tackling Plagiarism: a Teaching and Learning Perspective.* Unpublished paper presented at 'Tackling Plagiarism' Conference. University of Hertfordshire, Business School, 22 Mar. 2005.

J3 Archive material

If the author of a manuscript is not known, start with the title of the manuscript, or collection of manuscripts, (italics or underlined). Include any date or year of the manuscript, if known, plus the name of the archive collection and any reference number (also in italics or underlined). State the name and place of archive and add any additional relevant information to help others locate the material.

Examples:

- *LNWR plans* at West Yorkshire Archive Service, Kirklees, ref. KX272.
- Deposited Building Plans, no 10, 1 October 1886, West Yorkshire Archive Service, Leeds.

Table 9.J3i Archive papers (collection)

Harvard	APA
VICKRIDGE, A. *Correspondence of Alberta Vickridge 1917–1965*. Box 2. Letter to Vickridge from Agatha Christie, 12 Feb. 1918. University of Leeds, Brotherton Library.	Vickridge, A. *Correspondence of Alberta Vickridge 1917–1965*. Box 2. Letter to Vickridge from Agatha Christie, 12 February 1918. University of Leeds, Brotherton Library.
MLA	**Numerical**
Vickridge, A. Correspondence of Alberta Vickridge 1917–1965. Box 2. Letter to Vickridge from Agatha Christie, 12 Feb. 1918. U of Leeds, Brotherton Libr.	VICKRIDGE, A. *Correspondence of Alberta Vickridge 1917–1965*. Box 2. Letter to Vickridge from Agatha Christie, 12 Feb. 1918. University of Leeds, Brotherton Library.

Table 9.J3ii Single letter in a collection

Harvard	APA
Webb, Mary (1921). Letter to publisher requesting an advance on royalties, 21 Jan. 1921. Mary Webb Society.	Webb, Mary (1921). Letter to publisher requesting an advance on royalties, Jan. 21, 1921. Mary Webb Society.
MLA	**Numerical**
Webb, Mary. Letter to Publisher Requesting an Advance on Royalties. 21 Jan. 1921. Mary Webb Society	Webb, Mary. Letter to publisher requesting an advance on royalties, 21 Jan. 1921. Mary Webb Society.

Start with the name of the sender, give the year, state the nature of the letter (e.g. to whom was it sent, and its subject), specific date written, if shown, and give the name of the collection. If the collection in question has been given it a title, this can be italicized or underlined, but this is not necessary if you have given the document a title or description yourself.

J4 Unpublished proceedings of a meeting

Give names of contributors or presenters and full details of the meeting, including name and date of meeting, where it was held and details of any formal contribution made to the meeting by speakers or delegates.

Table 9.J4 Proceedings of a meeting

Harvard	APA
BONANNI, L. and C. VAUCELLE (2006) *A framework for Haptic psycho-therapy*. In Proceedings of IEEE ICPS Pervasive Health Systems Workshop, Lyon, France, 29 June 2006.	Bonanni, L. and Vaucelle, C. (2006, June 29) *A framework for Haptic psycho-therapy*. In Proceedings of IEEE ICPS Pervasive Health Systems Workshop, Lyon, France.
MLA	**Numerical**
Bonanni, Leonardo. and Cati Vaucelle. *A Framework for Haptic Psycho-therapy*. In Proceedings of IEEE ICPS Pervasive Health Systems Workshop, Lyon, France, 29 June 2006.	BONANNI, L. and C. VAUCELLE. *A framework for Haptic psycho-therapy*. In Proceedings of IEEE ICPS Pervasive Health Systems Workshop, Lyon, France, 29 June 2006.

K Cartographic material: maps and atlases

If you wish to use illustrations in any work that will be publicly accessible, e.g. in a journal article, you will need to seek permission from the people or organizations holding copyright.

For referencing purposes, treat any illustrated or cartographic material in the same way you would for books. If there is any named author, illustrator or photographer, start with this, if not start with the title of the item.

Atlases

Table 9.K1 Atlas

Harvard	APA
Atlas of the world 12th edn. (2004). Oxford: Oxford University Press.	*Atlas of the world* (12th ed.). (2004). Oxford: Oxford University Press.
MLA	**Numerical**
Atlas of the World. 12th ed. Oxford UP, 2004	*Atlas of the world* 12th edn. Oxford: Oxford University Press, 2004.

Maps

Include:

- Name of originators (e.g. Ordnance Survey)
- Year of publication
- Title of map (in italics or underlined)
- Sheet number and scale
- Series, (if applicable)
- Place of publication (and publisher, if different from originator).

Table 9.K2 Ordnance Survey

Harvard	APA
ORDNANCE SURVEY (1974). *Saxmundham and Aldeburgh* 156, 1:50 000. First series. Southampton: Ordnance Survey.	Ordnance Survey (1974). *Saxmundham & Aldeburgh* 156, 1:50 000. First series. Southampton: Ordnance Survey.
MLA	**Numerical**
Ordnance Survey. <u>Saxmundham and Aldeburgh</u> 156, 1:50 000. First series. Map. Southampton: OS, 1974.	ORDNANCE SURVEY. *Saxmundham and Aldeburgh* 156, 1:50 000. First series. Southampton: Ordnance Survey, 1974.

Maps for countries outside Britain should include title of map in the language of the country concerned, although a translation could be included if non-European characters have been used.

Table 9.K3 Map produced outside the UK

Harvard	APA
Wanderkarte Boppard (1996). M1: 25.000. Germany: Boppard, Tourist Information.	*Wanderkarte Boppard* (1996). M1: 25.000. Germany: Boppard, Tourist Information.
MLA	**Numerical**
<u>Wanderkarte Boppard</u>. M1: 25.000. Map. Germany: Boppard, Tourist Information, 1996.	*Wanderkarte Boppard*. M1: 25.000. Germany: Boppard, Tourist Information, 1996.

Table 9.K4 British Geological Survey map

Harvard	APA
BRITISH GEOLOGICAL SURVEY (1992). *Thirsk* (S&D) E52. 1:50 000. Nottingham: British Geological Survey.	British Geological Survey (1992). *Thirsk* (S&D) E52. 1:50 000. Nottingham: British Geological Survey.
MLA	**Numerical**
British Geological Survey. <u>Thirsk</u> (S&D) E52. 1:50 000. Map. Nottingham: BGS, 1992.	BRITISH GEOLOGICAL SURVEY. *Thirsk* (S&D) E52. 1:50 000. Nottingham: British Geological Survey, 1992.

It may be necessary to state the medium, i.e. satellite image.

Table 9.K5 Other example (satellite image)

Harvard	APA
PLANET OBSERVER (2006). European map. Satellite image. 1:8.000.000. USA: National Geographic Society.	*Planet Observer* (2006). European map Satellite image. 1:8.000.000. USA: National Geographic Society.
MLA	**Numerical**
<u>Planet Observer</u>. European Map. Satellite image. 1:8.000.000. USA: Nat. Geog. Soc. 2006.	*PLANET OBSERVER*. European map. Satellite image. 1:8.000.000. USA: National Geographic Society, 2006.

With old maps, give title, date (or use c: 'circa') and state where the map is located.

Table 9.K6 Old map

Harvard	APA
Map of the precincts of St Mary Graces, Tower Hill (c.1590). London: Guildhall Library.	*Map of the precincts of St Mary Graces, Tower Hill* (c.1590). London: Guildhall Library.
MLA	**Numerical**
Map of the Precincts of St Mary Graces, Tower Hill. London: Guildhall Libr. c.1590.	*Map of the precincts of St Mary Graces, Tower Hill*. London: Guildhall Library, c.1590.

L Graphs and charts

It is important to cite and reference all sources imported in, or used to construct graphs, tables and charts in your assignments. For example, with the constructed table shown below, the source, in Harvard style, is shown below the table. If more than one source as contributed to the compilation, show all these in the citation and list them separately in the references.

Table 9.L1 Population of Children in Tanzania (2002)

Age	Both sexes	Male	Female
Total Population	18,837,206	9,399,477	9,433,920
0–4 (per cent of total)	16.45	16.82	16.09
5–9 (per cent of total)	14.9	15.29	14.51
10–14 (per cent of total)	12.9	13.27	12.55
15–19 (per cent of total)	10.44	10.47	10.41

(Source: Canadian Cooperation Office 2003 p. 6)

The above table would be referenced, as follows:

Table 9.L2 Reference for source of Table 9.L1

Harvard	APA
CANADIAN COOPERATION OFFICE (2003). *Canadian government support to the education sector in Tanzania*. Dar es Salaam, Tanzania: as author.	Canadian Cooperation Office (2003). *Canadian government support to the education sector in Tanzania*. Dar es Salaam, Tanzania: Author.
MLA	**Numerical**
Canadian Cooperation Office. Canadian Government Support to the Education Sector in Tanzania. Dar es Salaam, Tanzania: as author, 2003.	CANADIAN COOPERATION OFFICE. *Canadian government support to the education sector in Tanzania*. Dar es Salaam, Tanzania: as author, 2003.

M Visual art and graphics

These can include original paintings, and any form of photographic or printed graphic illustration, including cartoons, line drawings, advertisements and postcards. You should state the artist's name, title of work, type of work and where the work can be located or viewed, e.g. book title, name of gallery, etc. If no artist name is shown, start with the title, in italics or underlined, and then give as much information as necessary to help others locate the source. British Standard guidelines show the full first name(s) of originator for visual sources for both Harvard and Numerical styles.

M1 Painting exhibited in a gallery

Table 9.M1 Painting exhibited in a gallery

Harvard	APA
KLIMT, Gustav. (1898). *Allegory of sculpture.* [Painting]. Salzburg: Galerie Welz.	Klimt, G. (1898). *Allegory of sculpture.* [Painting]. Salzburg: Galerie Welz.
MLA	**Numerical**
Klimt, Gustav. *Allegory of Sculpture.* Painting. Salzburg: Galerie Welz, 1898.	KLIMT, Gustav. *Allegory of sculpture.* [Painting]. Salzburg: Galerie Welz, 1898.

M2 Photographs

You should include:

* Name of photographer
* Year photograph taken, or approximate date, e.g. 'circa' or 'c'
* Title of photograph, or description, if no title. Titles should be in italics or underlined
* State medium, and enclose this description in square brackets, e.g. [Photograph]
* Name of publisher, or where photograph is to be viewed.

If it is a personal photograph, start the reference with a general description of the subject, but this does not need to be in italics or underlined. Then state the name of the photographer (if known), and the date, or approximate date, the photograph was taken. You also need to state who has ownership of the photographs.
   Examples:

* Alberta Vickridge, aged approximately 19 years. Photographer unknown. Circa 1911. In the private collection of Henry Vickridge, Otley, West Yorkshire.
* River Wharfe, near Bolton Abbey, North Yorkshire. Personal photograph by author. 22 June 2006.

Table 9.M2 Photograph in a public gallery

Harvard	APA
GRIFFITHS, Frances. (1920). *Frances and the leaping fairy*. [Photograph]. Bradford: National Museum Film and Photography.	Griffiths, F. (1920). *Frances & the leaping fairy*. [Photograph]. Bradford: National Museum Film and Photography.
MLA	**Numerical**
Griffiths, Frances. <u>Frances and the Leaping Fairy</u>. Photograph. Bradford: Natl. Mus. Film & Photo. 1920.	GRIFFITHS, Frances. *Frances and the leaping fairy*. [Photograph]. Bradford: National Museum Film and Photography, 1920.

M3 Book illustration

You should include:

- Name of the artist or illustrator, if known
- Date work originally completed (if known), or the year book was published
- Title of plate (if any)
- Author/editor of book, if different from artist
- Title of book and when published, if not already given. As this is the primary source, show this in italics or underlined
- Where published, and publisher.

Table 9.M3 Book illustration

Harvard	APA
FORSTER, Peter. (1999). Two illustrations for Romola. In S. Brett (Ed.) *An engraver's globe* (2002). London: Primrose Hill Press.	Forster, P. (1999). Two illustrations for Romola. In S. Brett (Ed.) *An engraver's globe* (2002). London: Primrose Hill Press.
MLA	**Numerical**
Forster, Peter. "Two Illustrations for Romola", 1999. Ed. Simon Brett, <u>An Engraver's Globe. London: Primrose Hill Press, 2002.</u>	FORSTER, Peter. Two illustrations for Romola. 1999. In Simon Brett (Ed.) *An engraver's globe*. London: Primrose Hill Press, 2002.

M4 Graphic art: cartoon (artist's name not shown)

If the artist's name is not shown, start with the name of the originator or title of the graphic. If the artist's name was shown, start with this. Make it clear what type of graphic art is referenced, e.g. advertisement, cartoon or poster, where it was publicly shown and give any other identifying information, e.g. title of the work.

Table 9.M4 Advertisement poster	
Harvard VODAFONE (2005). Advertisement on London Transport Underground. *Make the most of now – seize the day.*	**APA** Vodafone (2005). Advertisement on London Transport Underground. *Make the most of now – seize the day.*
MLA Vodafone. Advert. London Transport Underground. <u>Make the Most of Now – Seize the Day.</u> 2005.	**Numerical** VODAFONE. Advertisement on London Transport Underground. *Make the most of now – seize the day*, 2005.

(See also section R: 'Miscellaneous' in this chapter.)

N Audio-visual sources

This section includes any transmitted or produced visual and audio means of communication, including radio, television, music, cinema and other film productions (for live performances, see section O); also see 'electronic sources', section S in this chapter.

Radio and television

References to television and radio can contain the information that follows, depending on the context of the evidence presented. If you feel the names of authors/presenters and producers are not required, start with the title. It might be, for example, that the points made generally in a radio or television programme are more important to you than the details of people involved in the production.

However, if it is a work of fiction, or where the author/presenter's identity is associated with the programme, then you need to include this information. If someone has been interviewed (see television programme example below), and the interview is the basis for the citation and full reference entry, the reference should start with the name of the person interviewed.

Information that can be included:

- Writer of programme, if relevant to the evidence in question
- Producer of programme, if relevant to the evidence in question
- Title of the programme, in italics or underlined, and name of episode, if relevant
- Title of the series, if applicable
- Name of the radio or television network, e.g. BBC Radio 4
- Place of broadcast, if it is a regional station, e.g. Bradford: Pulse Radio
- Broadcast or transmission date.

If you miss them at the time of the broadcast, the names of the authors/presenter or producers can normally be found on the websites of the broadcast stations concerned, and many programmes can be replayed at a later date from the Internet (see section S in this chapter).

N1 Radio programmes

Table 9.N1i Radio programme

Harvard	APA
BBC Radio 4 (2003). *Analysis: future of work.* 12 May 2003.	BBC Radio 4 (2003, May 12). *Analysis: Future of work.*
MLA	**Numerical**
BBC Radio 4. "<u>Analysis: Future of Work</u>". 12 May 2003.	BBC Radio 4 (2003). *Analysis: future of work.* 12 May 2003.

Table 9.N1ii Radio programme

Harvard	APA
RICH, Emma. (2006). Interview with J. MURRAY. *Woman's Hour.* BBC Radio 4, 4 July 2006.	Rich, E. (2006, July 4). Interview with J. Murray. *Woman's hour.* BBC Radio 4.
MLA	**Numerical**
Rich, Emma. Interview with Jenni Murray. <u>Woman's Hour</u>. BBC Radio 4, 4 July 2006.	RICH, Emma. Interview with J. MURRAY. *Woman's Hour.* BBC Radio 4, 4 July 2006.

Table 9.N1iii Radio programme

Harvard	APA
LICHTAROWICZ, Ania. (Presenter). (2006). *Hip fractures.* BBC World Service, 4 July 2006.	Lichtarowicz, A. (Presenter). (2006, July 4). *Hip fractures.* BBC World Service.
MLA	**Numerical**
Lichtarowicz, Ania. (Presenter). <u>Hip Fractures</u>. BBC World Service. 4 July 2006.	LICHTAROWICZ, Ania. (Presenter). *Hip fractures.* BBC World Service. 4 July 2006.

N2 Television programmes

Table 9.N2i Television programme (1)

Harvard	APA
PORRIT, Jonathan. (1991). Interview by Jonathan DIMBLEBY on *Panorama.* BBC 1 television, 18 Mar. 1991.	Porrit, J. (1991, March 18). Interview by Jonathan Dimbleby on *Panorama.* BBC 1 television.
MLA	**Numerical**
Porrit, Jonathan. Interview with Jonathan Dimbleby on <u>Panorama</u>. BBC 1 TV, 18 Mar. 1991.	PORRIT, Jonathan. Interview by Jonathan DIMBLEBY on *Panorama.* BBC 1 television, 18 Mar. 1991.

Table 9.N2ii Television programme (2)

Harvard	APA
WOOD, Michael. (Presenter). (2006). *Gilbert White the nature man*. BBC4 television, 28 June 2006.	Wood, M. (Presenter). (2006, June 28). *Gilbert White the nature man*. BBC4 television.
MLA	**Numerical**
Wood, Michael. (Presenter). <u>Gilbert White the Nature Man</u>. BBC4 TV, 28 June 2006.	WOOD, Michael (Presenter). *Gilbert White the nature man*. BBC4 television, 28 June 2006.

Table 9.N2iii Television programme (3)

Harvard	APA
The Simpsons (2006). Episode. Bye-bye Nerdy. Channel 4 television, 28 June 2006.	*The Simpsons* (2006, June 28). Episode: Bye-bye Nerdy. Channel 4 television.
MLA	**Numerical**
<u>The Simpsons</u>. Episode: "Bye-bye Nerdy". Channel 4 TV, 28 June 2006	*The Simpsons*. Episode. Bye-bye Nerdy. Channel 4 Television broadcast, 28 June 2006.

N3 Audio productions on CD, tape and vinyl LPs

You can include:

- Name of writer, if applicable, e.g. song writer, composer, poet
- Title of item, in inverted commas or italics
- Specify the medium and (excepting MLA) enclose description within squared brackets, e.g. [CD-ROM]
- Track, side or position on medium
- Give name of producer, speaker, reader or performer(s), whoever is relevant to the evidence presented
- Where produced and publishers/producers of item, e.g. name of record label and any reference number
- Date (year) of copyright or production, if known.

The order in which you include items depends on the desired emphasis. You may, for example, want to call attention to the original writer, or to the performer, or to the title of the item. Examples:

Table 9.N3i Audio-CD

Harvard	APA
ROBERTS, Roland. (2000). *Passive music for accelerated learning*. [Audio-CD]. Carmarthen: Crown House Publishing.	Roberts, R. (2000). *Passive music for accelerated learning*. [Audio-CD]. Carmarthen: Crown House Publishing.

(Cont.)

MLA
Roberts, Roland. <u>Passive Music for Accelerated Learning</u>. Audio-CD. Carmarthen: Crown House, 2000.

Numerical
ROBERTS, Roland. *Passive music for accelerated learning*. [Audio-CD]. Carmarthen: Crown House Publishing, 2000.

Table 9.N3ii Audio-tape

Harvard
OWEN, Wilfred. *Anthem for doomed youth: selected poems and letters*. [Audio-cassette]. (1993). Side 2: poem: 'Disabled'. Read by Kenneth Branagh. London: Random House Audiobooks.

MLA
<u>Wilfred Owen: Anthem for Doomed Youth: Selected Poems and Letters</u>. [Audio-cassette]. Side 2: poem: "Disabled". Kenneth Branagh. London: Random House Audiobooks, 1993.

APA
Owen, W. *Anthem for doomed youth: Selected poems & letters*. [Audio-cassette]. (1993). Side 2: poem: 'Disabled'. Read by Kenneth Branagh. London: Random House Audiobooks.

Numerical
OWEN, Wilfred. *Anthem for doomed youth: selected poems and letters*. [Audio-cassette]. Side 2: poem: 'Disabled'. Read by Kenneth Branagh. London: Random House Audiobooks, 1993.

Table 9.N3iii Vinyl LP

Harvard
DELIUS, Frederick. (1982). *Delius*. Hallé Orchestra. [LP]. Hayes: Music for Pleasure, CFP 40373.

MLA
Delius, Frederick. <u>Delius</u>. Hallé Orchestra. LP. Hayes: Music for Pleasure, CFP 40373, 1982.

APA
Delius, F. (1982). *Delius*. Hallé Orchestra. [LP]. Hayes: Music for Pleasure, CFP 40373

Numerical
DELIUS, Frederick. *Delius*. Hallé Orchestra. [LP]. Hayes: Music for Pleasure, CFP 40373, 1982.

N4 Film sources

These include any film produced, on DVD, VHS or downloaded from the Internet for entertainment, interest or educational purposes. There is no set formula for listing elements, although both the APA and MLA offer examples in their respective style guides. However, in most instances you should include:

- The title, in italics or underlined
- Year of release (or production, if emphasizing DVD or VHS medium)
- Medium, e.g. [DVD] in squared brackets (exception of MLA)
- Volume, part number or episode (if in a set)
- Country of origin (where made)
- Place and name of distributor/movie studio.

The order in which these will appear will depend on the reason, or emphasis that you wish to place on their inclusion in your assignment. You may, for example, be discussing the work of the director generally, or referring to the playwright, in which case you would want to start with their names. Or, it might be the film itself: the themes, metaphors, dialogue, that interest you, so in this instance the title will feature first. Five examples:

Film: fiction

Table 9.N4i Fiction film

Harvard	APA
LOACH, Ken. (Director) and Sally HIBBIN (Producer). (1993). *Raining stones*. [DVD film]. London: Channel Four (FilmFour).	Loach, K. (Director) & Hibbin, S. (Producer). (1993). *Raining stones*. [DVD film]. London: Channel Four (FilmFour).
MLA	**Numerical**
Loach, Ken. (Director) and Sally Hibbin. (Producer). <u>Raining Stones</u>. DVD. London: Channel Four (FilmFour), 1993.	LOACH, Ken. (Director) and Sally HIBBIN (Producer). *Raining stones*. [DVD film]. London: Channel Four (FilmFour), 1993.

Table 9.N4ii Same film, but different emphasis

Harvard	APA
ALLEN, Jim (Screenplay). (1993). *Raining stones*. [DVD film]. London: Channel Four (FilmFour).	Allen, J. (Screenplay). (1993). *Raining stones*. [DVD film]. London: Channel Four (FilmFour).
MLA	**Numerical**
Allen, Jim (Screenplay). <u>Raining Stones</u>. DVD film. London: Channel Four (FilmFour), 1993.	ALLEN, Jim. (Screenplay). *Raining stones*. [DVD film]. London: Channel Four (FilmFour), 1993.

Table 9.N4iii Fiction film

Harvard	APA
SCHAFFER, Peter. (Playwright). (1977). *Equus*. Motion picture starring Richard Burton. [VHS]. Produced in Britain by MGM/United Artists Home Video.	Schaffer, P. (Playwright). (1977). *Equus*. Motion picture starring Richard Burton. [VHS]. Produced in Britain by MGM/United Artists Home Video.
MLA	**Numerical**
Schaffer, Peter. (Playwright). <u>Equus</u>. Motion picture starring Richard Burton. VHS. Prod. UK MGM/United Artists Home Video, 1977.	SCHAFFER, Peter. (Playwright). *Equus*. Motion picture starring RICHARD BURTON. [VHS]. Produced in Britain by MGM/United Artists Home Video, 1977.

Table 9.N4iv Fiction film

Harvard	APA
HANKS, Tom and Steven SPIELBERG (Producers). (2001). *Band of brothers: part 9: why we fight.* Television film series. Available on VHS. Vol. 4. USA: Warner Brothers: Warner Home Video.	Hanks, T. & Spielberg, S. (Producers). (2001). *Band of brothers: part 9: Why we fight.* Television film series [VHS Set] Vol. 4. USA: Warner Brothers: Warner Home Video.
MLA	**Numerical**
Hanks, Tom and Steven Spielberg (Producers). Band of Brothers: part 9: "Why We Fight". TV film series. Available VHS. Vol. 4. USA: Warner Bros. Home Video, 2001.	HANKS, Tom. and Steven SPIELBERG (Producers). *Band of brothers: part 9: why we fight.* Television film series. Available on VHS. Vol. 4. USA: Warner Brothers: Warner Home Video, 2001.

Table 9.N4v Fiction film

Harvard	APA
Twelve angry men. (1957). [Motion picture]. USA: MGM Studios	*Twelve angry men.* (1957). [Motion picture]. USA: MGM Studios
MLA	**Numerical**
Twelve Angry Men. Motion picture. USA: MGM Studios, 1957.	*Twelve angry men.* [Motion picture]. USA: MGM Studios, 1957.

Non-fiction film productions

It may be necessary to add postal or Internet contact details to help others locate the smaller, independent production companies. Two examples:

Table 9.N5 Non-fiction film with postal contact details

Harvard	APA
The presentation: a guide to effective speaking (n.d.). [VHS]. Bromley: TV Choice Productions [P.O. Box 597, Bromley, Kent BR2 OYB].	*The presentation: A guide to effective speaking* (n.d.). [VHS]. Bromley: TV Choice Productions [P.O. Box 597, Bromley, Kent BR2 OYB].
MLA	**Numerical**
The Presentation: a Guide to Effective Speaking. VHS. Bromley: TV Choice Productions [P.O. Box 597, Bromley, Kent, BR2 OYB], n.d.	*The presentation: a guide to effective speaking.* VHS. Bromley: TV Choice Productions [P.O. Box 597, Bromley, Kent BR2 OYB], n.d.

Table 9.N6 Non-fiction film

Harvard	APA
Guardians of the night (2005). [DVD]. USA: Janson Media.	*Guardians of the night* (2005). [DVD]. USA: Janson Media.
MLA	**Numerical**
Guardians of the Night. DVD. USA: Janson Media, 2005.	*Guardians of the night.* [DVD]. USA: Janson Media, 2005.

O Public performances and events (including theatre, dance, music, talks)

You may want to reference a live event or performance to discuss an aspect of the talk, performance or production, or to use an extract from it to make a particular point. You might also want to cite and reference an extract from a performance programme, and, if so, an example is given below (9.O1iii.)

01 Play

The scripts of plays are usually available in printed form, so you should be able to give details of the playwright and the publisher of the script, particularly when referring to dialogue, or to any themes and metaphors underpinning the dialogue. To reference dialogue in plays, start with the name of the playwright, then state year of publication, title of play (in italics or underlined). You also need to state the medium, e.g. 'play', unless it is obvious, and include details of the Act, Scene and/or page number, and publisher information.

If your emphasis is more concerned with the production, you can give more attention to this and less on other details. In this instance, you would start with the name of the play.

With performance arts sources, British Standard examples show full first name(s) of originator for Harvard and Numerical referencing.

Table 9.01i Emphasis on text in published script

Harvard	APA
KEMPINSKI, Tom. (1983). *Duet for one.* [Play]. Act 1, p.21. Script published London: Samuel French.	Kempinski, T. (1983). *Duet for one.* [Play]. Act 1, p.21. Script published London: Samuel French Inc.
MLA	**Numerical**
Kempinski, Tom. Duet for One. Play: Act 1, p.21. Script pub. London: S. French, 1983.	KEMPINSKI, Tom. *Duet for one.* [Play]. Act 1, p.21. Script published London: Samuel French, 1983

Table 9.01ii Emphasis on the production and cast

Harvard	APA
Duet for One by Tom KEMPINSKI (1980). [Play]. First produced 13 Feb. 1980 at Bush Theatre, London. Performers: Frances de la TOUR, David de KEYSER. Director: ROGER SMITH.	*Duet for one* by Kempinski, T. (1980, February 13). [Play]. First produced at Bush Theatre, London. Performers: Frances de la Tour, David de Keyser. Director: Roger Smith.
MLA	**Numerical**
Duet For One by Tom Kempinski. Play. Perfs. Frances de la Tour, David de Keyser. Dir. Roger Smith. First prod. Bush Theatre, London, 13 Feb. 1980.	*Duet for one* by Tom KEMPINSKI. [Play]. First Produced at Bush Theatre, London. Performers: Frances de la TOUR, David. de KEYSER. Director: Roger SMITH, on 13 Feb. 1980

Printed programme

You can reference theatrical or other programmes as these often contain useful information on the historical background to the production, details of performers, music details, etc.

- If the name of the writer is shown, start with this, and give the year of the production.
- If no writer's name is shown, start with the name of the production.
- State title of item in the programme, e.g. the sub-heading, and state the nature of the source, e.g. [Extract from theatre programme].
- Give details of place, name of theatre and dates of the performance.
- Give page numbers, if shown.

Table 9.01iii Extract from a theatre programme

Harvard	APA
LUDLOW, P. (1980). There is nothing like a Dame [Theatre programme]. *Jack and the beanstalk*, pp: 8–9. Bradford: Alhambra Theatre: 23 Dec.–21 Feb. 1980/81.	Ludlow, P. (1980/1 December 23–February 21). There is nothing like a Dame [Theatre programme]. *Jack and the beanstalk*, pp: 8–9 Bradford: Alhambra Theatre.
MLA	**Numerical**
Ludlow, Patrick. "There is Nothing Like a Dame". Theatre prog. <u>Jack and the Beanstalk</u>: 8–9. Bradford: Alhambra, 23 Dec.–21 Feb. 1980–81.	LUDLOW, P. There is nothing like a Dame, [Theatre programme]. *Jack and the beanstalk*, pp: 8–9, Bradford: Alhambra Theatre: 23 Dec.–21 Feb. 1980/81.

02 Dance

As with theatrical productions and film, the emphasis in the reference will depend on the context of the assignment and what is being discussed. The emphasis, for example, might be on the choreography and music, or on the main performers.

However, you would normally include:

- Title, in italics or underlined
- Details of medium (e.g. contemporary dance; ballet) unless obvious from the name of company
- Year of production
- Name of dance troop or company
- Place of company base, or place of performance.

You could include also names of performers, choreographer, musical composer or arranger and other details, as necessary.

Table 9.02i Ballet production

Harvard	APA
Wuthering Heights (2003). [Ballet]. David NIXON (Choreographer) Claude-Michel SCHÖNBERG (Music). Leeds: Northern Ballet.	*Wuthering Heights* (2003). [Ballet]. Nixon, D. (Choreographer), Schönberg, Claude-Michel (Music). Leeds: Northern Ballet.
MLA	**Numerical**
Wuthering Heights. Ballet. Choreog. David Nixon, David. Mus. Claude-Michel Schönberg. Leeds: Northern Ballet, 2003.	*Wuthering Heights*. [Ballet]. David NIXON (Choreographer). Claude-Michel SCHÖNBERG (Music). Leeds: Northern Ballet, 2003.

Table 9.02ii Other dance performance

Harvard	APA
Sacred monsters (2006). [Dance: kathak and ballet]. Performers: Akram KHAN and Sylvie GUILLEM. London: Sadler's Wells, 19–23 Sept. 2006.	*Sacred monsters* (2006, September 19–23). [Dance: kathak & ballet]. Performers: A. Khan & S. Guillem. London: Sadler's Wells.
MLA	**Numerical**
Sacred Monsters. Dance: kathak and ballet. Perfs: Akram Khan and Sylvie Guillem. London: Sadler's Wells, 19–23 Sept. 2006.	*Sacred monsters*. [Dance: kathak and ballet]. Performers: Akram KHAN and Sylvie GUILLEM. London: Sadler's Wells, 19–23 Sept. 2006.

03 Music

To reference a live music performance, you would normally start with the title of the work (in italics or underlined), followed by name of composer, then give details of the performance, including name of performers and place of performance. Other details can be included, if relevant, including name of conductor or leader, and names of soloists. It may be occasionally necessary to clarify that it is a music performance, if this is not obvious from other details supplied (see also section R1 'Music scores').

Three examples of live musical performances:

Table 9.03i Music

Harvard	APA
Double piano concerto. MOZART, Wolfgang (2006). London Mozart Players. Pianists: G. and S. PEKINEL. Leeds: Town Hall, 14 Oct. 2006.	*Double piano concerto*. Mozart. (2006, October 14). London Mozart Players. Pianists: G. & S. Pekinel. Leeds: Town Hall.
MLA	**Numerical**
Double Piano Concerto. Mozart, Wolfgang London Mozart Players. Pianists: Guher and Suher Pekinel. Leeds: Town Hall, 14 Oct. 2006.	*Double piano concerto*. MOZART, Wolfgang. London Mozart Players. Pianists: G. and S. PEKINEL. Leeds: Town Hall, 14 Oct. 2006.

Table 9.03ii Music

Harvard	APA
Jerry Springer, the opera (2006). Musical. Bradford: Alhambra Theatre, 22–27 May, 2006.	*Jerry Springer, the opera* (2006, May 22–27). [Musical]. Bradford: Alhambra Theatre.
MLA	**Numerical**
Jerry Springer, the Opera. Musical. Bradford: Alhambra, 22–27 May 2006.	*Jerry Springer, the opera.* Musical. Bradford: Alhambra Theatre, 22–27 May, 2006.

Table 9.03iii Music

Harvard	APA
The lark (2006). [Folk song]. Composer/Performer, Kate RUSBY. Chepstow Arts Festival, Chepstow Castle July 8, 2006.	*The lark* (2006, July 8). [Folk song]. Composer/Performer, Kate Rusby. Chepstow Arts Festival, Chepstow Castle.
MLA	**Numerical**
The Lark. Folk song. Comp./Perf. Kate Rusby. Chepstow Arts Festival, Chepstow Castle, July 8 2006.	*The lark.* [Folk song]. Composer/Performer, Kate RUSBY. Chepstow Arts Festival, Chepstow Castle, July 8, 2006.

04 Other live public event (e.g. talk, reading, address)

In most instances start with name of speaker, performer or principal person, title or type of event or performance, and the date of the event and its location. Add other detail that is relevant to the source and point being made in the assignment. If there was a title given to any speech or talk, this can be shown in italics or underlined.

Table 9.04i Speech

Harvard	APA
BENN, Tony. (2006). Speaker. Tolpuddle Martyrs' Festival. Dorset: Tolpuddle, 16 July 2006.	Benn, T. (2006, July 16). Speaker. Tolpuddle Martyrs' Festival. Dorset: Tolpuddle.
MLA	**Numerical**
Benn, Tony. Speaker. Tolpuddle Martyrs' Festival. Dorset: Tolpuddle, 16 July 2006.	BENN, Tony. Speaker. Tolpuddle Martyrs' Festival. Dorset: Tolpuddle, 16 July 2006.

Table 9.04ii Poetry reading

Harvard	APA
DUFFY, Carol, Ann. (2006). Poetry reading. West Sussex: Chichester Festival, 22 July 2006.	Duffy, C.A. (2006, July 22). Poetry reading. West Sussex: Chichester Festival.
MLA	**Numerical**
Duffy, Carol Ann. Poetry reading. West Sussex: Chichester Festival, 22 July 2006.	DUFFY, Carol, Ann. Poetry reading. West Sussex: Chichester Festival, 22 July 2006.

Table 9.04iii Talk

Harvard	APA
GREER, Germaine. (2004) Talk: *Shakespeare and sexual difference*. Perth: University of Western Australia, 7 Sept. 2004.	Greer, G. (2004, September 7) Talk: *Shakespeare and sexual difference*. Perth: University of Western Australia.
MLA	**Numerical**
Greer, Germaine. Talk: Shakespeare and Sexual Difference. Perth: U of Western Australia, 7 Sept. 2004.	GREER, Germaine. Talk: *Shakespeare and sexual difference*. Perth: University of Western Australia, 7 Sept. 2004.

P Referencing course lectures (see also section S1 'Online teaching material')

You can reference lectures from course tutors and visiting guest speakers, as they have made their points in a public and formal way. You can include:

- Name of lecturer
- Year
- Medium (lecture) and details of lecture, e.g. title or topic
- Module and course details, including academic year
- Place and name of institution
- Date of lecture.

You could include evidence from the lecture, e.g. handouts, as appendix items, if relevant.

Table 9.P1 Lecture

Harvard	APA
NEVILLE, C. (2005) *Lecture on academic writing*. Self-development module. First year undergraduate course 2005/6. Bradford: University of Bradford, 25 Nov. 2005.	Neville, C. (2005, November 25) *Lecture on academic writing*. Self-development module. First year undergraduate course 2005/6. Bradford: University of Bradford.
MLA	**Numerical**
Neville, Colin. (2005) Lecture on Academic Writing. Self-development module. First year undergraduate course 2005/6. U of Bradford, 25 Nov. 2005.	NEVILLE, C. *Lecture on academic writing*. Self-development module. First year undergraduate course 2005/6. Bradford: University of Bradford, 25 Nov. 2005.

Q Interviews and discussions, including telephone conversations

Personal communications, without supporting data, should be cited only in the text, or footnoted, but are not given a full reference. A citation-only in the text of an assignment might look like this: (Telephone conversation with author, 21 Oct. 2006).

However, if data has been collected and can be made accessible to others, e.g. interview notes, transcripts, completed interview questionnaires or recordings made, then a full reference can be given. Written data collected from interviews can be added as appendix items, if appropriate (check with your tutor).

If you include a full reference for this type of evidence, you need to include the family name of the interviewee, initials, year of interview, the purpose of the interview, place of interview, name of interviewer (if you are the interviewer: 'with author') and date of interview. You could also refer the tutor to the appropriate appendix item, as shown in the first example that follows.

You do not need to underline or italicize the title element of the full reference.

Table 9.Q1i Personal interview

Harvard	APA
BROWN, J. (2005). Personal interview. Marketing survey for MA project. At GKN, Leeds, with Jim CLARKE, 20 Mar. 2005 (see appendix item 2a).	Brown, J. (2005, March 20). Personal interview. Marketing survey for MA project. At GKN, Leeds, with Jim Clarke (see appendix item 2a).
MLA	**Numerical**
Brown, James. Personal Interview. Marketing survey for MA project. At GKN, Leeds, with Jim Clarke, 20 Mar. 2005 (see appendix item 2a).	BROWN, J. Personal interview. Marketing survey for MA project. At GKN, Leeds, with Jim CLARKE, 20 Mar. 2005 (see appendix item 2a).

Table 9.Q1ii Telephone interview

Harvard	APA
WALTERS, M. (2006). Telephone interview with author, 25 July 2006 (see appendix item 3).	Walters, M. (2006, July 25). Telephone Interview with author (see appendix item 3).
MLA	**Numerical**
Walters, Mark. Telephone interview with author, 25 July 2006 (see appendix item 3).	WALTERS, M. Telephone interview with author, 25 July 2006 (see appendix item 3).

You could also reference **published interviews** in journals, magazines or elsewhere. The sequence for this would be:

- Name of person interviewed (last or family name first, then initials)
- Year of interview

- Title of interview
- Explanation of interview
- Interviewer's name
- Title of publication (in italics or underlined)
- Publication details, including full date and page number.

Example of published interview (in Harvard style):

> TURNER, N. (2005). Turner's secret: the short-haul factor. Interview with Nigel Turner, BMI's new CEO, by Ben Flanagan. *The Observer (Business Section)*, 22 May 2005, p.18.

R Miscellaneous sources

R1 Music scores

Music scores are treated like books, except that the date of composition appears after the title. If there is no year of publication shown for the score, put 'no date' or 'n.d.'.

Table 9.R1 Music score	
Harvard	**APA**
BRUCH, Max. *Concerto in G Minor, Op. 26* (1867). New York: G. Schirmer. (n.d.).	Bruch, M. *Concerto in G Minor, Op. 26* (1867). New York: G. Schirmer. (n.d.).
MLA	**Numerical**
Bruch, Max. Concerto in G Minor, Op. 26 (1867). New York: G. Schirmer. n.d.	BRUCH, Max. *Concerto in G Minor, Op. 26* (1867). New York: G. Schirmer. (n.d.).

R2 Posters or wall-charts

Posters or wall-charts can contain useful information or may be of artistic, social or historical importance. In the text of the assignment you would normally outline your reasons for citing the poster or wall-chart, so the reference detail you supply is to help others identify the same source. Include name of designer or artist, if known, title or type of poster, year of publication, state medium, e.g. [wall-chart], details of the source or supplier, and exact date of issue, if, for example, it was issued as a supplement in a newspaper or magazine.

If the poster is on display in a public collection, state the place and name of the museum or gallery. In the example that follows, the poster does not have a title, so the description of the item (recruitment poster) is not in italics or underlined.

Table 9.R2i   Poster (no title)

Harvard	APA
LEETE, Alfred (1914) Recruitment poster. London: Imperial War Museum.	Leete, A. (1914) Recruitment poster. London: Imperial War Museum.
MLA	**Numerical**
Leete, Alfred. (1914) Recruitment poster. London: Imp. War Mus.	LEETE, Alfred. Recruitment poster. London: Imperial War Museum, 1914.

Table 9.R2ii   Poster (with title)

Harvard	APA
Ethel Waters (2006). [Poster]. In *Stars of the Harlem renaissance* series. USA: Emeryville: art.com.	*Ethel Waters* (2006). In *Stars of the Harlem renaissance* series [Poster]. USA: Emeryville: art.com.
MLA	**Numerical**
Ethel Waters (2006). Poster. In Stars of the Harlem Renaissance series. USA: Emeryville: art.com.	*Ethel Waters*. [Poster]. *Stars of the Harlem renaissance* series. USA: Emeryville: art.com, 2006.

Table 9.R2iii   Wall-chart

Harvard	APA
Whales (2006). [Wall-chart]. Supplement in *The Guardian*, 25 June 2006.	Whales (2006, June 25). [Wall-chart]. Supplement in *The Guardian*.
MLA	**Numerical**
"Whales". Wall-chart. Supp. Guardian, 25 June 2006.	Whales. [Wall-chart]. Supplement in *The Guardian*, 25 June 2006.

R3   Advertising

(See also section M4 in this chapter.)

Advertising can be of interest to students, for example, those with an interest in marketing, social history, cultural studies, graphic design or contemporary communications.

Include in the reference:

- Name(s) of the creators of the advertisement. This might be a named person, agency, or company, organization or institution promoting the goods or services concerned
- Year of origin of the advertisement, if known. If not known, put 'c' or 'circa' and an approximate decade, e.g. (circa 1930s)
- Title of the advertisement, or description of product/service
- Nature of the advertisement, e.g. [Radio advertisement]
- Name (and description, if necessary) of the host for the advertisement
- Date you heard or saw it, and time, if applicable
- Page number, if applicable.

Table 9.R3i Printed advertisement

Harvard	APA
VISIT GUERNSEY (2009). *Guernsey currency converter: £1 equals £1*. [Advertisement]. 'The Observer Magazine', 10 May 2009, p.35.	Visit Guernsey (2009, May 10). *Guernsey currency converter: £1 equals £1* [Advertisement]. 'The Observer Magazine', p.35.
MLA	**Numerical**
Visit Guernsey. "Guernsey Currency Converter: £1 Equals £1". Advert. 10 May 2009, Observer Mag, 35.	VISIT GUERNSEY. *Guernsey currency converter: £1 equals £1* [Advertisement]. 'The Observer Magazine', 10 May 2009, p.35.

Table 9.R3ii Television advertisement

Harvard	APA
CHANNEL 4 (2009). *'Adopt a child' appeal*. [TV advertisement]. 14 May, 10.00am.	Channel 4 (2009, May 14, 10.00am). *'Adopt a child' appeal* [TV advertisement].
MLA	**Numerical**
Channel 4. "Adopt a Child" appeal. TV advert, 14 May, 2009, 10.00am.	CHANNEL 4. *'Adopt a child' appeal*. [TV advertisement]. 14 May,2009, 10.00am.

Table 9.R3iii Radio advertisement

Harvard	APA
CLASSIC FM (2009). *Music Quest* [Radio advertisement]. 14 May, 10.15am.	Classic FM (2009, May 14, 10.15am). *Music Quest* [Radio advertisement].
MLA	**Numerical**
Classic FM. "Music Quest". Radio advert. 14 May, 10.15am, 2009.	CLASSIC FM. *Music Quest* [Radio advertisement]. 14 May, 10.15am., 2009.

For radio and television advertisements, include the time of the broadcast. You may need to give the advertisement a title of your own that summarizes the nature of the message or appeal.

R4 Postal items

First day issues, which are envelopes bearing the cancellation dates of the first day of issues of stamps, can be interesting as historical or design sources. They are usually mailed from the place where the stamp was first put into circulation. You should include country of origin, year, nature or type of first day cover, number (if it is a limited edition), design features of stamp, if relevant, and any significant markings or postal franking on envelope.

Table 9.R4 First day cover

Harvard	APA
CANADA (1928). *First flight cover via Amos to Siscoe.* 28th Oct. Bearing 'Amos', 'Quebec', 'New York', 'Siscoe' and other postmarks on illustrated envelope.	Canada (1928, October 28). *First flight cover via Amos to Siscoe.* Bearing 'Amos', 'Quebec', 'New York', 'Siscoe' and other postmarks on illustrated envelope.
MLA	**Numerical**
Canada. <u>First flight cover via Amos to Siscoe</u>. Bearing "Amos", "Quebec", "New York", "Siscoe" and other postmarks on illustrated envelope, 28 Oct. 1928.	CANADA. *First flight cover via Amos to Siscoe.* 28th Oct. Bearing 'Amos', 'Quebec', 'New York', 'Siscoe' and other postmarks on illustrated envelope. 28 Oct. 1928

R5 Postcards

Postcards can be useful historical sources. You would normally describe the features of the relevant postcard in the text of your assignment, so the full reference would just contain enough information to help the reader identify the location of the postcard, e.g. gallery, private collection, plus other relevant identifying features, i.e. reference number or title. These would include the name of the artist, or photographer, if known, and date, or estimated date, of first printing.

Unless there is a specific title, you do not need to italicize or underline the general description of the item (see first example below).

Table 9.R5i Postcard (artist known)

Harvard	APA
MCGILL, D. (1927). Seaside cartoon postcard. Ref.115. Holmfirth: Postcard Museum	McGill, D. (1927). Seaside cartoon postcard. Ref. 115. Holmfirth: Postcard Museum.
MLA	**Numerical**
McGill, Donald. (1927). Seaside cartoon postcard. 115. Holmfirth: Postcard Mus.	MCGILL, D. Seaside cartoon postcard. Ref.115. Holmfirth: Postcard Museum, 1927.

Table 9.R5ii Postcard (unknown photographer)

Harvard	APA
Picnic make believe (circa 1930s). Postcard. Photographer unknown. Private collection of Tom PHILLIPS.	*Picnic make believe* (circa 1930s). [Postcard]. Photographer unknown. Private collection of Tom Phillips.
MLA	**Numerical**
<u>Picnic Make Believe</u>. Postcard. Private Collection: Tom Phillips. Photogr. u/k (c. 1930s).	*Picnic make believe.* Postcard. Private collection of Tom PHILLIPS. Photographer unknown (circa 1930s).

R6 Displays and information panels

Display and information panels, in museums, galleries and elsewhere, can be a useful sources of information and so can be referenced. It is unlikely that the writer will be named, but if so start the full reference with this name. If the author is not identified, give the name of the **originator** of the information, e.g. the name of the gallery/museum. If the panel is dated, show the year, if not, give the year you looked at the information. State the title, either taken directly from the panel, or one that is your summation of the information shown, and indicate the nature of the source [Display panel]. Give the name of the museum, gallery etc. (if not used to start the reference) and its location, and the date you looked at the information.

Table 9.R6 Display panel

Harvard	APA
BRADFORD INDUSTRIAL MUSEUM (2009). *The Busby Family.* [Exhibition display]. 21 Jan. 2009. Bradford, West Yorkshire.	Bradford Industrial Museum (2009, January 21). *The Busby Family* [Exhibition display]. Bradford, West Yorkshire.
MLA	**Numerical**
Bradford Industrial Museum <u>The Busby Family.</u> Exhib. Display, 21 Jan. 2009. Bradford, West Yorks.	BRADFORD INDUSTRIAL MUSEUM. *The Busby Family.* [Exhibition display]. 21 Jan. 2009. Bradford, West Yorkshire.

R7 Sacred or classical texts

Sacred texts

These include the Bible, Talmud, Koran, Upanishads and major classical works, such as ancient Greek and Roman works. If you are simply quoting a verse or extract, you do not need to give full reference entries. Instead, you should include the detail in the text of your assignment, for example:

> The film script at this point echoes the Bible: 'And God looked upon the earth, and, behold, it was corrupt; for all flesh had corrupted his way upon the earth'.
>
> (Gen. 6:12)

However, if you were referring to a particular edition for a significant reason, it could be listed in full in the main references, e.g.:

Good News Bible (2004). Rainbow Edition. New York: Harper Collins.

Abbreviations

Abbreviations can be used in citations, e.g. Gen., for Genesis; Ezek., for Ezekiel. The online Journal of Biblical Studies has a useful website giving abbreviations for all biblical works likely to be cited (Search for 'Journal of Biblical Studies – Abbreviations').

Copies of *New Testament Studies* 34, 3 (1988): 476–79 and *Journal of Biblical Literature* 107, 3, can be consulted for abbreviations and the MLA Handbook also has a useful section (7.7) on abbreviations for literary and religious works.

Classical texts

Students studying the Classics are often given advice on referencing these texts by their tutors, but the format for citing sources in the text is normally, as follows:

- Name of author
- Title (italics or underlined)
- Details of book/poem
- Line number.

For example, Homer, *Iliad* 18.141–143.

If an author wrote only one work, e.g. Herodotus, you may omit the name of the work, i.e. *Histories*.

Page numbers should be from the translation or edition cited. However, citations to Plato and Plutarch should be included in the text using the Stephanus pagination, whenever possible. These works are divided into numbers, and each number will be divided into equal sections a, b, c, d and e. The numbers, however, must be used in conjunction with a title to make sense of them, e.g. *Republic*, 344a2.

The works of Aristotle are usually cited using the Bekker system of numbers. These numbers take the format of up to four digits, a letter for column 'a' or 'b', then the line number. These should be shown against the title of the particular work of Aristotle, e.g. Politics: 1252a1–4.

The full details of the book used should be included in the 'References', 'Bibliography' or 'Works cited' section.

S Referencing electronic sources

Electronic sources are very important to students. The Internet, for example, is quick, accessible and easy to use and, if the right keyword searches are made, can produce useful evidence for assignments.

However, there are drawbacks to using electronic sources and students often experience considerable difficulty in citing and referencing them. The apparent absence of authorship detail, dates, page numbers on some websites, plus length of some website addresses, can cause problems. Citation of sources in the text of an assignment can also cause difficulty, with students often uncertain what to put.

Common mistakes

- You should not put a www address as a citation. You always put the name of an author, or the source organisation, but never cite a uniform/universal resource locator (URL) or digital object identifier (DOI) address in the body of an assignment unless there is absolutely no other way of identifying the source.
- You do not need a separate list of www sites in your 'References', 'Works cited' or 'Bibliography' sections. In all referencing styles, Internet sites are incorporated along with other sources into one list at the end of the assignment.

- Another common mistake is to simply paste in a URL address to a list of references, without any other supporting information, such as the title of item, name of hosting organisation, or date the information was viewed.

Examples of a range of electronic sources will be presented later in this section. The examples are, of course, not exhaustive, but do offer examples of sources that students typically use in assignments. If you encounter sources not specifically illustrated in this book the following 'Basic principles' and 'What to include' sections of this chapter should help you to work out how to reference them.

If you are using APA and MLA referencing styles, you can also consult the respective style guides produced by these organizations, as both include chapters on citing and referencing electronic sources. The APA style guide to electronic sources was updated in 2007 and contains important information on the elements to include in references to electronic sources. This chapter will give electronic source examples for APA, but if you are required to use this particular style on a regular basis for your assignments, you may like to purchase the APA guide in question: available from http://books.apa.org/subpages/apastyle.cfm.

For Harvard and Numerical styles, the nearest thing to a benchmark guide are the British Standard referencing guidance recommendations, which contain examples of electronic sources. You should be able to download these free of charge via your institution library website.

Basic principles of referencing electronic sources

There are four main principles or guidelines to referencing electronic sources.

First, and this is common for all referencing styles, the citation should link with the full reference. What appears in the citation, either a name or a number, will connect with the full reference entry. So, in the case of a name–date in-text citation, the citation might be, as follows:

Citation: (Friends of the Earth 2005)
This would then link to the full list of references (in Harvard style):

Reference:
FRIENDS OF THE EARTH (2005). *Corporates: corporate power*. Available at http://www.foe.co.uk/campaigns/corporates/issues/corporate_power/ [Accessed 13/12/2005].

Second, tutors should be directed as closely as possible to the online information being cited and referenced. This usually means giving the complete URL addresses or DOI tags to take your tutors to the same screen you looked at, rather than leading them to just home or menu pages. Digital object identifiers offer a more permanent means of finding a source, as URLs are vulnerable to change if, for example, the site is moved to another host. Digital object identifiers sources are given an alpha-numeric label that will track sources and thus offer a more persistent and consistent way of locating them. If a DOI is shown, use this in your reference, in preference to a URL.

If access to a particular online database is restricted or password protected, there is no point in supplying a **full** URL address as others will not be able to access the source without a password. However, you need to state the name and give details of the database publisher and provide the website address of the home or menu page in question.

Third, ensure you show website addresses that work! There is nothing more frustrating than to type out the URL address given, only to find later that the address given is incorrect. Make sure you have copied them or pasted them in correctly.

Fourth, because sites do disappear without warning, it is wise to print out copies of sources used for citation purposes to show a tutor, if required, and some tutors will insist you do this. These copies can be included in an appendix, or a note included in the assignment for the reader to the effect that they can be made available to the tutor, if required.

What to include

Generally, the following elements are listed in the order in which they appear in a full reference entry. However, there may be occasional exceptions to this rule. This may be because of particular referencing style guidelines, or because of the nature of the source or the context in which it is to be used in an assignment.

You can include:

- Originator: the person or organization taking the main **responsibility** for the source
- Year of origin. This element is second listed in the case of Harvard, APA and MLA styles
- Title of work consulted
- Type of medium
- Publisher and place of publication
- Date of publication
- Online address or location within portable database
- Name of database, if applicable
- Other identifying features
- Date you looked at the information.

Table 9.SOi What these elements mean in practice

Main responsibility for message	This means the creator of the message. This can be name of the person, persons or corporate body responsible for writing or editing the document you looked at, including weblog (or 'blog') sites. This can include the name of an online site responsible for hosting the information, if no named author is shown. If a subsidiary company of a larger corporate body is responsibility, show the names of both
Title of work consulted	This means the main title(s) and subtitle(s) of the source you are citing or listing. Translations of title may be added, and these are usually enclosed in brackets. In practice, this can often mean a screen heading and relevant sub-heading. It is important to identify exactly what you looked at, as far as you are able

(Cont.)

Type of medium	The type of electronic medium should be indicated, e.g. CD-ROM; online database; computer program on disk; bulletin board online; electronic mail; etc.
Publisher and place of publication	This would apply particularly to documents on portable databases and refer to the organization responsible for preparing the data and/or the medium, and where they are located. One of the main aims of referencing is to help the reader locate the material, which includes knowing who the publisher is, and where they can be located. In the case of something that originally appeared in print, you need to show the name of the original publishers, as well as details of the online or portable database you looked at
Date of publication	This is any date of publication or copyright shown on the original work. For online material, show the last date of update or revision. If no dates are shown, put (n.d.), (no date) or (date unknown)
Online address, or location within portable database	Show full electronic online address and any other commands or methods of access to the document. This can be a URL or DOI address. This information is usually prefixed with a relevant term, e.g. 'Viewed', 'Available from . . .' or 'Retrieved from . . .' or by using angle brackets to enclose URL/DOI addresses (see MLA examples). However, see the next note 'Date you looked at the information'. In most cases of URL/DOI addresses, you would copy and paste in the full address to take the reader straight to the relevant data. In a portable database, give details of how and where to locate the relevant data, e.g. page numbers
Date you looked at the information	Electronic information can disappear or change very quickly, so it is important you state the date you looked at the source. With Harvard, and Numerical styles of referencing, British Standard guidelines show the term 'Viewed', e.g. [Viewed 10 June 2009]. However, there is some flexibility around this and most institutional guides are currently suggesting that the term 'Accessed', e.g. [Accessed 23 Aug. 2009] is used. MLA does not use any prefix term, and just gives a viewing date within angle bars (see examples). The current (2009) APA guidelines suggest that the term 'Retrieved', as in 'Retrieved 23 May 2009 from www . . .', but only for sources that are vulnerable to dislocation or change. A retrieval date is no longer required if a final or archival version of a source is being referenced. So sources, for example, with a DOI tag do not need the 'Retrieved' tag, as the source should be easily located by using the DOI
Other identifying features	The principle of helping readers identify location of sources must be kept in mind. This could mean including, for example, page, screen, paragraph or line number (if shown); any labelled part, section, table, graph, chart; any host-specific label or designation. If in doubt – include it.

The order these will appear will depend on the referencing style and type of source, but if you include all or most of this information you will not go far wrong.

Does the term 'online' need to go in the full reference?

The APA and MLA styles do not use the term 'online' in their references as a separate entity.

For Harvard, Numerical styles, the term 'online', can be included in the full reference entry [in brackets] to distinguish the source from the same item or material to be found elsewhere in other forms, e.g. printed. There may be, for example, some content differences between the printed and electronic versions, so the term 'online' indicates which version you looked at. Some online reference works already include the term in their titles, e.g. 'Times Online', but if in any doubt, include the term in your reference entry.

Table 9.SOii An example of an Internet site, shown in the four main referencing styles

Harvard	JISC PLAGIARISM ADVISORY SERVICE (2001). *Plagiarism – a good practice guide.* [Online]. Available at http://www.jiscpas.ac.uk/apppage.cgi?USERPAGE=6296 [Accessed 23 Aug. 2006].
APA	JISC Plagiarism Advisory Service (2001). *Plagiarism – a good practice guide.* Retrieved from http://www.jiscpas.ac.uk/apppage.cgi?USERPAGE=6296
MLA	JISC Plagiarism Advisory Service. Plagiarism – A Good Practice Guide. 2001. 23 Aug. 2006 <http://www.jiscpas.ac.uk/apppage.cgi?USERPAGE=6296>
Numerical	JISC PLAGIARISM ADVISORY SERVICE. *Plagiarism – a good practice guide*, 2001. Available at http://www.jiscpas.ac.uk/apppage.cgi?USERPAGE=6296 [Accessed 23 Aug. 2006].

Some hints

- Many Internet pages do not show an author's name. If this appears to be the case, it might be possible to identify an author by looking at the header of the HTML encoded text. To do this, click on the 'View' option in your browser and then either 'View Source' or 'Document Source'. If you cannot identify an author, cite the originator of the site/site name, or if this is not obvious, cite the title.
- If you find that, for some reason, an Internet URL address is not shown for the source concerned, you need then to give search terms to take others to the same source. The search terms can be entered after the URL address, and before the (Accessed–date) information.
- As mentioned earlier, you should cite the year the document was last updated. You can find this, if it exists, usually at the foot of the page.

Evaluating sites

As stated earlier, the Internet is a rich source of information for students. It is also, unfortunately, the unregulated host to sites that have been created by their authors as arenas for their ill-informed and biased opinions.

You should never let the ease of using the Internet replace using a library and using textbooks. Before an academic textbook reaches the library it has to go through a series of quality filters, including critical peer scrutiny and may have to go through a number of amendments until the publishers are satisfied with it. Not so with the Internet. Anyone can send out into the wide blue yonder uncorrected and opinionated junk. However, the Internet can and does provide a useful starting point for ideas and the pursuit of ideas.

Reliable Internet sites can certainly be used and cited in assignments. But how can you evaluate them? The use of DOIs now to track sources gives one indicator, at least, of their permanence. Munger and Campbell (2002) and Rumsey (2004) suggest the following questions should be asked of all sites to help evaluate their credibility:

Table 9.SOiii Evaluation questions

Author/purpose	Content	Design
• Who is taking 'ownership' of the information presented? • Why has this site been established – is it clear from the introduction? • Who is the sponsor of the site – who pays for it? • Who is the intended readership for the site? • Are there any biases or possible hidden agendas in the site? • Is it clear who is the originator or author for the item you want to cite? • Is there a link to any named author's Email address? • Does the author have any academic or professional affiliation?	• Were you linked to this site from a reliable source? • How comprehensive is the site in its coverage? • Is the site regularly updated? When was the site last updated? • How are sources referenced and documented? • Are the links provided working? (*A site that is not being updated, including the hyperlinks, should not be trusted.*) • On what basis are links selected? What rationale for the links is given?	• Does it **look** professional? • Is the site easy to navigate and use? • Does the resource follow good principles of design, proper grammar, spelling and style? If it does not, beware! • Does the site include advertising? If so, might this influence the range and objectivity of the material?

Quoting from the Internet

Quoting an author directly should always be done for a particular purpose, for example, to convey a sense of the 'voice' of a particular author or organisation
Example of an extract from a student essay (following Harvard):

> However, Howard Gardner regards the term 'domain' in a completely different way: 'The domain in a society can be thought of as the kinds of roles listed in the Yellow Pages of a phone book – anything from Accounting to Zoology'.
>
> (Gardner 2005)

The reference for this quotation, which was taken from the 'Frequently asked questions' (FAQ) section of the author's website, would be referenced, as follows (example shown in the Harvard style):

GARDNER, H. (2005). *Domains*. Howard GARDNER Homepages. FAQ, p.2, Available at www.howardgardner.com [Accessed 22 Apr. 05].

Secondary sources on the Internet

You will also encounter many Internet sources that summarize or quote indirectly the words of others. You treat these Internet sources as secondary sources. For example, on the 'Friends of the Earth' (FOE) Internet site, FOE quote the Executive Director of Corpwatch, Joshua Karliner, as saying that: '*51 of the 100 world's largest economies are corporations*'.

If you were unable to locate the **primary source** (i.e. Joshua Karliner), to check the accuracy of this quotation, you could cite the Friends of the Earth site, although this would not be as desirable as checking out the primary source for yourself. The citation and reference, following Harvard, would be as follows:

Citation:
(Friends of the Earth 2005, quoting Joseph Karliner); or (Joseph Karliner, as quoted by
   Friends of the Earth 2005)
Reference (Harvard):
FRIENDS OF THE EARTH (2005). *Corporates: corporate power.* Available at http://www.foe.co.uk/campaigns/corporates/issues/corporate_power/ [Accessed 13 Dec. 2005].

Examples of online references now follow.

S1 Online teaching material – virtual learning environments (VLE)

The range of online teaching materials (or VLE resources) is growing steadily, but here are a few examples that you may encounter.

To reference material:

- Start with the name of the tutor/author/originator of the material.
- Include the year of online publication.
- State title of item.
- Give (if applicable) course week number, if applicable, name of the course or module, the name of the institution.
- State the name of the VLE system, its login point.
- Give the date you accessed/retrieved the item.

Table 9.S1i Blackboard/Web CT

Harvard	APA
GREGORY, T. (2009). Regional trends: [course notes] week 6, *The changing world of work*: level 2 module. University of Bradford *Blackboard* [Online]. Available at http://blackboard.brad.ac.uk/ [Accessed 4 May 2009].	Gregory, T. (2009). Regional trends: [course notes] week 6, *The changing world of work*: level 2 module. University of Bradford. Retrieved from *Blackboard* May 4, 2009 from http://blackboard.brad.ac.uk/

(Cont.)

MLA

Gregory, Terry. "Regional Trends", wk. 6, module: The Changing World of Work. Course notes. U of Bradford, Blackboard. 4 May 2009 <http://blackboard.brad.ac.uk/>

Numerical

GREGORY, T. Regional trends: [course notes] week 6, *The changing world of work*: level 2 module. University of Bradford *Blackboard* [Online]. Available at http://blackboard.brad.ac.uk/ [Accessed 4 May 2009].

Table 9.S1ii Pebble Pad

Harvard

NEVILLE, C. (2009). *My CV*. Personal Development Planning, MBA, University of Bradford: *PebblePad*. [Online]. Available at http://www.pebblepad.co.uk/ [Accessed 4 May 2009].

MLA

Neville, Colin. My CV. U of Bradford: PDP-MBA, PebblePad, 4 May 2009 <http://www.pebblepad.co.uk/>

APA

Neville, C. (2009). *My CV*. Personal Development Planning, MBA, University of Bradford, Retrieved from *PebblePad* May 4 2009 from http://www.pebblepad.co.uk/

Numerical

NEVILLE, C. *My CV*. Personal Development Planning, MBA, University of Bradford, *PebblePad*. [Online]. Available at http://www.pebblepad.co.uk/ [Accessed 4 May 2009].

Table 9.S1iii Moodle

Harvard

HUNT, T. (2009). *How do you eat an elephant? Moodle: 'Planet Moodle'*. 8 Apr. 2009. Available at http://moodle.org/ [Accessed 4 May 2009].

MLA

Hunt, Tim. How Do You Eat an Elephant? 8 Apr. 2009. Moodle (Planet Moodle), 4 May 2009 <http://moodle.org/>

APA

Hunt, T. (2009). *How do you eat an elephant?* Retrieved from *Moodle: Planet Moodle* April 8 2009 from http://moodle.org/

Numerical

HUNT, T. *How do you eat an elephant? Moodle: 'Planet Moodle'*, 8 Apr. 2009. Available at http://moodle.org/ [Accessed 4 May 2009].

Screencast

A screencast is a screen capture of the actions on a user's computer screen, usually with accompanying audio commentary. They are becoming widely used in education to link tutors with students and can be used to give information in both audio and visual forms, e.g. feedback on marks, lectures and demonstrations of modelling applications.

To reference screencasts, start with the name of the lecturer, speaker or demonstrator, if applicable. If this is not given, start with the title. Then show year of production or broadcast, and the type of screencast, e.g. lecture, demonstration, feedback, etc. Then give name of the course, if applicable, institution, host or webpage. Give the full URL, and the date you accessed the site.

Table 9.S1iv Screencast

Harvard	APA
CAMPBELL, E. (2008). *What is a screencast?* [Screencast lecture] MSc TL10, Trinity College Dublin. Available at https://www.cs.tcd.ie/~campbeeo/web1/recorded_lecture.htm [Accessed 13 May 2009].	Campbell, E. (2008). *What is a screencast?* [Screencast lecture] MSc TL10, Trinity College Dublin. Retrieved from https://www.cs.tcd.ie/~campbeeo/web1/recorded_lecture.htm
MLA	**Numerical**
Campbell, Eoin. "What is a screencast?" Screencast lecture. MSc TL10, Trin. Coll. Dublin. 13 May 2009 <https://www.cs.tcd.ie/~campbeeo/web1/recorded_lecture.htm>	CAMPBELL, E. *What is a screencast?* [Screencast lecture] MSc TL10, Trinity College Dublin. Available at https://www.cs.tcd.ie/~campbeeo/web1/recorded_lecture.htm [Accessed 13 May 2009].

S2 Book online

Table 9.S2i Book online (complete book)

Harvard	APA
HARDY, T. (1887). *The Woodlanders.* [Online]. (Ed.) M. MONCUR. The Literature Page. Available at http://www.literaturepage.com/read/the-woodlanders.html [Accessed 25 July 2006).	Hardy, T. (1887). *The Woodlanders.* (Ed.) M. Moncur. The Literature Page. Retrieved from http://www.literaturepage.com/read/the-woodlanders.html
MLA	**Numerical**
Hardy, Thomas (1887). The Woodlanders. Ed. Michael Moncur. The Literature Page. 25 July 2006. <http://www.literaturepage.com/read/the-woodlanders.html>	HARDY, T (1887). *The Woodlanders.* [Online]. (Ed.) M. MONCUR. The Literature Page. Available at http://www.literaturepage.com/read/the-woodlanders.html [Accessed 25 July 2006).

- Note the indentation of second and subsequent lines in the APA and MLA entries.
- In this example, the whole book can be retrieved from the site. However, with APA style, the advice is to use 'Available from . . .' if the URL leads to information on how to obtain the cited material, rather than the full work, as is the case here.

Table 9.S2ii Online book in the British Library

Harvard	APA
CARROLL, Lewis (1864). *Alice's adventures under ground.* [Online]. British Library. Available at http://www.bl.uk/onlinegallery/ttp/alice/accessible/introduction.html [Accessed 15 May 2009].	Carroll, Lewis. (1864). *Alice's adventures under ground.* Retrieved from British Library at http://www.bl.uk/onlinegallery/ttp/alice/accessible/introduction.html
MLA	**Numerical**
Carroll, Lewis. Alice's Adventures Under Ground 1864. British Libr. 15 May 2009 <http://www.bl.uk/onlinegallery/ttp/alice/accessible/introduction.html>	CARROLL, Lewis. *Alice's adventures under ground* (1864). [Online]. British Library. Available at http://www.bl.uk/onlinegallery/ttp/alice/accessible/introduction.html [Accessed 15 May 2009].

S3 Specific part of an online book (as S2i above)

Give details of the chapter name or number and the page numbers concerned, and paste-in or copy out the URL address to take the reader to the relevant pages.

Table 9.S3 Part of an online book

Harvard	APA
HARDY, T. (1887). *The Woodlanders*. [Online]. (Ed.) M. MONCUR. The Literature Page. Ch. 18, pp. 139–41 Available at http://www.literaturepage.com/read/the-woodlanders-139.html [Accessed 25 July 2006).	Hardy, T. (1887). *The Woodlanders*. Ch. 18, pp.139–41 (Ed.) M. Moncur. The Literature Page. Retrieved from http://www.literaturepage.com/read/the-woodlanders-139.html
MLA	**Numerical**
Hardy, Thomas (1887). Ch. 18, 139–41 The Woodlanders. Ed. Michael Moncur. The Literature Page. 25 July 2006. <http://www.literaturepage.com/read/the-woodlanders-139.html>	HARDY, T. (1887). *The Woodlanders*. [Online]. (Ed.) M. MONCUR. The Literature Page. Ch. 18, pp. 139–41 Available at http://www.literaturepage.com/read/the-woodlanders-139.html [Accessed 25 July 2006).

S4 Online reference sources: three examples: reference book, encyclopedia, Wiki site

If an 'originator', i.e. the writer, author or site compiler or editor, is named, start with this. If not, start with the title of the site or reference work consulted. Include any date recorded against the entry, title of entry, name of online reference work and other relevant identifying features.

However, be cautious when using online reference sites. Try and ascertain what backing the site has from professional associations, universities and other reputable organizations; ask your tutors if they have a view on the site. It is also a good idea to check the entry against other online and printed reference works to verify the level of consistency and agreement there is among them.

The first example (Table 9.S4i) that follows has a named author and is taken from a free online source, so the URL address is given; the second (Table 9.S4ii) shows a restricted password-only subscription source with just the homepage address given.

Table 9.S4i Online reference book (author's name shown)

Harvard	APA
HALSALL, P. (2004). Byzantine studies on the Internet. *Online reference book for medieval studies*. Available at http://www.fordham.edu/halsall/byzantium/ [Accessed 30 July 2006].	Halsall, P. (2004). Byzantine studies on the Internet. *Online reference book for medieval studies*. Retrieved from http://www.fordham.edu/halsall/byzantium/
MLA	**Numerical**
Halsall, Paul. "Byzantine Studies on the Internet". Online Reference Book for Medieval Studies. July 30 2006, <http://www.fordham.edu/halsall/byzantium/>	HALSALL, P. Byzantine studies on the Internet. *Online reference book for medieval studies*. Available at http://www.fordham.edu/halsall/byzantium/ [Accessed 30 July 2006].

Table 9.S4ii Subscription site (no author's name shown)

Harvard	APA
Encyclopædia Britannica Online (2009). Definition of 'Conflict'. Available at http://www.britannica.com/ [Accessed July 29, 2009].	*Encyclopædia Britannica Online* (2009). Definition of 'Conflict'. Retrieved from http://www.britannica.com/
MLA	**Numerical**
Encyclopædia Britannica Online. "Conflict." 29 July 2009, <http://www.britannica.com/>	*Encyclopædia Britannica Online.* Definition of 'Conflict'. Available at http://www.britannica.com/ [Accessed July 29, 2009].

You should be cautious when using Wiki sites as sources in your assignments as some information presented on these can be inaccurate. Wiki sites are best used as secondary sources to help you to locate other more reliable sites and sources. However, if you need or want to reference a Wiki entry, it can be done in the way shown below. Start with the name of the site, the year of origin, and the title of the item referred to.

Table 9.S4iii Wiki sites

Harvard	APA
Wikipedia (2009). Parenthetical referencing. Available at http://en.wikipedia.org/wiki/Parenthetical_referencing [Accessed 20 Apr. 2009].	*Wikipedia* (2009). Parenthetical referencing. Retrieved April 20, 2009 from http://en.wikipedia.org/wiki/Parenthetical_referencing
MLA	**Numerical**
Wikipedia. "Parenthetical Referencing". 20 Apr. 2009, <http://en.wikipedia.org/wiki/Parenthetical_Referencing>	*Wikipedia.* Parenthetical referencing. Available at http://en.wikipedia.org/wiki/Parenthetical_referencing [Accessed 20 Apr. 2009].

S5 Academic journal articles

Academic journals are those containing scholarly articles that are usually peer reviewed – although you should always check this. Most articles are found within journal collections and are accessible via your institution library.

- Begin the reference entry with the name or names of the authors, and year of publication.
- State the title of the article, then give the name of the journal and details of volume, edition, and page numbers.
- With the Harvard, Numerical and MLA styles, include the name of the database, e.g. InterScience, but this is not required for APA style if a DOI is supplied.
- Give the DOI or URL, and (APA excepted) the date you accessed the site.

Table 9.S5i Academic article, via journal collections, with DOI assigned

Harvard	APA
McAULEY, C., P.J. PECORA, and J. K. WHITTAKER (2009). High risk youth: evidence on characteristics, needs and promising interventions. *Child & Family Social Work*, vol. 14, no. 2, pp: 129–131. *InterScience* [Online] doi: 10.1111/j.1365-2206.2009.00617.x [Accessed 22 Apr. 2009].	McAuley, C., Pecora, P.J. & Whittaker, J.K. (2009). High risk youth: evidence on characteristics, needs and promising interventions. *Child & Family Social Work*, 14 (2): 129–131. doi: 10.1111/j.1365-2206.2009.00617.x
MLA	**Numerical**
McAuley, Colette, Peter J. Pecora† and James K. Whittaker. "High Risk Youth: Evidence on Characteristics, Needs and Promising Interventions". Child & Family Social Work 14 .2 (2009): 129–131. Wiley InterScience. 22 Apr. 2009 doi: <10.1111/j.1365-2206.2009.00617.x>	McAULEY, C., P.J. PECORA, and J.K. WHITTAKER. High risk youth: evidence on characteristics, needs and promising interventions. *Child & Family Social Work*, vol. 14, no. 2, pp: 129–131. *Wiley InterScience* [Online] doi: 10.1111/j.1365-2206.2009.00617.x [Accessed 22 Apr. 2009].

- The following is an example of an online-only electronic journal (e-journal).
- If the final version of the article is being referenced, no retrieval date is necessary for the APA style entry.
- No page numbers are shown on the article, so it is important to use the exact URL to take the reader straight to the source.
- With open access sites, check to see what quality-control checks are in place on articles submitted, e.g. peer review; editorial teams.

Table 9.S5ii Academic e-journal article (no DOI, open access site)

Harvard	APA
SMITH, Sarah-Neel (2008). 'Nightcomers' at the 2007 Istanbul Biennial: revolution or counter-Revolution? *Art & Research*, vol. 2, no. 1. summer [Online]. Available at http://www.artandresearch.org.uk/v2n1/smith.html [Accessed 22 Apr. 2009]	Smith, Sarah-Neel (2008). 'Nightcomers' at the 2007 Istanbul Biennial: revolution or counter-revolution? *Art & Research*, 2(1), summer. Retrieved from http://www.artandresearch.org.uk/v2n1/smith.html
MLA	**Numerical**
Smith, Sarah-Neel. " 'Nightcomers' at the 2007 Istanbul Biennial: Revolution or Counter-Revolution?" Art & Research 2.1, summer (2008). 22 Apr. 2009. <http://www.artandresearch.org.uk/v2n1/smith.html>	SMITH, Sarah-Neel. 'Nightcomers' at the 2007 Istanbul Biennial: revolution or counter-revolution? *Art & Research*, vol. 2, no. 1. summer [Online]. Available at http://www.artandresearch.org.uk/v2n1/smith.html [Accessed 22 Apr. 2009].

- In the following example, the database for the journal, 'Proquest', is shown and the homepage is given. This database is accessible to most students through their institution library, but others would need to register to use it.
- The APA entry does not show a retrieval date because the final version of the article is found on the site. However, if in doubt about what version is shown, add the retrieval date, e.g. 'Retrieved 22 April 2009 from . . .'

Table 9.S5iii Academic journal article (no DOI, subscription site)

Harvard	APA
SCHAEFFER, R. (2009). Closing the medication safety loop. *Health Management Technology*. vol. 30, no. 3, pp. 30–33. [Online] *Proquest*. Available http://www.proquest.com/en-US/default.shtml [Accessed 22 Apr. 2009].	Schaeffer, R. (2009). Closing the medication safety loop. *Health Management Technology*, 30(3), 30–33. Retrieved from *Proquest* http://www.proquest.com/en-US/default.shtml
MLA	**Numerical**
Schaeffer, Richard. "Closing the Medication Safety Loop". Health Management Technology 30.2 (2009): 39–33. Proquest. 22 Apr. 2009 <http://www.proquest.com/en-US/default.shtml>	SCHAEFFER, R. Closing the medication safety loop. *Health Management Technology*. vol. 30, no. 3, pp. 30–33. [Online] *Proquest*]. Available at http://www.proquest.com/en-US/default.shtml [Accessed 22 Apr. 2009].

S6 Preprint of academic journal article or paper

A preprint is a draft, or work in progress, of a scientific paper that has not yet been published in a peer-reviewed journal. These are contained and maintained within repositories and digital copies (or eprints) are made accessible to others. Making their draft papers freely available, allows authors to receive early feedback from their peers to help them revise their work. Students can benefit from access to these papers to find out what research is in progress. However, they need to make it clear in the text of their assignments that the research in question is still unpublished work.

The first example below illustrates an example of a paper presented at a workshop and retrieved from an academic digital repository; the second, of an article accepted for publication, also from an academic digital repository; and the third a pre-publication version of an article from a personal website, hosted by an institution of higher education.

Table 9.S6i From a digital repository: paper presented at a workshop (awaiting acceptance for publication)

Harvard	APA
PAUL, S. (2009). The puzzle of neutron lifetime. Paper presented at *International Workshop on Particle Physics with Slow Neutrons* 29–31 May 2008 Institut Laue Langevin, Grenoble, France. *Arxiv* [Online] http://arxiv.org/abs/0902.0169v2 [Accessed 23 Apr. 2009].	Paul, S. (2009). The puzzle of neutron lifetime. Paper presented at *International Workshop on Particle Physics with Slow Neutrons* 29–31 May 2008 Institut Laue Langevin, Grenoble, France. Retrieved April 23, 2009 from *Arxiv* http://arxiv.org/abs/0902.0169v2
MLA	**Numerical**
Paul, Stephan. "The Puzzle of Neutron Lifetime". Paper presented at International Workshop on Particle Physics, 29–31 May 2008, Institut Laue Langevin, Grenoble, France. Arxiv: 23 Apr. 2009 <http://arxiv.org/abs/0902.0169v2>	PAUL, S. The puzzle of neutron lifetime. Paper presented at *International Workshop on Particle Physics with Slow Neutrons* 29–31 May 2008 Institut Laue Langevin, Grenoble, France. *Arxiv* [Online] http://arxiv.org/abs/0902.0169v2 [Accessed 23 Apr. 2009].

- Give details of the name (italicized or underlined; see examples), date and location of the workshop, symposium, or conference.
- The name of the digital repository should be shown (italicized/underlined).
- The retrieval date is shown in the APA style, as the final version of the paper is not used.

Table 9.S6ii From a digital repository: article accepted for publication

Harvard	APA
NG, I. and K.S. LEE (2008). Competition in the advanced sale of service capacity. Accepted for publication in *International Journal of Revenue Management*, vol. 2, no. 4, 2008. Available *University of Exeter* [Preprint] doi: 10.1504/ IJRM.2008.020724 [Accessed 23 Apr. 2009].	Ng, I. & K.S. Lee (2008). Competition in the advanced sale of service capacity. *International Journal of Revenue Management*. 2(4). Advance online publication. Retrieved April 23, 2009 from doi: 10.1504/IJRM.2008.020724
MLA	**Numerical**
Ng, Irene, Khai Lee. "Competition in the Advanced Sale of Service Capacity". Accepted for publication in International Journal of Revenue Management, 2.4 (2008). U of Exeter 23 Apr. 2009 doi: <10.1504/IJRM.2008.020724>	NG, I. and K.S. LEE. Competition in the advanced sale of service capacity. Accepted for publication in *International Journal of Revenue Management*, vol. 2, no. 4, 2008. Available *University of Exeter* [Preprint] doi: 10.1504/ IJRM.2008.020724 [Accessed 23 Apr. 2009].

- Give details of journal, including scheduled date of publication, volume and number.
- State the name of the repository; in this example, the University of Exeter.
- Use a DOI tag, if shown, as this will direct the reader to the latest version.
- Include the retrieval date in the APA style, unless you are sure the final version of the article is being accessed.

Table 9.S6iii Unpublished manuscript from personal web-pages

Harvard	APA
SPENCER, B. and M.W. JONES (2009). *Into the blue: better caustics through photon relaxation.* Unpublished manuscript. Available: Ben Spencer, Swansea University at http://cs.swan.ac.uk/ ~csbenjamin/ [Accessed 24 Apr. 2008].	Spencer, B. and Jones, M.W. (2009). *Into the blue: better caustics through photon relaxation.* Manuscript in preparation. Retrieved April 24 2009 from Ben Spencer, Swansea University: http://cs.swan.ac.uk/ ~csbenjamin/
MLA	**Numerical**
Spencer, Ben, Mark W. Jones. "Into the Blue: Better Caustics through Photon Relaxation". Ben Spencer: Swansea Univ. unpublished manuscript, 24 Apr. 2009 <http:// cs.swan.ac.uk/~csbenjamin/>	SPENCER, B. and M.W. JONES. *Into the blue: better caustics through photon relaxation.* Unpublished manuscript. Available: Ben Spencer, Swansea University at http:// cs.swan.ac.uk/~csbenjamin/ [Accessed 24 Apr. 2008].

- Start with the name(s) of author(s) of the manuscript.
- Title of manuscript.

- Name of personal website and, if applicable, name of website host institution.
- State type of source, e.g. unpublished manuscript, or manuscript in preparation.
- Give date of access/retrieval to the site.
- Give full URL address.

S7 Magazines

A magazine is a collection of news and features with a broad appeal, aimed either at a specialist readership or more general market.

Table 9.S7i Article in a magazine (originally printed, but found online)	
Harvard ENSERINK, M. (2006). Influenza: what came before 1918? Archaeovirologist offers a first glimpse. [Online]. *Science*: 23 June 2006, p 1725. Available at http://www.sciencemag.org/index.dtl [Accessed 23 April 2009].	**APA** Enserink, M. (2006, June 23, p. 1725). Influenza: What came before 1918? Archaeovirologist offers a first glimpse. Retrieved from *Science* http://www.sciencemag.org/index.dtl
MLA Enserink, Martin. "Influenza: What Came Before 1918? Archaeovirologist Offers a First Glimpse". *Science* 23 June 2006: 1725. 23 Apr. 2009 <http://www.sciencemag.org/index.dtl>	**Numerical** ENSERINK, M. Influenza: What came before 1918? Archaeovirologist offers a first glimpse. [Online]. *Science* 23 June 2006, p 1725. Available at http://www.sciencemag.org/index.dtl> [Accessed 23 April 2009].

- You should cite the name of author, if shown. If no author shown, start with name of originating source, e.g. title of magazine.
- Give full details of title, and edition number, and date of edition.
- Make it clear you looked at the online version, and give the URL of the source homepage.
- Give date of access to the source (APA excepted, if final version of article is shown).

Table 9.S7ii Article in an online magazine (not available in print form)	
Harvard *Microsoft Windows XP* (2006) 25 Best hidden programs. Issue 58, May. Available at http://www.windowsxpmagazine.co.uk/ [Accessed 19 July 2006].	**APA** *Microsoft Windows XP*. (2006, May). 25 best hidden programs, Issue 58. Retrieved from http://www.windowsxpmagazine.co.uk/
MLA Microsoft Windows XP. "25 Best Hidden Programs". 58, May 2006. 19 July 2006 <http://www.windowsxpmagazine.co.uk/>	**Numerical** *Microsoft Windows XP*. 25 Best hidden programs. Issue 58, May 2006. Available at http://www.windowsxpmagazine.co.uk/ [Accessed 19 July 2006].

- If there is no named author, start with name/title of originator, e.g. title of publication.

- Give the full URL to take the reader straight to the article in question.
- State the date of access/retrieval to the source.

S8 Newspaper article

Table 9.S8i Newspaper article

Harvard	APA
LISTER, S. (2006). Basic hygiene is failing in a third of NHS hospitals. *TimesOnline*. 22 Mar. 2006. Available at TimesOnlinehttp:// www.timesonline.co.uk/article/0,, 8122–2097936,00.html [Accessed 24 July 2006]	Lister, S. (2006, March 22). Basic hygiene is failing in a third of NHS hospitals. *TimesOnline*. Retrieved from http://www.timesonline.co.uk/ article/0,,8122–2097936,00.html

MLA	Numerical
Lister, Sam. "Basic Hygiene is Failing in a Third of NHS Hospitals". <u>TimesOnline</u>. 22 Mar. 2006. 24 July 2006. <http://www.timesonline.co.uk/ article/0,,8122–2097936,00.html>	LISTER, S. Basic hygiene is failing in a third of NHS hospitals. *TimesOnline*. 22 Mar. 2006. [Available at http://www.timesonline.co.uk/ article/0,,8122–2097936,00.html [Accessed 24 July 2006]

If the name of the journalist or writer is shown, start with this. If not, start with the name of the online newspaper site. Give the title and date of the item or article, and the URL address to take the reader to where the article can be found.

In example 9.S8i, shown above, the first date shown in the MLA reference is when the article was originally published, and the second date, which immediately precedes the URL address, is when the source was visited.

In example 9.S8ii, that follows, for the MLA entry, the date of publication, and when the site was visited, are the same.

Table 9.S8ii Newspaper article

Harvard	APA
TimesOnline (2006). On the flight path of dying Ibis. 24 July 2006. Available at http:// www.timesonline.co.uk/article/0,, 3–2282913,00.html [Accessed 24 July 2006].	*TimesOnline* (2006, July 24). On the flight path of dying ibis. Retrieved from http:// www.timesonline.co.uk/article/ 0,,3–2282913,00.html

MLA	Numerical
<u>TimesOnline</u>. "On the Flight Path of Dying Ibis". 24 July 2006. <http://www.timesonline.co.uk/ article/0,,3–2282913,00.html>	*TimesOnline*. on the flight path of dying Ibis. 24 July 2006. Available at http:// www.timesonline.co.uk/article/ 0,,3–2282913,00.html [Accessed 24 July 2006].

S9 Online reports or guidelines

- You need to include the name(s) of the authors, and the full title, including any subtitles, in italics or underlined.

- Include the name of sponsoring organization, if shown, i.e. Lancaster University (see example 9.S9i), and give the full URL address information.
- If no author is named, start with the name of the organization sponsoring the report or guidelines (see example 9.S9ii).

Table 9.S9i Online report (author named)

Harvard	APA
INTRONA, L. et al. (2003). *Cultural attitudes towards plagiarism*. Lancaster University. [Online]. Available at http://www.jiscpas.ac.uk/images/bin/lancsplagiarismreport.pdf [Accessed 24 Apr. 2009].	Introna, L., Hayes, N., Blair, L., & Wood, E. (2003). *Cultural attitudes towards plagiarism*. Retrieved from http://www.jiscpas.ac.uk/images/bin/lancsplagiarismreport.pdf
MLA	**Numerical**
Introna, Lucas, et al. Cultural Attitudes Towards Plagiarism. 24 Apr. 2009, U. of Lancaster <http://www.jiscpas.ac.uk/apppage.cgi?USERPAGE=7508>	INTRONA, L. et al. *Cultural attitudes towards plagiarism*. Lancaster University [Online] Available at http://www.jiscpas.ac.uk/apppage.cgi?USERPAGE=7508 [Accessed 24 April 2009].

Table 9.S9ii Online guidelines (no named author)

Harvard	APA
THE AMERICAN PHYTOPATHOLOGICAL SOCIETY (2006). *B&C tests: guidelines for preparing reports*. Available at http://www.apsnet.org/online/BCTests/guidelines/ [Accessed 27 July 2006].	The American Phytopathological Society (2006). *B&C tests: Guidelines for preparing reports*. Retrieved July 27, 2006 from http://www.apsnet.org/online/BCTests
MLA	**Numerical**
The American Phytopathological Society. B&C Tests: Guidelines for Preparing Reports. 27 July 2006. <http://www.apsnet.org/online/BCTests/guidelines/>	THE AMERICAN PHYTOPATHOLOGICAL SOCIETY. *B&C tests: guidelines for preparing reports*. Available at http://www.apsnet.org/online/BCTests/guidelines/ [Accessed 27 July 2006].

- APA style: show the retrieval date if there is a likelihood of the guidelines changing or merging with other agencies.

S10 Online company reports

- If there is a named writer, start with his or her name, if not state the company name and year of publication.
- Give the title of the report.
- Show the URL and date you accessed the site (APA excepted, if the final version of the report is shown).

Table 9.S10i Individual company report

Harvard	APA
BROWNE BROTHERS (2009), *Browne Brothers Company Report 2008*. Available at www.brownebros.com [Accessed 12 May 2009].	Browne Brothers (2009). *Browne Brothers Company Report 2008*. Retrieved from www.brownebros.com
MLA	**Numerical**
Browne Brothers "Browne Brothers Company Report 2009". 12 May 2009. <www.brownebros.com>	BROWNE BROTHERS, *Browne Brothers Company Report 2008*. Available at www.brownebros.com [Accessed 12 May 2009].

Compilation of company reports

The following example illustrates referencing a collection of reports from a subscriber database. You might, for example, prepare a graph or chart, in the main body or appendix of your report, which gives an overview of these reports.

- Start with the name of the publisher of the database, the year of publication of reports. If the reports are drawn from between a number of years, show this as (2007–9)
- State the nature of the reports and list the companies involved.
- Give name of the database and homepage address.
- Give date of access to site (APA excepted, if final versions of reports shown).

Table 9.S10ii Compilation

Harvard	APA
BUREAU VAN DIJK (2006). Compilation from company annual reports 2005: PC World, Currys, and UniEuro, *FAME* [Online]. Available at http://www.Bvdep.com [Accessed 22 Apr. 2006].	Bureau Van Dijk (2006). Compilation from company annual reports 2005: PC World, Currys, and UniEuro, Retrieved from *FAME* www.Bvdep.com
MLA	**Numerical**
Bureau Van Dijk Compilation from Co.annual reports 2005: PC World, Currys, and UniEuro, 22 Apr. 2006. FAME database, <http://www.Bvdep.com>	BUREAU VAN DIJK (2006). Compilation from company annual reports 2005: PC World, Currys, and UniEuro, *FAME* [Online]. Available at http://www.Bvdep.com [Accessed 22 Apr. 2006].

S11 Online dissertation (extract from a university website)

If the work was available from a dissertation database (or commercial organization), give details of the database after the title of thesis, and any accession number, and/or relevant search path or file name information.

Table 9.S11i Abstract

Harvard	APA
DAY, S.J. (2002). *Studies of controlled substances and the enhancement of fingerprints: analysis of drugs of abuse in latent and cyanoacrylate-fumed fingerprints using raman spectroscopy.* Unpublished doctoral thesis. University of Bradford. Abstract [Online]. Available at http://ipac.brad.ac.uk/#focus Search: Chemistry; Day; 2002. [Accessed 4 Aug. 2006].	Day, S.J. (2002). *Studies of controlled substances and the enhancement of fingerprints: Analysis of drugs of abuse in latent and cyanoacrylate-fumed fingerprints using raman spectroscopy.* Unpublished doctoral thesis. University of Bradford. Abstract retrieved from http://ipac.brad.ac.uk/#focus Search: Chemistry; Day; 2002.

MLA	Numerical
Day, Sara, J. "Studies of Controlled Substances and the Enhancement of fingerprints: Analysis of Drugs of Abuse in Latent and Cyanoacrylate-fumed Fingerprints Using Raman Spectroscopy". Unpub. diss. U. of Bradford. A043 Day. Abstract. 4 Aug. 2006 <http://ipac.brad.ac.uk/#focus> Path: Chemistry; Day; 2002.	DAY, S.J. *Studies of controlled substances and the enhancement of fingerprints: analysis of drugs of abuse in latent and cyanoacrylate-fumed fingerprints Using raman spectroscopy.* Unpublished doctoral thesis, 2002. University of Bradford. Abstract [Online]. Available at http://ipac.brad.ac.uk/#focus Search: Chemistry; Day; 2002. [Accessed 4 Aug. 2006].

- For referencing the full thesis, follow the format in the example above, but omit 'Abstract' and give chapter or section number or title and page numbers, if referring to a specific part of the thesis.

Table 9.S11ii Example of an abstract of a dissertation available online via a database

Harvard	APA
HARRIS, C.D. (2006). *Organizational change and intellectual production: the case study of Hohokam archaeology.* Unpublished doctoral thesis. [Online] University of Arizona, via *ProQuest Digital Dissertations* Abstract available at http://wwwlib.umi.com/dissertations/fullcit/3206908 [Accessed 4 Aug. 2006].	Harris, C.D. (2006). *Organizational change and intellectual production: The case study of Hohokam archaeology.* Unpublished doctoral thesis. University of Arizona. Abstract retrieved from ProQuest Digital Dissertations at http://wwwlib.umi.com/dissertations/fullcit/3206908

MLA	Numerical
Harris, Cory, D. (2006). Organizational Change and Intellectual Production: The Case Study of Hohokam Archaeology. Unpub. diss. U of Arizona. ProQuest Digital Dissertations. Abstract. 4 Aug. 2006 <http://wwwlib.umi.com/dissertations/fullcit/3206908>	HARRIS, C.D. *Organizational change and intellectual production: the case study of Hohokam archaeology.* Unpublished doctoral thesis. 2006. [Online] University of Arizona, via ProQuest Digital Dissertation. Abstract available at http://wwwlib.umi.com/dissertations/fullcit/3206908 [Accessed 4 Aug. 2006].

S12 Conference paper (or manuscript) available online

Reference should include name of presenter, title of paper, status of paper (unpublished manuscript; working paper), unpublished report, name and place of conference, date delivered, URL details, date you accessed the site, and any relevant page numbers.

Table 9.S12 Manuscript

Harvard	APA
ROSS, M. (2005). *Is democracy good for the poor?* Unpublished manuscript. Annual meeting American Political Science Association, Washington. 1 Sept. 2005. [Online] Available at http://convention2.allacademic.com/one/apsa/apsa05/index.php?click_key=1 [Accessed 2 Aug. 2006].	Ross, M. (2005, September 1). *Is democracy good for the poor?* Unpublished manuscript presented at Annual meeting American Political Science Association, Washington. Retrieved from http://convention2.allacademic.com/one/apsa/apsa05/index.php?click_key=1
MLA	**Numerical**
Ross, Michael. "Is Democracy Good for the Poor?". Unpubl. ms. Annual meeting APSA. Washington, DC. 1 Sept. 2005. 2 Aug. 2006. <http://convention2.allacademic.com/one/apsa/apsa05/index.php?click_key=1>	ROSS, M. *Is democracy good for the poor?* Unpublished manuscript. Annual meeting American Political Science Association, Washington. 1 Sept. 2005. [Online] Available at http://convention2.allacademic.com/one/apsa/apsa05/index.php?click_key=1 [Accessed 2 Aug. 2006].

S13 Government or other statistics online

If no author name is shown, start with the name of the publishing agency or organization. Include then, the year the data was originally published, title of the statistics, plus full URL address. It may also be necessary to state the country of origin, as the same name of the government agency may be used in different countries, e.g. the title, 'National Bureau of Statistics' is used by more than one country.

In example 9.S13i that follows, the source for just one set of UK statistics is shown (but see the note following the example shown here).

Table 9.S13i Government statistics

Harvard	APA
OFFICE FOR NATIONAL STATISTICS (UK). (2005). *Employment: rate rises to 74.9 per cent in 3 months to Sept 05.* [Online]. Available at http://www.statistics.gov.uk/CCI/nugget.asp?ID=12 [Accessed 14 Dec. 2005].	Office for National Statistics (UK). (2005). *Employment: Rate rises to 74.9 per cent in 3 months to Sept 05.* from http://www.statistics.gov.uk/CCI/nugget.asp?ID=12
MLA	**Numerical**
Office for National Statistics (UK). Employment: Rate Rises to 74.9 per cent in 3 Months to Sept 05. 14 Dec. 2005 <http://www.statistics.gov.uk/CCI/nugget.asp?ID=12>	OFFICE FOR NATIONAL STATISTICS (UK). *Employment: rate rises to 74.9 per cent in 3 months to Sept 05.* [Online] Available at http://www.statistics.gov.uk/CCI/nugget.asp?ID=12 [Accessed 14 Dec. 2005].

However, referencing is not always this easy! Students often gather statistics relating to different topics from one major source, e.g. national offices or bureaus of statistics, but may then be unsure how to cite and reference the different parts of the same site in the text of their assignment. In this situation, the important point and principle of referencing to remember is to make it easy for your reader to locate the same source, which may mean you have to list a range of slightly different URL addresses in your references.

However, if you are using Harvard, APA or MLA referencing styles, your citations can separate out the relevant parts of a single source by the use of prefix letters.

For example, if you wanted to refer to three different parts of the National Bureau of Statistics (China):

a. Regulations on the Composition of Gross Wages
b. Regulations on the National Economic Census
c. Statistical Bulletin on the Input of Science and Technology, 2002.

Your citations in the text of your assignment (in the Harvard style) would be shown respectively as:

- (NBOS (China) 2006**a**)
- (NBOS (China) 2006**b**)
- (NBOS (China) 2006**c**).

Do not forget, you can use abbreviations in your citations, i.e. NBOS, as this can reduce your word count. However, in the full reference details you need to start with the abbreviation and then explain it to the reader (see examples that follow).

With the APA style, you would give the full title of the organization the first time it is mentioned in the assignment, but it can be abbreviated thereafter. The full reference entry would show the full title of the organization

---

Table 9.S13ii Full reference details (Harvard style)

NBOS (China): NATIONAL BUREAU OF STATISTICS OF CHINA (2006**a**). *Regulations on the composition of gross wages*. [Online]. Available at http://www.stats.gov.cn/english/lawsandregulations/statisticalregulations/t20020801_2413.htm [Accessed 23 July 2006].

NBOS (China): NATIONAL BUREAU OF STATISTICS OF CHINA (2006**b**). *Regulations on the national economic census*. [Online]. Available at http://www.stats.gov.cn/english/lawsandregulations/statisticalregulations/t20050110_402222113.htm [Accessed 23 July 2006].

NBOS (China): NATIONAL BUREAU OF STATISTICS OF CHINA (2006**c**). *Statistical bulletin on the input of science and technology*, 2002. [Online]. Available at http://www.stats.gov.cn/english/newrelease/statisticalreports/t20031111_119097.htm [Accessed 23 July 2006].

S14 Public/archival records and documents online

Detail should include name of country, if not obvious, record or source, title of specific document or list, reference number, if applicable, locality information (if applicable)

and other identifying features of source, plus name of any database, or URL address, and the date the information was accessed or retrieved. If referring to a specific named person, start with this (see following example 9.S14iii).

Table 9.S14i Census record

Harvard
UK CENSUS 1881: *Residents of Bolton Union workhouse, Fishpool, Farnworth, Lancashire.* Available from Census Online at http://users.ox.ac.uk/~peter/workhouse/Bolton/Bolton1881.html [Accessed 8 Aug. 2006].

APA
UK Census 1881: *Residents of Bolton Union workhouse, Fishpool, Farnworth, Lancashire.* Retrieved from Census Online at http://users.ox.ac.uk/~peter/workhouse/Bolton/Bolton1881.html

MLA
UK Census 1881: Residents of Bolton Union Workhouse, Fishpool, Farnworth, Lancashire. 8 Aug. 2006, Census Online <http://users.ox.ac.uk/~peter/workhouse/Bolton/Bolton1881.html>

Numerical
UK CENSUS 1881: *Residents of Bolton Union workhouse, Fishpool, Farnworth, Lancashire.* Available from Census Online http://users.ox.ac.uk/~peter/workhouse/Bolton/Bolton1881.html [Accessed 8 Aug. 2006].

Table 9.S14ii National archives

Harvard
UK NATIONAL ARCHIVES (2006). *Records of the Admiralty, Naval Forces, Royal Marines, Coastguard, and related bodies.* Ref. ADM 188/360. [Online]. Available http://www.nationalarchives.gov.uk/documentsonline/details-result.asp?queryType=1&resultcount=1&Edoc_Id=6929949 [Accessed 10 Aug. 2006].

APA
UK National Archives (2006). *Records of the Admiralty, Naval Forces, Royal Marines, Coastguard, and related bodies.* Ref. ADM 188/360. Retrieved from http://www.nationalarchives.gov.uk/documentsonline/details-result.asp?queryType=1&resultcount=1&Edoc_Id=6929949

MLA
UK National Archives. Records of the Admiralty, Naval Forces, Royal Marines, Coastguard, and related bodies. Ref. ADM 188/360. 10 Aug. 2006 <http://www.nationalarchives.gov.uk/documentsonline/details-result.asp?queryType=1&resultcount=1&Edoc_Id=6929949>

Numerical
UK NATIONAL ARCHIVES. *Records of the Admiralty, Naval Forces, Royal Marines, Coastguard, and related bodies.* Ref. ADM-188/360. [Online]. Available http://www.nationalarchives.gov.uk/documentsonline/details-result.asp?queryType=1&resultcount=1&Edoc_Id=6929949 [Accessed 10 Aug. 2006].

Table 9.S14iii Military records

Harvard
BIRKS, F. (2nd Lieut. VC). (2006). *Military record.* Australian Military Units. Australian War Memorial. [Online]. Available at http://www.awm.gov.au/units/people8228.asp [Accessed 11 Aug. 2006].

APA
Birks, F. (2nd Lieut. VC). (2006). *Military record.* Australian Military Units. Australian War Memorial. Retrieved from http://www.awm.gov.au/units/people8228.asp

(Cont.)

MLA	Numerical
Birks, Frederick (2nd Lieut. VC). <u>Military Record</u>. Australian Military Units. Australian War Memorial. 11 Aug. 2006. <http://www.awm.gov.au/units/people8228.asp>	BIRKS, F. (2nd Lieut. VC). *Military record*. Australian Military Units. Australian War Memorial. [Online]. Available at http://www.awm.gov.au/units/people8228.asp [Accessed 11 Aug. 2006].

Table 9.S14iv Letter

Harvard	APA
THOMAS OF YORK (1105). *Letter from Thomas of York to Lanfranc*. British Library: Collection of Letters [Online]. Available at http://www.bl.uk/onlinegallery/onlineex/illmanus/cottmanucoll/a/011cotvese00006u00205v00.html [Accessed 15 May 2009].	Thomas of York (1105). *Letter from Thomas of York to Lanfranc*. British Library: Collection of Letters. Retrieved from http://www.bl.uk/onlinegallery/onlineex/illmanus/cottmanucoll/a/011cotvese00006u00205v00.html
MLA	**Numerical**
Thomas of York. <u>Letter from Thomas of York to Lanfranc</u>. 1105. British Libr: Coll. of Letters, 15 May, 2009 <http://www.bl.uk/onlinegallery/onlineex/illmanus/cottmanucoll/a/011cotvese00006u00205v00.html>	THOMAS OF YORK. *Letter from Thomas of York to Lanfranc* (1105). British Library: Collection of Letters [Online]. Available at http://www.bl.uk/onlinegallery/onlineex/illmanus/cottmanucoll/a/011cotvese00006u00205v00.html [Accessed 15 May 2009].

S15 Personal communications: emails/twitters and tweets/text messages/faxes

Personal emails

Significant personal email messages can be referenced – but be cautious. Wherever possible, you should obtain permission from the sender to use personal email correspondence, particularly if the correspondence will appear in the public domain. You may also need to save a copy of the correspondence to enable a tutor to read it (consult with your tutor on this).

If the message is included as a reference, do not give the email address of the sender, as this would be a breach of confidentiality and might lead to unwarranted correspondence being sent to the sender.

The following format is recommended:

- Name of sender
- Year communication received
- Medium (email)
- Title or subject of message
- Name of recipient – this may be your name
- Date communication received.

Table 9.S15i Personal email

Harvard	APA
BROWN, J. (2005) Email to C. HARRIS re. marketing survey, 12 Dec. 2005.	Brown, J. (2005, December 12) Email to C. Harris re. marketing survey.
MLA	**Numerical**
Brown, John. Email to Chris Harris re. marketing survey, 12 Dec. 2005.	BROWN, J. Email to C. HARRIS re. marketing survey, 12 Dec. 2005.

Twitter/tweets

Twitter is a networking service allowing users to send and read very short messages. Messages (tweets) can be displayed on a user's profile page/blog and/or delivered to others who have subscribed to them. The user's own blog can be referenced, or if not applicable, the Twitter home page. You may also need to save a copy of the correspondence to enable a tutor to read it, if necessary (consult with your tutor on this).

The suggested format for referencing tweets is:

- Name or pseudonym of sender
- Year
- Medium (tweet)
- Brief description of topic
- Date of message
- Where available
- Date of access/retrieval.

Table 9.S15ii Twitter/tweets

Harvard	APA
FRY, S. (2009). Tweet message: re. death of Jade Goody. 23 Mar. 2009. Available at http://www.stephenfry.com [Accessed 5 May 2009].	Fry, S. (2009, Mar 23). Tweet message: re. death of Jade Goody. Retrieved 5 May 2009 http://www.stephenfry.com
MLA	**Numerical**
Fry, Stephen. Tweet message: re. Death of Jade Goody. 23 Mar. 2009. 5 May 2009 <http://www.stephenfry.com	FRY, S. Tweet message: re. death of Jade Goody. 23 Mar. 2009. Available at http://www.stephenfry.com [Accessed 5 May 2009].

Text messages

The transient nature of text messages is a problem and, unless saved, the lack of a permanent record of the message makes it difficult to record them in the list of references, as the reader will not be able to look at the original source. One way around this situation would be for you to save the text, copy the message into print form and then ask a neutral and objective third party, preferably the tutor marking the assignment, to witness and confirm the accuracy of the copied or summarized message. The transcribed message could then be included as an appendix item and be fully referenced. The name of the sender should come first, description of medium, name of receiver and date received.

Table 9.S15iii Text message

Harvard	APA
DESAI, S. (2006). Text message to J. Jones, 12 Dec. 2006.	Desai, S. (2006, December 12). Text message to J. Jones.
MLA	**Numerical**
Desai, Shoeb. Text message to Janet Jones, 12 Dec. 2006.	DESAI, S. Text message to J. Jones, 12 Dec. 2006.

Faxes

Faxes produce a paper record, which can be kept and included as an appendix item, if required.

Table 9.S15iv Fax message

Harvard	APA
JONES, J. (2006) Fax message to S. DESAI, 13 Dec. 2006.	Jones, J. (2006, December 13) Fax message to S. Desai.
MLA	**Numerical**
Jones, Janet. Fax message to Shoeb Desai, 13 Dec. 2006.	JONES, J. Fax message to S. DESAI, 13 Dec. 2006.

S16 Networking and public communication sites

This section covers:

- Discussion groups/bulletin boards/lifestyle sharing
- Blogs and related sites.

Networking and public communication sites allow individuals to communicate, rapidly and globally, with others. Discussion sites can be easily established or users can create online individual profiles and make these accessible within a particular grouping, e.g. an employing organization; or externally to all comers.

Why might you want to reference such a site? Sites are becoming important points of origin for ideas, information (or misinformation), and advice. They are also increasingly the subject of academic study, e.g. in communication studies; information technology, sociology, etc.

For referencing purposes:

- Start with the name (including just initials or nickname) of the originator of the item being referenced (If not shown start with name of site)
- Give year the site was established or updated, if shown
- Title of message/item in question
- Name of site/name of person featured
- Specific date of message
- URL (log-in page)
- Date the message was retrieved/accessed.

It may be necessary to search for an old item via the search facility on the site's home page.

Because of the ephemeral nature of material on these sites, it may be necessary to make a printed copy of the source to include as an appendix item with your assignment (consult with your tutor). Here are some referencing examples of sites.

Discussion groups/bulletin boards/lifestyle sharing

Although emails on discussion lists and bulletin boards are entered by their senders into a limited public domain, you should, wherever possible, notify the contributors, and preferably seek their permission to use their correspondence, particularly if you are hoping to publish your work. Cite the author's name, if known, or the author's login name, nickname or nomenclature, followed by the subject of the discussion. Then state the name and address of the discussion list, or the protocol and address of the newsgroup. You should also include the date the message was posted and the date it was read by you.

Table 9.S16i Discussion group

Harvard	APA
SMITH, J. (2005). Re. skills audit. LDHEN discussion list, 25 Nov. 2005 [Online]. Available at LDHEN@Jiscmail.ac.uk [Accessed 4 Oct. 2006].	Smith, J. (2005, November 25). Re. skills audit. LDHEN discussion list. Retrieved October 4, 2006 LDHEN@Jiscmail.ac.uk.
MLA	**Numerical**
Smith, John. "Re. Skills Audit". 25 Nov L.2005. DHEN Discussion List. <LDHEN@Jiscmail.ac.uk>.	SMITH, J. Re. skills audit. LDHEN discussion list, 25 Nov. 2005 [Online]. Available at LDHEN@Jiscmail.ac.uk [Accessed 4 Oct. 2006].

There are an increasing number of social networking/sharing sites; each has its own particular emphasis. Here are some examples:

Table 9.S16ii Lifestyle sharing

Harvard
JJ (2009). Oprah says hair is real, has photos to prove it. *Zimbio* 25 Apr. 2009. Available at http://www.zimbio.com/Oprah+Winfrey/articles/444/Oprah+Says+Hair+Real+Photos+Prove [Accessed 27 Apr. 2009].

MLA
JJ. Oprah Says Hair is Real, Has Photos to Prove It. 25 Apr. 2009. Zimbio 27 Apr. 2009 <http://www.zimbio.com/Oprah+Winfrey/articles/444/Oprah+Says+Hair+Real+Photos+Prove>

APA
JJ (2009, April 25). Oprah says hair is real, has photos to prove It. Retrieved 27 April 2009 from *Zimbio* http://www.zimbio.com/Oprah+Winfrey/articles/444/Oprah+Says+Hair+Real+Photos+Prove

Numerical
JJ. Oprah says hair is real, has photos to prove It. *Zimbio* 25 Apr. 2009. Available at http://www.zimbio.com/Oprah+Winfrey/articles/444/Oprah+Says+Hair+Real+Photos+Prove [Accessed 27 Apr. 2009].

Table 9.S16iii Weblog/blog

Harvard
BYFORD, P. (2006). Networking. *Phil Byford's website*. 26 July 2006. Available at http://www.byford.com/ [Accessed 27 July 2006]

MLA
Byford, Phil. "Networking". Phil Byford's website. 26 July 2006. 27 July 2006 <http://www.byford.com/>

APA
Byford, P. (2006, July 26). Networking. *Phil Byford's website*. Retrieved July 27, 2006 from http://www.byford.com/

Numerical
BYFORD, P. Networking. *Phil Byford's website*. 26 July 2006. Available at http://www.byford.com/ [Accessed 27 July 2006]

Table 9.S16iv Facebook

Harvard
MIDGLEY, J. (2009). Isle of Mull. *Facebook: Judy Midgley*, 28 Apr. 2009. Available at http://www.facebook.com/ [Accessed 5 May 2009].

MLA
Midgley, Judy. "Isle of Mull". Facebook: Judy Midgley 28 Apr. 2009. 5 May 2009 <http://www.facebook.com>

APA
Midgley, J. (2009, April 28). Isle of Mull. *Facebook: Judy Midgley*. Retrieved May 5, 2009 from http://www.facebook.com/

Numerical
MIDGLEY, J. Isle of Mull. *Facebook: Judy Midgley*, 28 Apr. 2009. Available at http://www.facebook.com/ [Accessed 5 May 2009].

Table 9.S16v MySpace

Harvard
OBAMA, B. (2009). The President's Weekly Address: a budget equal to the task before us. *MySpace* 24 Mar. 2009. Available at http://www.myspace.com/ [Accessed 5 May 2009].

APA
OBAMA, B. (2009, March 24). The President's Weekly Address: a budget equal to the task before us. *MySpace: Barack Obama*. Retrieved from http://www.myspace.com/

(*Cont.*)

MLA	Numerical
Obama, Barack. "The President's Weekly address: A Budget Equal to the Task Before Us". 24 Mar. 2009. 5 May 2009, <u>MySpace: Barack Obama</u> <http://www.myspace.com/>	OBAMA, B. The President's Weekly Address: a budget equal to the task before us. *MySpace* 24 Mar. 2009. Available at http://www.myspace.com/ [Accessed 5 May 2009].

Table 9.S16vi YouTube

Harvard	APA
BROWN, G. (2009). Gordon Brown's New Year Message 2009. *YouTube* 1 Jan. 2009. Available at http://www.youtube.com/watch?v=jkMNxpcvm8I [Accessed 5 May 2009].	Brown, G. (2009, January 1). Gordon Brown's New Year Message 2009. *YouTube*. Retrieved May 5, 2009 from http://www.youtube.com/watch?v=jkMNxpcvm8I

MLA	Numerical
Gordon, Brown. "Gordon Brown's New Year Message 2009". 1 Jan. 2009. 5 May 2009, <u>YouTube</u> <http://www.youtube.com/watch?v=jkMNxpcvm8I>	Brown, G. Gordon Brown's New Year Message 2009. *YouTube* 1 Jan. 2009. Available at http://www.youtube.com/watch?v=jkMNxpcvm8I [Accessed 5 May 2009].

S17 Audio and vision downloads

Archived sound and vision media files can be downloaded onto personal computers, phones and/or other mobile devices, and can be referenced.

As with all references, start with the name of the originator of the source. For audio/vision programmes and productions, this can be the editor or commissioning editor or, if not shown, the lead commentator or presenter. If this information is not available, start with the name of sponsoring organization, e.g. History Channel. Give details of date of original broadcast or production, title of work, the nature of the download, e.g. audio podcast. Supply the full URL and the date you downloaded the information. If there is a transcript, check with your tutor if this is required as an appendix item.

Table 9.S17i Audio download

Harvard	APA
FINK, S. (2006). Aids in Papua New Guinea. 29 May 2006. *BBC world news: health/HIV Aids.* [Audio podcast] Available at http://www.theworld.org/health/aids.shtml [Accessed 1. Aug. 2006).	Fink, S. (2006, May 29). AIDS in Papua New Guinea. *BBC world news: Health/HIV aids.* Retrieved from http://www.theworld.org/health/aids.shtml

MLA	Numerical
Fink, Sheri. "AIDS in Papua New Guinea". <u>BBC World News: Health/HIV Aids</u>. 29 May 2006. 1 August 2006. <http://www.theworld.org/health/aids.shtml>	FINK, S. Aids in Papua New Guinea. 29 May 2006. *BBC world news: health/HIV Aids.* [Audio download] Available at http://www.theworld.org/health/aids.shtml [Accessed 1 Aug. 2006).

Table 9.S17ii Vision download

Harvard	APA
WALKER, D. (Ed.). (2009). Find me a family, episode 1. *Channel 4*, 11 May 2009. [Podcast]. Available at http://www.channel4.com/programmes/find-me-a-family/catch-up#2917354 [Accessed 15 May 2009].	Walker, D. (Editor). (2009, May 11). Find me a family, episode 1. Television podcast retrieved from *Channel 4* http://www.channel4.com/programmes/find-me-a-family/catch-up#2917354
MLA	**Numerical**
Walker, Dominique (Ed.). "Find Me a Family", ep.1. Channel 4 11 May 2009. Podcast 15 May 2009. <http://www.channel4.com/programmes/find-me-a-family/catch-up#2917354	WALKER, D. (Ed.). Find me a family, episode 1. *Channel 4*, 11 May 2009. [Podcast]. Available at http://www.channel4.com/programmes/find-me-a-family/catch-up#2917354 [Accessed 15 May 2009].

Phonecast

Phonecasts are audio or vision downloads on demand to a subscriber's mobile phone.

Table 9.S17iii Podcast

Harvard	APA
SMITH, M. (2009). London Marathon live. [Phonecast] 26 Apr. 2009 *ipadio*. Available at http://www.ipadio.com/phlog.asp?section=&phlogid=16&phlogcastId=495 [Accessed 13 May 2009].	Smith, M. (2009, April 26). London Marathon live. Phonecast retrieved May 13, 2009 from *ipadio* http://www.ipadio.com/phlog.asp?section=&phlogid=16&phlogcastId=495
MLA	**Numerical**
Smith, Mark. "London Marathon Live". Phonecast 26 Apr. 2009 ipadio 13 May 2009 <http://www.ipadio.com/phlog.asp?section=&phlogid=16&phlogcastId=495	SMITH, M. London Marathon live. [Phonecast] 26 Apr. 2009 *ipadio*. Available at http://www.ipadio.com/phlog.asp?section=&phlogid=16&phlogcastId=495 [Accessed 13 May 2009].

S18 Visual material online (maps, photographs, drawings, three-dimensional art etc.)

If an author/artist/photographer or other named originator is shown, start with this. If a pseudonym or nickname is given, use this. If no author name is shown, start with the name of organisation hosting or organising the site.

You should include the title of work, in italics or underlined, and state the medium, if not obvious, and enclose this description in squared brackets e.g. [photograph].

You should also include other relevant source/publication/collection information, the URL, and the date you visited the site. British Standard examples show full names of originators for visual sources for Harvard and Numerical styles of referencing.

Table 9.S18i Online map

Harvard
MULTIMAP.COM (2006). *Map of Poland.*
Available at http://www.multimap.com/map/
browse.cgi?lat=51.6301&lon=17.068&scale
=2000000&icon=x [Accessed 2 Aug. 2006].

MLA
MultiMap.Com. Map of Poland. 2 Aug. 2006
  <http://www.multimap.com/map/browse.
cgi?lat=51.6301&lon=17.068&scale=
2000000&icon=x >

APA
MultiMap.Com (2006). *Map of Poland.*
  Retrieved from http://www.multimap.com/map/
  browse.cgi?lat=51.6301&lon=17.068&scale
  =2000000&icon=x

Numerical
MULTIMAP.COM. *Map of Poland.* Available
http://www.multimap.com/map/browse.
cgi?lat=51.6301&lon=17.068&scale=
2000000&icon=x [Accessed 2 Aug. 2006].

Table 9.S18ii Photograph in a museum collection

Harvard
CAMERON, Julia. (1864). *Suspense.*
[Photograph]. National Museum Film and
Photography. Available at http://
www.nmpft.org.uk/insight/col-
lectiononline_group.asp?exid=44 [Accessed 12
Aug. 2006].

MLA
Cameron, Julia. Suspense. Photo. 1864. Nat.
  Mus. Film and Photogr. 12 Aug. 2006, <http://
  www.nmpft.org.uk/insight/
  collectiononline_group.asp?exid=44>

APA
Cameron, J. (1864). *Suspense.* [Photograph].
  National Museum Film & Photography.
  Retrieved from http://www.nmpft.org.uk/
  insight/collectiononline_group.asp?exid=44

Numerical
CAMERON, Julia. *Suspense.* (1864).
  [Photograph]. National Museum Film and
  Photography. Available at http://
  www.nmpft.org.uk/insight/
  collectiononline_group.asp?exid=44
  [Accessed 12 Aug. 2006].

Table 9.S18iii Photograph in other collections, e.g. Flickr

Harvard
TANNER, Kate. (2008). *Miar Glacier.*
[Photograph]. *Flickr.* [Online] Available at http://
www.flickr.com/photos/katetanner1/
3083702446/ [Accessed 13 May 2009].

MLA
Tanner, Kate. "Miar Glacier". Photograph. Flickr
  13 May 2009, <http://www.flickr.com/photos/
  katetanner1/3083702446/ >

APA
Tanner, K. (2008). *Miar Glacier.* [Photograph].
  Retrieved May 13 2009 from *Flickr* at http://
  www.flickr.com/photos/katetanner1/
  3083702446/

Numerical
TANNER, Kate. *Miar Glacier.* 2008.
  [Photograph]. *Flickr.* [Online]. Available at
  http://www.flickr.com/photos/katetanner1/
  3083702446/ [Accessed 13 May 2009].

Table 9.S18iv Painting

Harvard	APA
KLEE, Paul. (1937). *Legend of the Nile*. [Painting]. Kunstmuseum Bern. Available at WebMuseum http://www.sai.msu.su/wm/paint/auth/klee/ [Accessed 16 Aug. 2006].	Klee, P. (1937). *Legend of the Nile*. [Painting]. Kunstmuseum Bern. Retrieved from WebMuseum http://www.sai.msu.su/wm/paint/auth/klee/
MLA	**Numerical**
Klee, Paul. "Legend of the Nile". Painting. 1937. Kunstmuseum Bern. <u>WebMuseum</u> 16 Aug. 2006 <http://www.sai.msu.su/wm/paint/auth/klee/>	KLEE, Paul. *Legend of the Nile*. [Painting]. 1937. Kunstmuseum Bern. Available at WebMuseum http://www.sai.msu.su/wm/paint/auth/klee [Accessed 16. Aug. 2006].

Table 9.S18v Cartoon

Harvard	APA
BELL, Steve. (2006). The Government energy review. [Cartoon]. *The Guardian* 12 July 2006. Available at http://www.guardian.co.uk/cartoons/stevebell/0,,1818593,00.html [Accessed 30 July 2006].	Bell, S. (2006, July 12). The government energy review. [Cartoon]. *The Guardian* Retrieved from http://www.guardian.co.uk/cartoons/stevebell/0,,1818593,00.html
MLA	**Numerical**
Bell, Steve. "The Government Energy Review". Cartoon. <u>Guardian</u> 12 July 2006. 30 July 2006. <http://www.guardian.co.uk/cartoons/stevebell/0,,1818593,00.html>	BELL, Steve. The Government energy review. [Cartoon]. *The Guardian* 12 July 2006. Available at http://www.guardian.co.uk/cartoons/stevebell/0,,1818593,00.html [Accessed 30 July 2006].

Three-dimensional art work (e.g. sculpture)

If the URL is very long, you can use the home or search page address, but include a relevant search term or terms to guide others to the online source.

Table 9.S18vi Three-dimensional art work

Harvard	APA
SWINBURNE, Elizabeth. (1991). *Life cycles* [Glass sculpture]. London: V & A Museum, ref. C.8-1994. Available at http://images.vam.ac.uk/ixbin/hixclient.exe?_IXSESSION_=&submit-button=search&search-form=main/index.html [Search terms: glass, Swinburne, Life Cycles]. [Accessed 1 Aug. 2006].	Swinburne, E. (1991). *Life cycles* [Glass sculpture]. London: V & A Museum, ref. C.8-1994. Retrieved from http://images.vam.ac.uk/ixbin/hixclient.exe?_IXSESSION_=&submit-button=search&search-form=main/index.html [Search terms: glass, Swinburne, Life Cycles]. *(Cont.)*

MLA	Numerical
Swinburne, Elizabeth. Life Cycles [Glass sculpture] 1991.London: V & A Mus. ref. C.8-1994. 1 Aug. 2006 <http://images.vam.ac.uk/ixbin/hlxclient.exe?_IXSESSION_=&submit-button=search&search-form=main/index.html> Path: glass; Swinburne; Life Cycles	SWINBURNE, Elizabeth. *Life cycles* [Glass sculpture]. London: V & A Museum, ref. C.8-1994. Available at http://images.vam.ac.uk/ixbin/hixclient.exe?_IXSESSION_=&submit-button=search&search-form=main/index.html [Search terms: glass, Swinburne, Life Cycles]. [Accessed 1 Aug. 2006].

S19 Portable databases (DVD/CD-ROM)

Detail to include:

- Author/editor
- Year of production
- Title of work, in italics or underlined
- Title and type of database, e.g. DVD
- Volume, edition, and item number
- Other identifying features
- Place of publication and name of publisher
- Page numbers, if applicable.

If no author is shown, start with the title of item. However, you do not need to include the terms, 'Accessed' or 'Retrieved', with date, as you would with an online source.

Table 9.S19i DVD (no named author)

Harvard	APA
Sports injuries (2006). 2nd edn. [DVD]. Wigan: Open Software Library.	*Sports injuries* (2006). (2nd ed.) [DVD]. Wigan: Open Software Library.
MLA	**Numerical**
Sports Injuries. 2nd ed. DVD. Wigan: Open Software Libr. 2006.	*Sports injuries* (2006). 2nd edn. [DVD]. Wigan: Open Software Library.

Table 9.S19ii CD-ROM (name(s) of author(s) shown)

Harvard	APA
MERRITT, F.S., M.K. LOFTIN, and J.T. RICKETTS (1995). *Merritt's standard handbook of civil engineering*. 4th edn. [CD-ROM]. New York: McGraw Hill.	Merritt, F.S., Loftin, M.K. & Ricketts, J.T. (1995). *Merritt's standard handbook of civil engineering*. (4th ed.) [CD-ROM]. New York: McGraw Hill.
MLA	**Numerical**
Merritt, Frederick. S., M. Kent Loftin, and Jonathan T. Ricketts. Merritt's Standard Handbook of Civil Engineering. 4th ed. CD-ROM. New York: McGraw Hill, 1995.	MERRITT, F.S., M.K. LOFTIN, and J.T. RICKETTS. *Merritt's standard handbook of civil engineering*. 4th edn. [CD-ROM]. New York: McGraw Hill, 1995.

Appendix 1

Answers to the quiz on understanding when to reference

	Yes	No
1. When you include tables, photos, statistics and diagrams in your assignment. These may be items directly copied or a source of data collation which you have used	✓	
2. When describing or discussing a theory, model or practice associated with a particular writer	✓	
3. When you summarize information drawn from a variety of sources about what has happened over a period, and the summary is unlikely to be a cause of dispute or controversy		✓
4. To give weight or credibility to an argument that you believe is important	✓	
5. When giving emphasis to a particular idea that has found a measure of agreement and support among commentators	✓	
6. When pulling together a range of key ideas that you introduced and referenced earlier in the assignment		✓
7. When stating or summarizing obvious facts, and when there is unlikely to be any significant disagreement with your statements or summaries		✓
8. When including quotations	✓	
9. When you copy and paste items from the Internet and where no author's name is shown	✓	
10. When paraphrasing or summarizing (in your own words) another person's work that you feel is particularly significant, or likely to be a subject of debate	✓	

Appendix 2

Plagiarism quiz 2 answers

The answer to all questions, apart from 6, 8 and 12 is **'yes'**.

6.	**No** However, be cautious when doing this and always try to establish the name of the original author. If an author's name is shown, this must be cited. If the idea is an **original** one (as opposed to 'interesting'), it would be wise to reference the website if no author's name is shown.
8.	**No** It is not plagiarism if you present a summary of what has happened in the past, providing you draw from a range of sources and there is no significant dispute between commentators on the events you describe. However, if you just use one source, or you quote directly, or paraphrase, from any particular source, the author(s) should be cited and referenced.
12.	**No** Plagiarism is to **knowingly** take and use another person's work and claim it directly or indirectly as your own. This is an example of carelessness and you could be criticized for this, but it is not plagiarism. However, you should always check out ideas as thoroughly as you can before claiming any originality for them. You could, for example, discuss your ideas with your tutor, as the tutor is likely to know if others have published ideas similar or identical to your own.

Appendix 3

Exercise: Is it plagiarism?

Example 4.1

This is a clear example of worst-case plagiarism. The extract from the article has been copied directly into the essay without any attempt to acknowledge the source.

Example 4.2

This is plagiarism. Although the original authors are cited, the article has been copied, with only very minor changes, directly into the essay. Copying on this scale, even if the source is acknowledged, will be regarded by most UK universities as plagiarism.

Example 4.3

This is plagiarism. Although an attempt has been made to summarize in part the original article, the authors are not acknowledged. The extract contains important background information that cannot be regarded as 'common knowledge', particularly the last sentence, so the authors and original source should have been cited.

Example 4.4

This is plagiarism. Although the authors have been cited, and some of their words directly quoted, the student simply copies a large part of the original, and the implication is that the sections outside the quotations are the student's own words – which they are not.

Example 4.5

This is not plagiarism. The original source is acknowledged and the student has made a reasonable effort to summarize the extract in his or her own words.

Example 4.6

This is not plagiarism. The original source is acknowledged and the student has made a very good effort to summarize the extract in his or her own words.

Example 4.7

This is plagiarism. Although this is a very good summary of the original extract, it is plagiarism, as the original authors are not cited. The original work containing the ideas of authors must be acknowledged. It is only if knowledge becomes publicly well known (or 'common knowledge') that summaries of generally undisputed facts can be presented without referencing the sources. Sentences two and three can be regarded as common knowledge, as the information in these could be derived from a general reference book. However, the following paraphrased sentences reflect the specialist work of the authors, who should have been cited at the end of this section:

> Since 1979, China has loosened opened and stimulated its economy by foreign direct investment (FDI), international technology transfer (ITT) – and from the influence of multinational enterprises (MNEs). However, these developments have also focused attention on the issue of intellectual property rights (IPR) and until recently in China there has been no effective system of intellectual property protection (IPP).

If in doubt, always cite the source.

Recommended reading on referencing

APA: AMERICAN PSYCHOLOGICAL ASSOCIATION (2005). *Concise rules of APA style*. Washington, DC: American Psychological Association.

APA: AMERICAN PSYCHOLOGICAL ASSOCIATION. (2007). APA style guide to electronic references. Available at www.apa.org/books/ [Accessed 20 Feb 2009].

COUNCIL OF SCIENCE EDITORS (CSE) (2006). *Scientific style and format: the CSE manual for authors, editors, and publishers*. 7th edn. Reston (VA): CSE.

FRENCH, D. (1996). *How to cite legal authorities*. London: Blackstone.

GRAFTON, A. (1997). *The footnote: a curious history*. London: Faber and Faber.

LEVIN, P. (2004). *Write great essays!* Maidenhead: Open University Press.

MAIMON, E.P., J.H. PERITZ and K.B. YANCEY (2007). *A writer's resource: A handbook for writing and research*. New York: McGraw Hill.

MHRA: MODERN HUMANITIES RESEARCH ASSOCIATION (2002). *A handbook for authors, editors, and writers of thesis*. London: as author.

MLA: (2009). *The MLA handbook for writers of research papers*. 7th edn. New York: Modern Language Association of America.

OXFORD STANDARD FOR CITATION OF LEGAL AUTHORITIES (2005). http://denning.law.ox.ac.uk/published/oscola.shtml). [Accessed 10 Jan. 2006].

PEARS, R. and G. SHIELDS (2008). *Cite them right: the essential guide to referencing and plagiarism*. Newcastle upon Tyne: Pear Tree Books.

TURABIAN, K.L. (2007). *A manual for writers of research papers, theses, and dissertations*, 7th edn. Revised by Wayne C. Booth et al. Chicago: University of Chicago Press.

WALKER, J.R. and T. TAYLOR (1998). *The Columbia guide to online style*. New York: Columbia University Press.

WILLIAMS, K. and J. CARROLL (2009). *Referencing and understanding plagiarism*. Basingstoke: Palgrove Macmillan (Pocket Study Skills).

References

AGGARWAL, R. et al. (2002). A study of academic dishonesty among students at two pharmacy schools. *The Pharmaceutical Journal*, Vol. 269, 12 October.

AKHTAR, N. (2007). Indexing Asian names. *The Indexer*, Vol. 25, no. 4, C3: pp:12–14.

ANGÉLIL-CARTER, S. (2000). *Stolen language? Plagiarism in writing*. Harlow: Pearson education.

APA: AMERICAN PSYCHOLOGICAL ASSOCIATION (2005). *Concise rules of APA style*. Washington, DC: American Psychological Association.

APA: AMERICAN PSYCHOLOGICAL ASSOCIATION (2007). *APA style guide to electronic references*. Available at www.apa.org/books/ [Accessed 20 Feb. 2009].

APA: AMERICAN PSYCHOLOGICAL ASSOCIATION (2009). *Publication Manual of the American Psychological Association*. 6th edn. Washington, DC: American Psychological Association.

ASHTON, D. and D. FIELD (1976) *Young workers*. London: Hutchinson and Co.

BARRETT, R. and J. MALCOLM (2006). Embedding plagiarism in the assessment process. *International Journal for Educational Integrity* [online], Vol. 2, no. 1. Available at http://www.ojs.unisa.edu.au/journals/index.php/IJEI [Accessed 28 Aug. 2006].

BOWERS, W.J. (1964). *Student dishonesty and its control in a college*. New York: Bureau of Applied Social Research, Columbia University.

BRITISH COUNCIL (2006). *IELTS band and descriptions*. Available at http://www.britishcouncil.org/taiwan-exams-ielts-ielts-bank-and-descriptions.htm [Accessed 28 Aug. 2006].

BRITISH STANDARD INSTITUTION (BS) (1989). *Recommendation for references to published materials*. BS 1629:1989. London: BS.

BRITISH STANDARD INSTITUTION (BS) (1990). *Recommendations for citing and referencing published material*. BS 5605: 1990. London: BS.

BRITISH STANDARD INSTITUTION (BS) (2000). *Copy preparation and proof correction – part 1: Design and layout of documents*. BS5261–1:2000. London: BS.

BUTCHER, D. (1991). *Official publications in Britain*. 2nd edn. London: Library Association.

CABLE, J. (2001). *Harold Freeman and his nine novels*. Colchester: Bloozoo Publishing.

CARROLL, J. (2005). Institutional issues in deterring, detecting and dealing with student plagiarism. Available at www.jisc.ac.uk/uploaded_documents/plagFinal.doc [Accessed 15 Mar. 2006].

CHERNIN, E. (1988). The 'Harvard system': a mystery dispelled. *British Medical Journal*, vol. 297, pp. 1062–63.

COHEN, J. (2007). *Using Turnitin as a formative writing tool*. Report presented at CETL Research Symposium: 'Opening The Gateway: Keys to Understanding Student Learning and Writing'. Liverpool Hope University 26 June 2007.

COUNCIL OF SCIENCE EDITORS (CSE) (2006). *Scientific style and format: the CSE manual for authors, editors, and publishers*. 7th edn. Reston (VA): CSE.

CULWIN, F. et al. (2002). *Source code plagiarism in UK HE computing schools: issues attitudes and tools*. London: South Bank University, SCISM Technical Report 2000–2001.

THE CHICAGO MANUAL OF STYLE. 15th edn. (2003). Chicago: University of Chicago Press.

DALY, J.A. and L. STAFFORD (1984). Correlates and consequences of social-communicative anxiety. In J.C. McCROSKEY and J.A. DALY (Eds.) *Avoiding communication: shyness, reticence, and communication apprehension*. London: Sage Publications.

DENNIS, L.A. (2005). Student attitudes to plagiarism and collusion within computer science. University of Nottingham. Available at http://eprints.nottingham.ac.uk/archive/00000319/. [Accessed 15 Mar. 2006].

DORDOY, A. (2002). *Cheating and plagiarism: staff and student perceptions at Northumbria.* Working Paper presented Northumbrian Conference: 'Educating for the Future', Newcastle 22 Oct. 2003.

EISENSTEIN, E.L. (1983). *The printing revolution in Early Modern Europe.* New York: Cambridge Univ. Press.

FRENCH, D. (1996). *How to cite legal authorities.* London: Blackstone.

GIBALDI, J. (2003) *The MLA handbook for writers of research papers.* 6th edn. New York: Modern Language Association of America.

GRAFTON, A. (1997). *The footnote: a curious history.* London: Faber and Faber.

GUSTAVII, B. (2003). *How to write and illustrate a scientific paper.* Cambridge: Cambridge University Press.

HA, PHAN LE (2006). Plagiarism and overseas students: stereotypes again? *ELT Journal*, Vol. 60, no. 1, pp.76–78.

HAMPDEN-TURNER, C. and F. TROMPENAARS (2000). *Building cross-cultural competence.* New York: John Wiley and Sons.

HANDY, C. (1995). *Beyond certainty. The changing worlds of organisations.* London: Hutchinson.

HANSEN, J. (2005). *Is there still time to avoid 'dangerous anthropogenic interference' with global climate?* A tribute to Charles David Keeling. Presentation given 6 Dec. 2005 at the American Geophysical Union, San Francisco.

HART, M. and T. FRIESNER (2004). Plagiarism and poor academic practice – a threat to the extension of e-learning in higher education? Academic Conferences Limited. Available at www.ejel.org (Accessed 13 Mar. 2006).

HOPKINS, J.D. (2005). *Common knowledge in academic writing.* Guidance to students, University of Tampere, FAST Area Studies Program, Department of Translation Studies, Finland. Available at http://www.uta.fi/FAST/PK6/REF/commknow.html [Accessed 26 Oct. 2006].

HOUNSEL, D. (1984). Essay writing and the quality of feedback. In T.E. RICHARDSON, M.W. EYSENCK and D.W. PIPER (eds.), *Student learning: research in education and cognitive psychology* (pp: 109–119). Milton Keynes: Open University Press.

HOWARD, R.M. (1995). Plagiarisms, authorships, and the academic death penalty. *College English.* No. 57, pp. 788–806.

HOWARD, R.M. (1999). The new abolitionism comes to plagiarism. In L. BURANEN and R. ROY (Eds.). *Perspectives on plagiarism and intellectual property in a postmodern world* (pp.87–95). Albany: State University of New York Press.

ICMJE: INTERNATIONAL COMMITTEE OF MEDICAL JOURNAL EDITORS (2006). *Uniform requirements for manuscripts submitted to biomedical journals: sample references.* Available at http://www.icmje.org/ [Accessed 14 Oct. 2006].

IEEE: INSTITUTE OF ELECTRICAL AND ELECTRONICS ENGINEERS (2006). *Transactions, journals, and letters: information for author.* Available online from http://www.ieee.org/web/publications/authors/transjnl/index.html [Accessed 20 Aug. 2006].

INTRONA, L. et al. (2003). *Cultural attitudes towards plagiarism.* Report. Lancaster: Lancaster University (Dept of Organisation, Work and Technology).

JONES, K.O. et al. (2005). *Student plagiarism and cheating in an IT age.* Paper presented at International Conference on Computer Systems and Technologies – CompSysTech 2005, 16–17 June 2005.

KELLY, G. (1955). *The psychology of personal constructs.* Two vols. New York: Norton.

LAKE, J. (2004). EAP writing: the Chinese challenge; new ideas on plagiarism. *Humanising Language Teaching*, year 6, iss.1, January. Available at http://www.hltmag.co.uk/jan04/mart4.htm [Accessed 27 Aug. 2006].

LENSMIRE, T.J. and D.E. BEALS (1994). Appropriating others' words: traces of literature and peer culture in a third-grader's writing. *Language in Society*, Vol. 23, pp. 411–25.

LEVIN, P. (2004). *Write great essays*. Maidenhead: Open University Press.

LI, X. and N.B. CRANE. (1996). *Electronic styles: a handbook for citing electronic information*. Medford (N.J.): Information Today.

Mc CROSKEY, J.C. and V.P. RICHMOND (1987). Willingness to communicate. In J.C. MCCROSKEY and J.A. DALY (Eds.). *Personality and interpersonal communication*. (pp.129–156). London: Sage Publications.

Mc CROSKEY, J.C. et al. (1977). Studies of the relationship between communication apprehension and self-esteem. *Human Communication Research*, Vol. 3, no. 3, pp.269–277.

McGRATH, A. (2006). RefWorks investigated – an appropriate bibliographic management solution for health students at Kings College London? *Library and Information Research*, Vol. 30, no. 94, pp.66–73.

MAIMON, E.P., J.H. PERITZ and K.B.YANCEY (2007). *A writer's resource: a handbook for writing and research*. New York: McGraw Hill.

MAIZELS, J. (1970) *Adolescent needs and the transition from school to work*. London: Athlone Press.

MHRA: MODERN HUMANITIES RESEARCH ASSOCIATION (2002). *A handbook for authors, editors, and writers of theses*. London: as author.

MHRA: MODERN HUMANITIES RESEARCH ASSOCIATION (2008). *A handbook for authors, editors, and writers of theses*. 2nd edn. London: as author.

MLA: MODERN LANGUAGES ASSOCIATION (2009). *The MLA handbook for writers of research papers*. 7th edn. New York: Modern Language Association of America.

MUNGER, D. and S. CAMPBELL. (2002). *Researching Online*. 5th edn. New York: Pearson Education.

NEVILLE, C. (2007). *The complete guide to referencing and avoiding plagiarism*. Maidenhead: Open University Press.

NEVILLE, C. (2009a). *How to improve your assignment results*. Maidenhead: McGraw Hill/Open University Press.

NEVILLE, C. (2009b). Student perceptions of referencing – a research report. University of Bradford/LearnHigher CETL. Available at http://www.learnhigher.ac.uk/learningareas/referencing/resourcesforstaff.htm [Accessed 17 Oct. 2009].

NORTON, L.S. (1990). Essay-writing: what really counts? *Higher Education*, Vol. 20, pp. 411–442.

OXFORD STANDARD FOR CITATION OF LEGAL AUTHORITIES (2005). Available at http://denning.law.ox.ac.uk/published/oscola.shtml [Accessed 10 Jan. 2006].

PENNYCOOK, A. (1996). Borrowing others' words: text, ownership, memory and plagiarism. *TESOL Quarterly*, Vol. 30, no. 2, Summer, pp. 210–23.

RICHMOND, V.P. (1984). Implication of quietness: Some facts and speculations. In J.C. Mc CROSKEY and J.A. DALY (Eds.). *Avoiding communication: shyness, reticence, and communication apprehension*. (pp. 145–155). London: Sage Publications.

RUMSEY, S. (2004). *How to find information: a guide for researchers*. Maidenhead: Open University Press.

SCOTT, C.R. and S.C. ROCKWELL. (1997). The effect of communication, writing, and technology apprehension on likelihood to use new communication technologies. *Communication education*. Vol. 46, pp.44–62.

SHAPLAND, M. (1999). *Evaluation of reference management software on NT (comparing Papyrus with ProCite, Reference Manager, Endnote, Citation, GetARef, Biblioscape, Library Master, Bibliographica, Scribe, Refs)*. University of Bristol. Updated Apr. 2001. Available at http://eis.bris.ac.uk/~ccmjs/rmeval99.htm [Accessed 28 April, 2009].

SHERMAN, J. (1992). Your own thoughts in your own words. *ELT Journal*. Vol. 46, no. 2, pp. 190–198.

STEVENS, S. (2008). *RefWorks – a pilot study*. Unpublished report, University of Birmingham, Library Services.

TAYLOR, G. (1989) *The Student's Writing Guide for the Arts and Social Sciences*. Cambridge: Cambridge University Press.

THES: TIMES HIGHER EDUCATION SUPPLEMENT (2006). Polls find elite top cheats list. 17 Mar. 2006, p.9.

THOMPSON, C. (2005). Authority is everything: A study of the politics of textual ownership and knowledge in the formation of student writer identities. *International Journal for Educational Integrity*, Vol. 1, no. 1 (12 pages). Available at http://www.ojs.unisa.edu.au/journals/index.php/ IJEI [Accessed 29 Aug. 2006].

TURABIAN, K.L. (2007). *A manual for writers of research papers, theses, and dissertations*. 7th edn. Revised by Wayne C. Booth et al. Chicago: University of Chicago Press.

UNIVERSITY OF QUEENSLAND (2006). *Handbook of university policies and procedures*, policy number 3.40.12, subsection 2.4 'Common Knowledge'. University of Queensland, Australia.

UNIVERSITY OF QUEENSLAND (2006). *Policy no. 3.40.12 Academic integrity and plagiarism*. Available at http://www.uq.edu.au/hupp/index.html?page=25128 [Accessed 25 Aug. 2006].

WALKER, J.R. and T. TAYLOR (1998). *The Columbia guide to online style*. New York: Columbia University Press.

WINCHCOMBE, A. (1978). *Thomas Hardy: a wayfarer*. Dorchester: Dorset County Library and the Thomas Hardy Society.

YANG, D. (2005). Culture matters to multinationals' intellectual property businesses. *Journal of World Business*, Vol. 40, pp.281–301.

YANG, D. and P. Clarke (2004). Review of the current intellectual property system in China. *International Journal Technology Transfer and Commercialisation*. Vol. 3, no. 1, pp.12–37.

ZEEGERS, P. and L. GILES (1996). Essay writing in biology: an example of effective student learning? *Research in Science Education*. Vol. 26, no. 4, pp. 437–459.

Index

WRITING UP YOUR UNIVERSITY ASSIGNMENTS AND RESEARCH PROJECTS
A PRACTICAL HANDBOOK

Neil Murray and Geraldine Hughes

- What is good academic writing?
- How should I present my written work?
- How can I improve my written work?

Academic writing can be a daunting prospect for new undergraduates and postgraduates alike, regardless of whether they are home or overseas students. This accessible book provides them/ students with all they need to know to produce excellent written work.

Based on their many years of experience, the authors have structured the book so as to build students' confidence in their own writing ability whilst at the same time respecting conventional ideas of what is, and what is not, acceptable in the academic domain. To reinforce student learning, the material is presented using a wealth of clear examples, hands-on tasks with answers, and logical sequences that build on earlier chapters. The first two sections of the book address the preparation and writing of assignments and research projects, while the third provides a useful toolkit containing reference materials on areas including punctuation, grammar and academic terminology.

The book includes numerous tips and insights and comprehensively covers issues such as:

- Reading around a new topic
- The need for coherence and how to achieve it
- Structure and organisation
- Plagiarism, quoting and citing sources
- The main sections of a typical research project
- Writing style
- Finding your own voice
- Examiner expectations

Contents
Foreword – A guide to the book's icons: What do they mean? – Part 1: The fundamentals of academic writing – Introduction – What are the key functions in academic writing? – How should I structure my writing? – What do I need to know about writing style? – Approaching your writing project: Tips and strategies – Part 2: Putting together your research project – Understanding the research and writing process – What are the different components of a research project? – . . . And when it's all over: Publishing and presenting your research – Part 3: Toolkit – Punctuation basics: A brief guide to the correct use of punctuation – Glossary of key terms – The academic word list – Appendix – Index.

2008   256pp
978–0–335–22717–4 (Paperback)   978–0–335–22718–1 (Hardback)